La Jolla Cooks Again

A collection of favorite recipes
from the community of
La Jolla Country Day School

Dedication

This book is dedicated to the children of La Jolla Country Day School—yesterday's, today's, and tomorrow's.

This cookbook is a collection of favorite recipes, which are not necessarily original recipes.

Published by
La Jolla Country Day School Parents' Association

Copyright © 1998 by
La Jolla Country Day School Parents' Association
9490 Genesee Avenue, La Jolla, California 92037

Cover Photography: Jon Lyons Photography

ISBN: 0-9614176-1-7

Designed, Edited, and Manufactured by
Favorite Recipes® Press
an imprint of

FRP™

P.O. Box 305142, Nashville, Tennessee 800-358-0560

Art Director: Steve Newman
Project Manager: Georgia Brazil

Manufactured in the United States of America
First Printing: 1998   7,500 copies

To order additional copies of **La Jolla Cooks** and **La Jolla Cooks Again** contact:
La Jolla Country Day School Parents' Association, 9490 Genesee Avenue,
La Jolla, California 92037 or use the order forms in the back of the book.

This cookbook is a project of The La Jolla Country Day School Parents' Association. All proceeds from the sale of the cookbook are contributed to the school for the benefit of the children.

La Jolla Cooks Again!

This cookbook contains over three hundred and fifty interesting and diverse recipes all contributed by the students, parents, grandparents, friends, and extended families of La Jolla Country Day School. It is actually a sequel to **La Jolla Cooks**, their first cookbook, published in 1987. Again it offers a fabulous collection of high-quality dishes handed down from one generation to the next, so important in preserving our culinary history.

These time-tested recipes provide a marvelous selection of old family favorites perfect for planning menus for parties and everyday meals as well. Many of the recipes also include suggestions, tips, and techniques to help you modify them for anyone interested in lighter fare.

Food fashion is an ever changing scene. Culinary trends constantly tend to come and go. However, we are always the most completely satisfied with dishes we remember fondly from childhood. These comfort foods can easily be updated to meet the needs of contemporary nutritional guidelines without losing any of their fabulous, old-timey flavor and texture.

La Jolla Cooks Again is a veritable treasure chest filled with valuable heirloom recipes sure to delight even the most discerning members of your family!

Jeanne Jones
Internationally acclaimed cookbook author
and syndicated columnist of **Cook It Light**

Preface

As La Jolla Country Day School celebrates seventy years of serving our community with academic excellence, the La Jolla Country Day School Parents' Association embarked upon its second cookbook project in 1996. Following the highly successful publication of **La Jolla Cooks** in 1985, this new book was conceived to commemorate the school that has given so generously to our children. It was easy to capture the culinary talents of our La Jolla Country Day family, past and present, in pursuit of our goal to provide a long-term fundraiser to help meet the Parents' Association commitment to the school. With the profits from this cookbook, the Parents' Association will continue to fund special projects, programs, and purchases that enhance and benefit the children's educational experience at La Jolla Country Day School.

We collected over 700 recipes from former and current students, parents, teachers, staff, trustees, grandparents, and special friends of the Country Day community. Professionals from the culinary industry hand selected the recipes included in this book. The cookbook in your hands is not just another collection of recipes; it is a compilation of timeless treasures, each one distinctive and diverse. Each one demands your attention, and hopes to become a family favorite of yours.

Throughout the cookbook you will be drawn to the unique and provocative sculpture titled "The Unfinished Man," located on the beautiful La Jolla Country Day School campus. Education and learning, like the sculpture, are an unfinished and evolving process. So too, the joys of cooking continue to develop as new ideas and recipes are shared between family and friends.

The Parents' Association invites you to experience the unique and intrinsic flavors that comprise each and every recipe in this cookbook. We promise each ingredient will command your taste buds' attention, as each individual contribution is a favored culinary selection.

Shelley A. Patton

Shelley Ackerberg-Patton
Cookbook Editor

Contents

Acknowledgements

The Parents' Association extends a special thanks to the following persons whose efforts and commitment made this book possible.

John Neiswender, Headmaster
Linda Moyer, Assistant to the Headmaster
Mark Marcus, Business Manager
Mary Doyle, Director of Public Relations
Izzy Leverant, Parents' Association President 1996–1997
Joan Mann Chesner, Parents' Association President 1997–1998
Susan Morris, Parents' Association President 1998–1999

The Parents' Association of La Jolla Country Day School wishes to thank Shelley Ackerberg-Patton, Editor and Project Supervisor of this cookbook for her incredible dedication and hard work. Without her efforts, the cookbook would have remained just another good idea. Shelley rallied the entire school community to participate, an enormous undertaking which she pursued with passion. The result speaks for itself! Shelley, thank you so much.

The Parents' Association would like to express appreciation and gratefully acknowledge the gifted chefs and culinary experts who unselfishly donated their time to hand select recipes for this book.

Maureen Clancy Shiftan, Former Food Editor of the San Diego **Union-Tribune**. Currently, a food and wine columnist at the **Union-Tribune** and Editor of the **Zagat Survey of Restaurants for San Diego**.

Michel Malécot, Professional French Chef, founder and owner of The French Gourmet, Inc. Trained in France, he has worked as a chef in Paris, London, Germany, and throughout the United States. In 1994 he received national awards for Caterer of the Year and the Gold Key Award for Food and Beverage Person of the Year. His bakery, restaurants, and full-service catering have earned numerous local and national awards.

Ricard G. Kauffmann, Executive French Pastry Chef at The French Gourmet since 1982. Professionally trained in France, he has worked in Australia, Germany, Switzerland, and Canada as a renowned pastry chef.

Lesa Heebner, Cookbook author, television chef and professional speaker. Founder and owner of Garlic & Sapphires.

Jeffrey Strauss, Executive Chef and owner of Pamplemousse Grill, has delighted the palates of the world's most powerful business brokers, socialites, United States presidents and countless American and foreign dignitaries. From "Chef to the Stars" to his acclaimed restaurant, his eclectic personal touch is the inspiration for quality food that delights all the senses.

a special thank you to Jeanne Jones, an internationally recognized leader in the field of light cuisine and the acclaimed author of more than 30 cookbooks. Jeanne Jones is affectionately known as the "Dear Abby" of the food pages. Her internationally syndicated Cook It Light recipe makeover column reaches over 30 million people weekly. Your thoughtful insight and kind encouragement will surely inspire the readers of this book.

and a final thank you to Jon Lyons, owner of Jon Lyons Photography, San Diego, California, for his skilled lens and artistic cover photography. He captured the essence of beautiful La Jolla, home to our extraordinary campus. Jon has a Master's Degree in Photography and for 23 years has excelled in portrait work. His association with La Jolla Country Day School for the past 12 years is truly appreciated.

Appetizers

Learn as though you would never be able to
master it; hold onto it as though you
be in fear of losing it.

Confucius,
Analects (6th C.B.C.)

Appetizers

Hot Artichoke Dip 9
Hot Bean Dip 9
Spicy Black Bean Dip 10
Cheese Dip 10
Chili Dip for Chips 11
Cheese and Artichoke Dip 11
Crab Dip Olé 12
Guacamole 12
Sour Cream Guacamole 13
Guadalajara Guacamole 13
Hummus 14
Pesto Dip 14
The Best Seven-Layer Dip 15
Homemade Mexican Salsa 15
Mango and Papaya Salsa 16
Saucy Dip for Shrimp or
   Vegetables 16
Basil Dijon Dip for Veggies 17
Liptauer Cheese Spread 17
Baked Brie with Apples and
   Pecans 18
Crab Meat Appetizer Spread 19

Olive Pecan Spread 19
Salmon Cheese Pâté 20
Smoked Trout Pâté 20
Tuna Spread 21
Mushroom Starter 21
Gravlax 22
Sausage and Sauerkraut 23
Chicken and Cheese Roll-Ups 23
Curried Chicken Wraps 24
Vietnamese Gio Lua (Chicken
   Roll) 24
Cheesy Crab Toasts 25
Crab Pizza 25
Baja Scallop Cocktail 26
Spinach Rolls 26
Country French Wrap 27
Monterey Artichoke Bake 27
Artichoke Frittatas 28
Baked Pecans 28
Tiropetes 29
Cold Dolmathes (Stuffed Vine
   Leaves) 30

Hot Artichoke Dip

Yield:
40 tablespoons

1 (14-ounce) can artichoke hearts
1/2 cup mayonnaise

1/2 cup grated Parmesan cheese
2 teaspoons lemon juice

Approx
Per Tablespoon:
Cal 30
Prot 1 g
Carbo 1 g
T Fat 3 g
76% Calories
from Fat
Chol 3 mg
Fiber 1 g
Sod 45 mg

Drain the artichokes and cut into quarters. Combine the mayonnaise, Parmesan cheese and lemon juice in a 1-quart microwave-safe bowl and blend well. Mix in the artichokes. Microwave, tightly covered, on Medium-High for 2 minutes. Mix well. Microwave for 2 to 3 minutes longer or until heated through. Serve hot.

Jana Hirschenbein 1990 and Seth Hirschenbein 1993

Hot Bean Dip

Yield:
100 tablespoons

1 (8-ounce) can bean dip
1 envelope taco seasoning mix
1 cup sour cream
8 ounces cream cheese, softened
20 drops of Tabasco sauce

1/4 cup chopped onion
1 1/2 cups shredded Cheddar cheese
1 1/2 cups shredded Monterey Jack
cheese

Approx
Per Tablespoon:
Cal 31
Prot 1 g
Carbo 1 g
T Fat 2 g
72% Calories
from Fat
Chol 7 mg
Fiber <1 g
Sod 89 mg

Combine the bean dip, seasoning mix, sour cream, cream cheese and Tabasco sauce in a bowl and blend well. Mix in the onion. Spread half the mixture in a baking dish sprayed with nonstick cooking spray. Mix the cheeses together. Sprinkle half the cheese mixture over the sour cream mixture. Spread the remaining sour cream mixture over the cheese layer. Top with the remaining cheese. Bake at 350 degrees for 20 minutes or until hot and bubbly. Serve with tortilla chips.

Debbie Moyneur
Wife of Chris Moyneur
Superintendent of Buildings and Grounds, 1993 to present

Spicy Black Bean Dip

Yield:
100 tablespoons

3 (15-ounce) cans black beans, drained
1/2 cup chopped cucumber
1/4 cup chopped cilantro
2 tablespoons minced red bell pepper
2 tablespoons minced yellow bell pepper
2 tablespoons minced green bell pepper
2 tablespoons minced red onion
2 tablespoons lime juice
1 jalapeño, seeded
2 teaspoons dried basil
1 teaspoon pepper
1/2 teaspoon garlic powder
1/2 teaspoon ground cumin
1/4 teaspoon salt
1/4 teaspoon hot pepper sauce
1/4 cup shredded Cheddar cheese

Approx
Per Tablespoon:
Cal 11
Prot 1 g
Carbo 2 g
T Fat <1 g
15% Calories
from Fat
Chol <1 mg
Fiber 1 g
Sod 47 mg

Place the beans in a food processor. Add the cucumber, cilantro, bell peppers, onion, lime juice, jalapeño and seasonings. Process until puréed. Spoon into a lightly greased 1 1/2-quart casserole. Refrigerate, covered, overnight. Bake, covered, at 350 degrees for 15 to 20 minutes or until heated through. Sprinkle with the cheese. Serve with chips.

Charlotte Garfield
Parent, Brian 2008 and Jim 1996

Cheese Dip

Yield:
140 tablespoons

12 ounces Monterey Jack cheese
12 ounces Cheddar cheese
1 bunch green onions
1 bunch cilantro
1 tomato
1 (4-ounce) can chopped mild green chiles
1 (16-ounce) bottle zesty Italian salad dressing

Approx
Per Tablespoon:
Cal 31
Prot 1 g
Carbo <1 g
T Fat 3 g
79% Calories
from Fat
Chol 5 mg
Fiber <1 g
Sod 95 mg

Shred the cheeses finely. Chop the green onions, cilantro and tomato. Combine the cheeses, green onions, cilantro, tomato and green chiles in a large bowl and toss to mix. Add the salad dressing and toss lightly. Serve with tortilla chips.

Kelly Justus
Accounts Receivable Accountant and Financial Aid Coordinator, 1993 to present

Chili Dip for Chips

This tastes much better than it looks. Serve with blue corn tortilla chips.

Yield:
60 tablespoons

8 ounces cream cheese, softened
1 (15-ounce) can chili without beans

1 (8-ounce) jar mild salsa

Approx
Per Tablespoon:
Cal 27
Prot 1 g
Carbo 1 g
T Fat 2 g
77% Calories
from Fat
Chol 6 mg
Fiber <1 g
Sod 65 mg

Heat the cream cheese in a saucepan over low heat for 1 to 2 minutes or until melted. Add the chili and salsa. Heat until well mixed and heated through, stirring constantly. Serve immediately.

Sue Waggener
Parent, Casey 2002 and Scott McCracken 2004

Cheese and Artichoke Dip

Yield:
40 tablespoons

1 (6-ounce) jar marinated artichoke
 hearts
8 ounces cream cheese, softened
1 (4-ounce) can chopped green
 chiles

1/2 cup sour cream
1/2 cup shredded Cheddar cheese
2 tablespoons hot sauce, or to taste

Approx
Per Tablespoon:
Cal 37
Prot 1 g
Carbo 1 g
T Fat 3 g
81% Calories
from Fat
Chol 9 mg
Fiber <1 g
Sod 101 mg

Place the artichoke hearts in a strainer and rinse under running water to remove the marinade. Pat dry with a paper towel and chop. Combine the cream cheese, chiles, sour cream, Cheddar cheese and hot sauce in a medium bowl and mix well. Mix in the artichokes. Spoon into a lightly greased 1-quart casserole. Bake at 350 degrees for 20 to 25 minutes or until bubbly. Serve hot with tortilla chips.

Gaylee Rogers
Parent, Sam 2008 and Mollie 2011

Crab Dip Olé

Yield:
90 tablespoons

2 (6-ounce) cans crab meat, drained
2 green onions, minced
1/2 cup minced cucumber
1/2 cup minced red onion
1 medium tomato, chopped
2 tablespoons minced cilantro
1/4 cup lime juice

1/4 cup lemon juice
1/4 cup orange juice
Salt and pepper to taste
16 ounces cream cheese, softened
1/4 cup reduced-fat mayonnaise
1 avocado, chopped

Approx
Per Tablespoon:
Cal 28
Prot 1 g
Carbo 1 g
T Fat 2 g
72% Calories
from Fat
Chol 8 mg
Fiber <1 g
Sod 28 mg

Combine the crab meat, green onions, cucumber, red onion, tomato and cilantro in a bowl. Mix the juices together and add to the crab meat mixture. Add salt and pepper and mix well. Refrigerate, covered, overnight. Blend the cream cheese and mayonnaise in a small bowl. Spread evenly over the bottom of a serving platter. Add a layer of avocado. Drain the crab meat mixture, pressing out as much liquid as possible. Spread over the avocado layer. Serve with tortilla chips. For a hotter dip, add minced jalapeños to the crab meat mixture.

Charlotte Garfield
Parent, Brian 2008 and Jim 1996

Guacamole

Yield:
60 tablespoons

4 avocados
1/4 cup finely chopped onion
1 1/2 tomatoes, finely chopped

1/2 to 1 whole serrano chile
Salt to taste

Approx
Per Tablespoon:
Cal 23
Prot <1 g
Carbo 1 g
T Fat 2 g
76% Calories
from Fat
Chol 0 mg
Fiber 1 g
Sod 2 mg

Cut the avocados into halves and scoop out the pulp; reserve the pits. Combine the avocado pulp, onion, tomatoes and chile in a bowl and mash with a potato masher until well mixed. Add salt. Place the pits in the avocado mixture to prevent browning. Cover tightly with plastic wrap and refrigerate until serving time.

Kris Ochoa-Keane
Parent, Christofer 1998 and Annette Ochoa 2008

Sour Cream Guacamole

Yield:
50 tablespoons

7 cloves of garlic
1 teaspoon (or more) salt
3 avocados
1/2 cup low-fat sour cream

Juice of 1 lemon
1 tomato, finely chopped
6 green onions, finely chopped
1 teaspoon (or more) Tabasco sauce

Approx
Per Tablespoon:
Cal 24
Prot <1 g
Carbo 1 g
T Fat 2 g
70% Calories
from Fat
Chol 1 mg
Fiber 1 g
Sod 50 mg

Chop the garlic finely and mash with the salt in a medium bowl. Cut the avocados into halves and scoop out the pulp; reserve an avocado pit. Mash the avocado pulp with the garlic mixture. Add the sour cream and lemon juice and mix well. Stir in the tomato, green onions and Tabasco sauce. Place the reserved avocado pit in the mixture to prevent browning. Cover tightly with plastic wrap and refrigerate until serving time. Serve with tortilla chips or taquitos. This dip is not for the timid.

Sam Goldberg
Parent, Aaron 2003 and Emily 2008

Guadalajara Guacamole

Yield:
32 tablespoons

3 avocados
2 tablespoons lemon or lime juice
1 teaspoon salt
1/2 medium onion, finely chopped

1 1/2 medium tomatoes, finely chopped
2 tablespoons (or more) green chile salsa

Approx
Per Tablespoon:
Cal 33
Prot <1 g
Carbo 2 g
T Fat 3 g
73% Calories
from Fat
Chol 0 mg
Fiber 1 g
Sod 82 mg

Cut the avocados into halves and scoop out the pulp; reserve an avocado pit. Mash the avocados in a bowl until slightly chunky. Add the lemon juice, salt, onion, tomatoes and salsa and mix well. Place the reserved avocado pit in the mixture to prevent browning. Cover tightly with plastic wrap and refrigerate until serving time. Serve with tortilla chips.

Gail Finegold
Parent, Jared 1997

Hummus

Yield:
100 tablespoons

2 (15-ounce) cans garbanzo beans
1 to 1¹/2 cups tahini
Juice of 3 to 4 lemons
2 to 3 teaspoons ground cumin

1 teaspoon (about) garlic salt
2 tablespoons olive oil
¹/2 to ³/4 cup water

Approx
Per Tablespoon:
Cal 35
Prot 1 g
Carbo 3 g
T Fat 3 g
60% Calories
from Fat
Chol 0 mg
Fiber 1 g
Sod 44 mg

Process the garbanzo beans in a food processor until puréed. Add the tahini, lemon juice, cumin and garlic salt gradually, tasting frequently to adjust the seasonings. Add the olive oil. Add the water ¹/4 cup at a time, processing until thick and smooth, not runny. Spoon into a serving bowl. Refrigerate, tightly covered, for several hours to overnight to allow flavors to meld. Serve with pita bread cut into quarters and assorted bite-size fresh vegetables for dipping. Garnish with parsley.

Moira Solomon
Parent, Jesse 1997 and Quinn 1999

Pesto Dip

Yield:
30 tablespoons

¹/4 cup grated Parmesan cheese
2 large cloves of garlic
¹/3 cup chopped parsley
2 sprigs of fresh basil
1 teaspoon salt

¹/2 teaspoon pepper
2 eggs
2 tablespoons lemon juice
¹/2 cup olive oil
¹/2 cup vegetable oil

Approx
Per Tablespoon:
Cal 74
Prot 1 g
Carbo <1 g
T Fat 8 g
94% Calories
from Fat
Chol 15 mg
Fiber <1 g
Sod 98 mg

Combine the cheese, garlic, parsley, basil, salt and pepper in a food processor and pulse until mixed. Add the eggs, lemon juice and 1 tablespoon of the olive oil and process until mixed. Add the remaining oil in a fine stream, processing constantly until the mixture is the consistency of mayonnaise. Spoon into a serving bowl. Refrigerate, tightly covered, for several hours. Serve with assorted bite-size fresh vegetables for dipping. May use egg substitute for fresh eggs but the thickness of the dip will be slightly reduced.

Rebecca Wood, 1970

The Best Seven-Layer Dip

Yield:
80 tablespoons

1 (12-ounce) carton frozen
  guacamole, thawed
1/2 envelope taco seasoning mix
1 cup sour cream
1 cup shredded mild Cheddar cheese
1 cup shredded Monterey Jack
  cheese

2 or 3 Roma tomatoes, finely
  chopped
Tops of 2 green onions, finely
  chopped
1/4 cup sliced black olives

Approx
Per Tablespoon:
Cal 24
Prot 1 g
Carbo 1 g
T Fat 2 g
73% Calories
from Fat
Chol 4 mg
Fiber <1 g
Sod 39 mg

Spread the guacamole evenly in a shallow serving dish. Blend the seasoning mix with the sour cream and spread over the guacamole layer. Add layers of the cheeses, tomatoes, green onions and olives. Serve immediately or cover tightly with plastic wrap and refrigerate until serving time. Serve with tortilla chips.

Barbara Mulligan
Parent, Matthew 2007 and Amanda 2009

Homemade Mexican Salsa

Yield:
64 tablespoons

1 large onion, chopped
1/2 cup (or more) fresh lemon juice
1/4 teaspoon salt

1/4 small head cabbage, chopped
3/4 cup chopped cilantro
4 tomatoes, chopped

Approx
Per Tablespoon:
Cal 4
Prot <1 g
Carbo 1 g
T Fat <1 g
8% Calories
from Fat
Chol 0 mg
Fiber <1 g
Sod 10 mg

Place the onion in a bowl. Add the lemon juice and salt and mix well. Let stand for 30 minutes or longer. Add the cabbage, cilantro and tomatoes. Add additional lemon juice if desired. Mix well and store, tightly covered, in the refrigerator. Serve with tacos, enchiladas or other Mexican dishes or with tortilla chips.

Cameron Volker, 1972
Parent, John 2010

Mango and Papaya Salsa

Serve with tortilla chips, as a topping for scrambled eggs or Mexican omelet, or as an accompaniment with grilled chicken or fish.

Yield:
64 tablespoons

Approx
Per Tablespoon:
Cal 8
Prot <1 g
Carbo 1 g
T Fat <1 g
46% Calories
from Fat
Chol 0 mg
Fiber <1 g
Sod 79 mg

2 (4-ounce) cans chopped green chiles
3 medium tomatoes, peeled, seeded, chopped
1/2 papaya, peeled, seeded, chopped
1/2 mango, peeled, chopped
4 large green onions with tops, chopped

2 tablespoons olive oil
1 tablespoon red wine vinegar
1 teaspoon salt
1 teaspoon ground cumin
3 large cloves of garlic, minced
1/2 cup chopped cilantro

Combine the green chiles, tomatoes, papaya, mango, green onions, olive oil, vinegar, salt, cumin and garlic in a medium bowl and mix well. Refrigerate, tightly covered, until serving time. Stir in the cilantro just before serving.

Rebecca Wood, 1970

Saucy Dip for Shrimp or Vegetables

Yield:
30 tablespoons

1 cup mayonnaise
2 teaspoons lemon juice
1 teaspoon curry powder
1/2 onion, finely minced
1/2 teaspoon Worcestershire sauce

1/2 teaspoon Tabasco sauce
1/4 cup chili sauce
1/4 teaspoon (or more) salt
Pepper to taste

Approx
Per Tablespoon:
Cal 57
Prot <1 g
Carbo 1 g
T Fat 6 g
94% Calories
from Fat
Chol 5 mg
Fiber <1 g
Sod 91 mg

Blend the mayonnaise with the lemon juice in a small bowl. Add the curry powder, onion, Worcestershire sauce, Tabasco sauce, chili sauce, salt and pepper and mix well. Refrigerate, tightly covered, until serving time. Serve with cooked shrimp or bite-size fresh vegetables.

Don Leavenworth
Parent, Laurie 1970 and Julie 1973
Headmaster, 1957 to 1972

Basil Dijon Dip for Veggies

Yield:
50 tablespoons

1/4 cup red wine vinegar
2 tablespoons balsamic vinegar
1/2 cup olive oil
1 teaspoon salt
1 teaspoon cracked pepper

2 teaspoons Dijon mustard
3 or 4 cloves of garlic
2 cups fresh basil leaves
2 cups (about) fat-free sour cream

Approx
Per Tablespoon:
Cal 43
Prot 2 g
Carbo 4 g
T Fat 2 g
49% Calories
from Fat
Chol 0 mg
Fiber 2 g
Sod 61 mg

Combine the vinegars, olive oil, salt, pepper, mustard and garlic in a blender container. Process for several seconds. Add the basil leaves and process until puréed. Blend the desired amount of basil mixture with the desired amount of sour cream. Serve with assorted bite-size fresh vegetables.

Gloria Salem
Friend, Sanders 2001, Charlie 2004, and Amy Patton

Liptauer Cheese Spread

Yield:
20 tablespoons

8 ounces whipped cream cheese
1/2 teaspoon grated onion

Paprika to taste
1 (2-ounce) can flat anchovies

Approx
Per Tablespoon:
Cal 43
Prot 2 g
Carbo <1 g
T Fat 4 g
82% Calories
from Fat
Chol 15 mg
Fiber 0 g
Sod 139 mg

Combine the cream cheese, onion and paprika in a small bowl and mix well. Reserve 3 of the anchovies. Chop the remaining anchovies and mix into the cheese mixture. Spoon into a small serving dish. Decorate with the reserved anchovies. Refrigerate, tightly covered, until serving time.

Vera and Harry Rotenberg
Grandparents, David 1996 and Steven Seidman 2001

Baked Brie with Apples and Pecans

Yield:
50 servings

4 large Granny Smith apples
1/4 cup unsalted butter
6 ounces pecan pieces
3/4 cup packed light brown sugar
1/2 teaspoon cinnamon
1 (2-pound) round Brie cheese
6 sheets phyllo dough
4 to 6 tablespoons melted unsalted butter

Approx
Per Serving:
Cal 131
Prot 4 g
Carbo 7 g
T Fat 10 g
69% Calories
from Fat
Chol 24 mg
Fiber 1 g
Sod 114 mg

Peel the apples and cut into 1/8-inch slices. Melt 1/4 cup butter in a large skillet. Add the apples and pecans. Sprinkle with brown sugar and cinnamon and stir gently until the apples and pecans are coated. Cook over medium-high heat until the apples are tender and the apples and pecans are caramelized. Remove from heat and set aside. Wrap the Brie in 1 sheet of phyllo at a time, brushing with melted butter between sheets and turning the Brie over to wrap evenly. Do not be concerned if the edges are ragged. Place the wrapped Brie in a baking dish suitable for serving. Be sure that the dish is at least as deep as the side of the Brie. The Brie may be prepared in advance to this point and refrigerated before baking. Bake at 375 degrees for 12 to 15 minutes or until the Brie is soft and warm but not runny. Cover the Brie on top and around the side with the apple mixture. Serve immediately with croissant crackers or baguette slices.

Amy Haimsohn, 1984 to 1989

Crab Meat Appetizer Spread

Yield:
40 tablespoons

8 ounces cream cheese, softened
1 (6-ounce) can crab meat, drained
1/2 cup chili sauce

1 (4-ounce) can chopped green
chiles

Approx
Per Tablespoon:
Cal 28
Prot 1 g
Carbo 1 g
T Fat 2 g
64% Calories
from Fat
Chol 10 mg
Fiber <1 g
Sod 110 mg

Place the cream cheese on a serving plate. Combine the crab meat, chili sauce and chiles in a small bowl and mix well. Spoon over the cream cheese. Serve with plain crackers.

Pat Stickels
Nursery Teacher, 1991 to present

Olive Pecan Spread

Yield:
40 tablespoons

6 ounces cream cheese, softened
1/2 cup (or less) mayonnaise
1/2 cup chopped pecans
1 cup chopped pimento-stuffed
olives

2 tablespoons olive juice
Pepper to taste

Approx
Per Tablespoon:
Cal 49
Prot 1 g
Carbo <1 g
T Fat 5 g
92% Calories
from Fat
Chol 7 mg
Fiber <1 g
Sod 116 mg

Mash the cream cheese with a fork in a small bowl. Add the mayonnaise and blend well. Add the pecans, olives, olive juice and pepper and mix well. Place in a covered container in the refrigerator. The mixture will become firm with chilling and will keep well if you can find somewhere to hide it. Serve with crackers.

Mrs. Ralph S. Michael, Jr.
Grandparent, Kenner 2002

Salmon Cheese Pâté

Yield:
32 tablespoons

1 (7-ounce) can red salmon
8 ounces cream cheese, softened
1/4 cup crumbled bleu cheese
1 tablespoon grated onion
2 tablespoons chopped parsley

1 tablespoon lemon juice
1 teaspoon Worcestershire sauce
1/8 teaspoon garlic powder
1/8 teaspoon pepper

Approx
Per Tablespoon:
Cal 40
Prot 2 g
Carbo <1 g
T Fat 3 g
77% Calories
from Fat
Chol 13 mg
Fiber <1 g
Sod 64 mg

Drain and rinse the salmon if desired. Flake the salmon in a small bowl. Add the cheeses, onion, chopped parsley, lemon juice, Worcestershire sauce, garlic powder and pepper and mix well. Press the mixture into a small bowl or decorative mold lined with plastic wrap. Chill for several hours or until firm. Invert onto a serving plate and remove the plastic wrap carefully. Garnish with parsley sprigs. Serve with crackers, toast rounds or rye bread.

Dorothy Trexel
Grandparent, Mandy 2010

Smoked Trout Pâté

This is a good substitute for gefilte fish at Passover.

Yield:
6 servings

1/2 red onion
3 hard-cooked eggs
4 (4-ounce) smoked trout fillets
1/2 cup mayonnaise

1 tablespoon minced fresh dill
Juice of 1/2 lemon
1 teaspoon Worcestershire sauce
2 tablespoons horseradish

Approx
Per Serving:
Cal 319
Prot 25 g
Carbo 2 g
T Fat 23 g
66% Calories
from Fat
Chol 179 mg
Fiber <1 g
Sod 1658 mg

Chop the onion in a food processor. Add the eggs and trout and process until finely chopped. Place in a medium bowl. Add the mayonnaise, dill, lemon juice, Worcestershire sauce and horseradish and mix well. Spoon into a small bowl or mold lined with plastic wrap and press firmly. Refrigerate, covered tightly with plastic wrap, for 24 hours. Unmold onto a serving plate and remove the plastic wrap carefully. Serve with matzo or plain crackers.

Julie Goldberg
Parent, Aaron 2003 and Emily 2008

Tuna Spread

Yield:
40 tablespoons

2 (6-ounce) cans water-pack tuna, drained
8 ounces cream cheese, softened
1 tablespoon chopped green onions

2 tablespoons chopped parsley
2 tablespoons chili sauce
1/2 teaspoon (about) Tabasco sauce

Approx
Per Tablespoon:
Cal 30
Prot 3 g
Carbo <1 g
T Fat 2 g
61% Calories
from Fat
Chol 9 mg
Fiber <1 g
Sod 57 mg

Combine the tuna, cream cheese, green onions, parsley, chili sauce and Tabasco sauce in a blender or food processor. Process until smooth. Spoon into a mold or small bowl lined with plastic wrap. Refrigerate, tightly covered, for three hours to overnight. Unmold onto a serving plate and remove the plastic wrap carefully. Serve with thin slices of Italian bread or crackers.

Gail Finegold
Parent, Jared 1997

Mushroom Starter

This is a perfect appetite enhancer from France. It is stimulating to the taste buds but you must enjoy garlic! Use a mixture of different mushrooms or just one type.

Yield:
6 servings

3 cups thinly sliced rinsed mushrooms
1 cup sour cream
1 teaspoon lemon juice

6 to 8 medium cloves of garlic, grated
Cracked pepper to taste

Approx
Per Serving:
Cal 97
Prot 2 g
Carbo 5 g
T Fat 8 g
73% Calories
from Fat
Chol 17 mg
Fiber 1 g
Sod 23 mg

Combine the mushrooms, sour cream, lemon juice, garlic and pepper in a bowl and mix gently. Refrigerate, covered, for 2 to 4 hours. Spoon onto small salad plates. Garnish with fresh parsley.

Joy Davis
Associate Director of Admissions, 1991 to present

Gravlax

This very Scandinavian dish is commonly eaten at midsummer. It is usually served as a part of a smorgasbord or an appetizer in two- or three-slice portions.

Yield:
variable

3 pounds center-cut salmon fillet,
  cut in half lengthwise
1 large bunch fresh dill
1/4 cup coarse salt

1/4 cup sugar
2 tablespoons crushed white or
  black peppercorns
Mustard Dill Sauce

Nutritional information for Gravlax is not available.

Place half the salmon skin side down in a deep glass dish. Rinse the dill and pat dry. Place on the salmon. Mix the salt, sugar and crushed peppercorns in a small bowl. Sprinkle evenly over the dill. Top with the remaining salmon skin side up. Cover with foil. Place a platter on top and add weights. Marinate in the refrigerator for 3 days, turning the salmon every 12 hours and basting with the juices. Remove the seasonings. Slice the salmon diagonally into thin slices. Serve with Mustard Dill Sauce.

Mustard Dill Sauce

Yield:
12 tablespoons

1/4 cup spicy dark prepared mustard
1 teaspoon dry mustard
3 tablespoons sugar

2 tablespoons white vinegar
1/3 cup vegetable oil
3 tablespoons chopped fresh dill

Approx
Per Tablespoon:
Cal 80
Prot <1 g
Carbo 6 g
T Fat 6 g
71% Calories
from Fat
Chol <1 mg
Fiber <1 g
Sod 68 mg

Combine the prepared and dry mustards in a small bowl and blend well. Add the sugar and vinegar and mix until a thick paste forms. Add the oil gradually, whisking until a thick mayonnaise-like emulsion forms. Stir in the dill. Refrigerate, tightly covered, for several days. Mix well before serving with gravlax or other cold seafood.

Diane and Peter Mothander
Parents, Matthew 2001, Eric 2005 and David 2009
Diane, Director of Admissions, 1996 to present

Sausage and Sauerkraut

Yield:
12 servings

2 pounds kielbasa or sweet Polish
  sausage
1 large onion, coarsely chopped
1½ pounds bacon, cut into 1-inch
  pieces

1½ heads green cabbage, shredded
3 to 4 tablespoons water
2 cups dark raisins

**Approx
Per Serving:
Cal 323
Prot 13 g
Carbo 27 g
T Fat 19 g
52% Calories
from Fat
Chol 40 mg
Fiber 4 g
Sod 705 mg**

Slice the sausage into ⅛-inch slices and place in a large saucepan with water to cover. Bring to a simmer. Simmer over medium heat for 15 to 18 minutes. Drain and set aside to cool. Combine the onion and bacon in a Dutch oven. Cook until the onion is transparent and the bacon is cooked but not crisp. Drain well. Add the cabbage to the bacon mixture. Stir in 3 to 4 tablespoons water or more if necessary. Cook for 30 minutes, stirring frequently. Add the raisins and mix well. Cook for 15 minutes. Add the sausage and mix well. Heat to serving temperature. Spoon into a large serving bowl. Serve with small plates and forks with assorted mustards on the side.

Rita Gittes
Parent, Robert 1999

Chicken and Cheese Roll-Ups

Yield:
24 servings

16 ounces cream cheese, softened
½ cup shredded Cheddar cheese
1 bunch green onions, chopped
4½ ounces black olives, chopped

2½ ounces chopped green chiles
2 cups chopped cooked chicken
12 flour tortillas

**Approx
Per Serving:
Cal 220
Prot 8 g
Carbo 21 g
T Fat 11 g
46% Calories
from Fat
Chol 32 mg
Fiber 2 g
Sod 333 mg**

Combine the cream cheese, Cheddar cheese, green onions, olives and green chiles in a bowl and mix well. Stir in the chicken. Spread the chicken mixture on the tortillas and roll up as for a jellyroll to enclose the filling. Arrange on a plate and cover with a damp towel. Wrap tightly in plastic wrap. Refrigerate for several hours. Cut into ½-inch slices just before serving and arrange on a serving plate. Serve at room temperature.

Jenn Buckner
Parent, Hillary 2007 and Trent 2010

Curried Chicken Wraps

Yield:
12 servings

3/4 cup mayonnaise
1 1/2 tablespoons fresh lemon juice
1 1/2 teaspoons curry powder
1/2 teaspoon salt
1/4 teaspoon pepper
2 cups coarsely chopped cooked
  chicken breast

1/2 cup chopped green onions
1/2 cup chopped green bell pepper
1/2 cup golden raisins
6 (10-inch) flour tortillas
1/2 cup chopped peanuts
1 cup alfalfa sprouts

Approx
Per Serving:
Cal 310
Prot 12 g
Carbo 27 g
T Fat 17 g
50% Calories
from Fat
Chol 30 mg
Fiber 2 g
Sod 363 mg

Combine the mayonnaise, lemon juice, curry powder, salt and pepper in a medium bowl and mix well. Stir in the chicken, green onions, green pepper and raisins. Spread the mixture on the tortillas, leaving a 1/2-inch border around the edges. Sprinkle with the peanuts and alfalfa sprouts. Roll as for a jellyroll to enclose the filling. Wrap in plastic wrap. Refrigerate for several hours. Cut into 3/4-inch slices using a serrated knife. Arrange on a serving plate.

Vina Saycocie
Director, Finance and Administration, 1982 to 1984

Vietnamese Gio Lua (Chicken Roll)

Yield:
12 servings

2 pounds boneless skinless chicken
  breasts
2 teaspoons sugar

2 teaspoons baking powder
1/4 cup fish sauce
1 tablespoon cornstarch

Approx
Per Serving:
Cal 89
Prot 16 g
Carbo 2 g
T Fat 2 g
19% Calories
from Fat
Chol 42 mg
Fiber <1 g
Sod 581 mg

Grind the chicken or cut into very small cubes. Combine with the sugar, baking powder, fish sauce and cornstarch in a bowl and mix well. Refrigerate, covered, for 3 hours. Place the mixture in a food processor and process until very sticky. Shape into a roll on plastic wrap, wrap in foil and tie securely with cotton string. Place on a rack over boiling water. Steam, covered, for 45 minutes. Cool. Store in the refrigerator. Slice or cut into cubes to serve as a cold meat.

Meiling C. Hager
Secretary, Lower School, 1991 to present

Cheesy Crab Toasts

Yield:
48 appetizers

1 (5-ounce) jar Old English cheese spread
1 (6-ounce) can crab meat, drained
1/2 cup butter, softened
Garlic powder to taste
Pepper to taste
6 English muffins
Minced parsley to taste

Approx
Per Appetizer:
Cal 45
Prot 2 g
Carbo 3 g
I Fat 3 g
56% Calories
from Fat
Chol 10 mg
Fiber <1 g
Sod 109 mg

Combine the cheese spread, crab meat, butter, garlic powder and pepper in a bowl and mix well. Split the muffins. Spread with the crab meat mixture and sprinkle with parsley. Cut into quarters and arrange on a baking sheet. Bake at 350 degrees for 5 minutes. Broil for 5 minutes or until light brown and bubbly. May freeze the muffin halves and store in plastic bags for later use. Cut into quarters, bake at 350 degrees for 10 minutes, then broil for 5 minutes.

Ellen Person
Parent, Jeff 2000

Crab Pizza

Yield:
12 servings

1/2 cup mayonnaise
1 teaspoon lemon juice
1/4 teaspoon curry powder
1/4 teaspoon salt
6 ounces crab meat, flaked
1 cup shredded Swiss cheese
1 (11-inch) baked pizza crust
1 tablespoon chopped green onions

Approx
Per Serving:
Cal 176
Prot 7 g
Carbo 9 g
T Fat 12 g
63% Calories
from Fat
Chol 25 mg
Fiber <1 g
Sod 235 mg

Combine the mayonnaise, lemon juice, curry powder and salt in a bowl and mix well. Add the crab meat and cheese. Place the pizza crust on a lightly greased baking sheet. Spread with the crab meat mixture. Sprinkle with the green onions. Bake at 450 degrees for 10 minutes or until the topping is puffed and brown. Cut into wedges and serve immediately.

Sally B. Huzyak, 1967

Baja Scallop Cocktail

Whitefish such as halibut or sea bass can be used for the scallops. For the squeamish, the scallops can be lightly parboiled before marinating.

Yield:
4 servings

8 ounces fresh scallops
1/2 cup fresh lemon juice
4 scallions
1 large avocado
2 tomatoes, seeded, coarsely
   chopped

1 jalapeño, finely chopped
1 bunch cilantro, coarsely chopped
3 to 4 ounces clam juice
Hot sauce to taste
Salt to taste
1 lime, cut into quarters

Approx
Per Serving:
Cal 160
Prot 7 g
Carbo 12 g
T Fat 11 g
56% Calories
from Fat
Chol 9 mg
Fiber 4 g
Sod 192 mg

Cut sea scallops into 1/4-inch dice; bay scallops may be left whole. Combine the scallops with the lemon juice. Marinate in the refrigerator overnight. Rinse the scallops, drain and pat dry. Slice the scallions diagonally into 1/4-inch pieces. Cut the avocado into 1/4-inch dice. Combine the scallops, scallions, avocado, tomatoes, jalapeño and chopped cilantro in a large bowl. Add the clam juice, hot sauce and salt and mix gently. Spoon into stemmed glasses. Add a lime wedge and garnish with cilantro leaves.

Dr. Terry Gulden and Renee Comeau
Parents, Stacey Gulden 2003

Spinach Rolls

Yield:
12 servings

1 cup sour cream
1 cup mayonnaise
1 1/2 ounces bacon bits
6 green onions, chopped

2 (10-ounce) packages frozen
   chopped spinach, thawed
6 (10-inch) flour tortillas

Approx
Per Serving:
Cal 317
Prot 7 g
Carbo 23 g
T Fat 22 g
62% Calories
from Fat
Chol 24 mg
Fiber 3 g
Sod 432 mg

Blend the sour cream and mayonnaise in a bowl. Add the bacon bits and green onions. Drain the spinach and squeeze dry. Add to the sour cream mixture and mix well. Spread the mixture over the tortillas and roll as for a jellyroll to enclose the filling. Wrap in plastic wrap. Refrigerate for 3 hours to overnight. Cut into slices and arrange on a serving plate.

Karen Stewart
Parent, Ty 1980 to 1993 and Tara 1999
Pre-Kindergarten Teacher, 1984 to present

Country French Wrap

This recipe was created at the request of Chicken of the Sea for their gourmet tuna by The French Gourmet.

Yield:
2 servings

2 teaspoons whole grain mustard
2 tablespoons mayonnaise
1 teaspoon chopped fresh basil
1 teaspoon chopped fresh dill
1 teaspoon chopped fresh rosemary

1 teaspoon chopped fresh parsley
1 (6-ounce) can tuna in olive oil, drained
1 (6-inch) whole wheat tortilla

Approx
Per Serving:
Cal 309
Prot 26 g
Carbo 10 g
T Fat 18 g
53% Calories
from Fat
Chol 25 mg
Fiber 1 g
Sod 527 mg

Blend the mustard and mayonnaise in a medium bowl. Add the herbs and mix well. Add the tuna and toss lightly; the tuna should remain in chunks. Spread on the tortilla and roll up to enclose the filling. Cut into bite-size pieces and place on a serving plate. Garnish with avocado slices, spinach leaves and chopped red tomato.

Michel and Lesa Malécot
Parents, Joshua Royle 2002

Monterey Artichoke Bake

Yield:
36 servings

2 (6-ounce) cans marinated artichoke hearts
1 small onion, finely chopped
1 clove of garlic, crushed
4 eggs, beaten
2 cups shredded Monterey Jack cheese

1/4 cup fine dry bread crumbs
2 tablespoons chopped green chiles
1/4 teaspoon salt
1/4 teaspoon each crushed dried basil leaves and oregano leaves
1/8 teaspoon pepper

Approx
Per Serving:
Cal 45
Prot 3 g
Carbo 2 g
T Fat 3 g
63% Calories
from Fat
Chol 29 mg
Fiber <1 g
Sod 113 mg

Drain the artichokes, reserving 1 tablespoon of the marinade. Sauté the onion and garlic in the reserved marinade in a skillet until tender. Mix the artichokes, sautéed mixture, eggs and remaining ingredients. Spoon into a greased 8-inch-square baking pan. Bake at 325 degrees for 25 to 30 minutes or until golden brown and firm. Cut into squares. Serve hot or cold.

Keith Heldman
Parent, Jennifer 1982, Sean 1985 and Noah 1990
Director, Fine Arts Department, 1968 to present

Artichoke Frittatas

In the sixties when LJCDS was located on Fay I purchased artichoke frittatas from the C & M Market on Girard. This is my version of those tasty delights.

Yield:
75 appetizers

2 (8-ounce) cans artichokes
Juice of 1 lemon
3 slices bread, toasted
10 eggs
1/4 cup milk

Salt and pepper to taste
1 onion, chopped
1/4 cup chopped parsley
1/2 cup grated Parmesan cheese
Vegetable oil for deep-frying

Approx
Per Appetizer:
Cal 20
Prot 1 g
Carbo 1 g
T Fat 1 g
43% Calories
from Fat
Chol 29 mg
Fiber <1 g
Sod 46 mg

Combine the artichokes and lemon juice in a saucepan. Simmer just until the artichokes are tender. Drain and cool. Cut the toast into 1/4-inch cubes. Cut the artichokes into 1/4-inch pieces. Beat the eggs with the milk, salt and pepper. Add the toast, artichokes, onion, parsley and cheese and mix well. Preheat oil in a deep pan. Drop the artichoke mixture by spoonfuls into hot oil. Deep-fry until brown, turning as necessary. Drain on paper towels.

Nutritional information does not include oil for deep-frying.

Janice Batter, 1965
Parent, Juliet 2001 and Jeremy 2005
Board of Trustees, 1989 to 1998

Baked Pecans

Yield:
8 servings

1 pound pecan halves
1/4 cup butter

Salt to taste

Approx
Per Serving:
Cal 429
Prot 5 g
Carbo 10 g
T Fat 44 g
87% Calories
from Fat
Chol 16 mg
Fiber 4 g
Sod 59 mg

Spread the pecans in a single layer in a 9x13-inch baking pan. Bake at 325 degrees for 30 minutes or until dry. Dot the pecans with the butter. Bake until the butter melts and sprinkle with salt. Bake for 1 hour longer, stirring the pecans and sprinkling with additional salt every 15 minutes. Spread on paper towels to cool.

Jo Ann DeMartini
Director of Athletics and Physical Education, 1992 to present

Appetizers

Tiropetes

This recipe is presented in honor of my mother, Nota Solomos, who teaches Greek cooking classes.

Yield:
100 appetizers

8 ounces phyllo dough
1 cup melted butter
Four-Cheese Filling

Approx
Per Appetizer:
Cal 39
Prot 1 g
Carbo 1 g
T Fat 3 g
71% Calories
from Fat
Chol 17 mg
Fiber <1 g
Sod 78 mg

Let the wrapped phyllo stand at room temperature. Unwrap, cover with waxed paper and a damp towel to prevent drying. Place 1 sheet of phyllo at a time on the work surface and brush with melted butter. Cut the phyllo horizontally into 5 strips. Place a small spoonful of Four-Cheese Filling at the end of a strip, fold the phyllo over the filling about 1/2 inch and roll up; the finished roll should resemble a cigar. Place on a baking sheet and brush with additional melted butter. Repeat with the remaining phyllo, filling and melted butter. Bake at 375 degrees for 20 minutes or until golden brown. Tiropetes may be frozen before baking. Use waxed paper between layers to prevent sticking together.

Four-Cheese Filling

4 eggs
8 ounces feta cheese, crumbled
8 ounces dry curd cottage cheese
4 ounces bleu cheese, crumbled
1/4 cup grated Parmesan or Romano cheese
1/8 teaspoon pepper

Beat the eggs in a large mixer bowl. Add the cheeses and pepper and mix well. Note that there is no salt required; the cheeses provide enough.

Ann Brizolis
Parent, Alex 2001

Cold Dolmathes (Stuffed Vine Leaves)

You must use olive oil to avoid the flavor of congealed butter or other fat. It is best to prepare dolmathes the day before and store in a cool place outside the refrigerator. This Greek dish is relatively easy to prepare and a unique appetizer. The secret is to make them as small as possible with little wrapping.

Yield: 100
appetizers

1 jar California vine leaves
Rice Stuffing
2 cups stock or water

Juice of 1/2 lemon
1 tablespoon tomato purée

Approx
Per Appetizer:
Cal 19
Prot <1 g
Carbo 2 g
T Fat 1 g
52% Calories
from Fat
Chol 0 mg
Fiber <1 g
Sod 31 mg

Rinse the leaves by dropping into hot water quickly to remove the brine and drain well. Reserve any torn or undesirable leaves. Cover the bottom of a large skillet with some of the reserved leaves. Place a teaspoon of Rice Stuffing on each of the remaining leaves. Roll up into a neat roll about 1 1/2 inches long and 1 inch in diameter, tucking in the leaf edges while rolling. Arrange in the prepared skillet, packing tightly to avoid movement while cooking and adding reserved leaves to separate layers of dolmathes. Add the stock. Cover the layers with a plate and then cover the skillet with the lid. Cook over very low heat for 2 hours. Serve cold with net-wrapped lemon halves or sprinkle with fresh lemon juice to taste just before serving.

Rice Stuffing

1/2 cup olive oil
2 onions, chopped
1 cup rice
1 cup boiling water
1 tablespoon tomato purée
1 tablespoon currants

1 tablespoon pine nuts
1 tablespoon chopped fresh mint
1 teaspoon chopped fresh sage
1 teaspoon sugar
Salt and pepper to taste

Heat the olive oil in a medium skillet. Add the onions and sauté until light brown. Add the rice. Cook over low heat for 20 minutes, stirring frequently. Add the water, tomato purée, currants, pine nuts, mint, sage, sugar, salt and pepper and mix well. Cook, covered, for 20 minutes or until the liquid is absorbed. Let stand in the skillet until completely cooled.

Patricia Wild
History, Middle School, 1977 to present

Salads and Soups

No one can "get" an education, for of necessity,
education is a continuing process.

Louis L'Amour,
Education of a Wandering Man, (1989)

Salads and Soups

Mandarin Orange Gelatin Salad

Yield:
10 servings

1 (6-ounce) package orange gelatin
2 cups boiling water
1 (12-ounce) can frozen orange
    juice concentrate, thawed

2 (9-ounce) cans crushed pineapple
2 (11-ounce) cans mandarin
    oranges
1/4 cup lemon juice

Approx
Per Serving:
Cal 195
Prot 3 g
Carbo 49 g
T Fat <1 g
1% Calories
from Fat
Chol 0 mg
Fiber 1 g
Sod 44 mg

Dissolve the gelatin in the boiling water in a large bowl. Mix the orange juice concentrate with the undrained crushed pineapple. Stir into the dissolved gelatin. Drain the mandarin oranges, reserving 1 1/4 cups of the juice. Stir the oranges, reserved juice and lemon juice into the gelatin mixture. Chill until firm.

Cheryl Stewart
Parent, Meredith 2001 and Philip 2007

Special Raspberry Gelatin

Yield:
4 servings

1 cup applesauce
1 (3-ounce) package raspberry
    gelatin

1 (10-ounce) package frozen
    raspberries, thawed

Approx
Per Serving:
Cal 176
Prot 3 g
Carbo 44 g
T Fat <1 g
1% Calories
from Fat
Chol 0 mg
Fiber 4 g
Sod 50 mg

Heat the applesauce to the boiling point in a large saucepan. Add the gelatin and stir until dissolved. Remove from the heat. Stir in the raspberries. Pour into a gelatin mold. Chill until firm. Unmold onto a serving plate.

Sandra Peavey
Parent, Ryan 2001

Walt's Waldorf Salad

My dad made this up for Thanksgiving one year and it has become a favorite.

Yield:
12 servings

1 lemon
3 red apples
3 green apples
5 ribs celery, chopped
6 ounces walnuts, chopped

2 oranges, peeled, chopped
6 dates, pitted, chopped
1/4 cup cream cheese, softened
1/4 cup sour cream
2 tablespoons sugar

Approx
Per Serving:
Cal 187
Prot 3 g
Carbo 21 g
T Fat 12 g
52% Calories
from Fat
Chol 7 mg
Fiber 4 g
Sod 33 mg

Cut a slice from the lemon and add to about 2 cups water in a large bowl. Juice the remaining lemon and set aside. Core the apples, cut into bite-size pieces and place in the lemon water to prevent browning. Drain the apples and combine with the celery, walnuts, oranges and dates in a large bowl. Blend the cream cheese with the sour cream and sugar in a small bowl. Add the lemon juice to taste and mix well. Pour over the salad and toss to mix. Chill, tightly covered, until serving time.

Julie Sanderson
Parent, Jesse 1998 and Amy 1999

California Chicken Salad

Yield:
4 servings

1 large tomato, cut into wedges
2 cups torn greens
1 medium green bell pepper, cut
   into rings
1 1/2 cups cooked chicken strips
1 1/2 cups cooked green peas

1 teaspoon salt
Pepper to taste
1 small red onion, sliced
1 cup mayonnaise
1 teaspoon sugar

Approx
Per Serving:
Cal 572
Prot 18 g
Carbo 17 g
T Fat 48 g
76% Calories
from Fat
Chol 79 mg
Fiber 5 g
Sod 935 mg

Layer the tomato wedges, 1 cup of the greens, green pepper rings, chicken and peas in a 2 1/2-quart salad bowl. Sprinkle with salt and pepper. Separate the onion slices into rings and arrange over the layers. Add the remaining greens. Spread the mayonnaise over the greens, sealing to the bowl. Sprinkle with sugar. Chill, covered, overnight. Toss well just before serving.

Elizabeth Hill
Grandmother, Andrew 2009

Tropical Chicken

Yield:
3 servings

3 (6-ounce) chicken breasts
2 avocados
2 mangoes

Salt and pepper to taste
3/4 cup reduced-fat mayonnaise

Approx
Per Serving:
Cal 627
Prot 38 g
Carbo 43 g
T Fat 36 g
50% Calories
from Fat
Chol 108 mg
Fiber 9 g
Sod 396 mg

Cook the chicken in simmering water to cover for 40 minutes or until tender. Let cool for 10 minutes. Drain the chicken. Cut the chicken into 1-inch cubes, discarding the skin and bones. Cut the avocados into 1/2-inch cubes and the mangoes into bite-size pieces. Combine the chicken, avocados, mangoes, salt and pepper and mayonnaise in a bowl and toss to mix. Chill until serving time. Serve with your favorite bread and the cold version of Hot or Cold Carrot Soup (page 58).

Joel Salberg
Supervisor, Custodial Service, 1982 to present

Chicken and Cabbage Salad

Yield:
6 servings

1 large head cabbage, shredded
1 (3-ounce) package ramen noodles, crushed
1 bunch cilantro, chopped
1 bunch green onions, slivered
5 (4-ounce) boneless skinless chicken breast halves, cooked

1/2 cup vegetable oil
1/4 cup vinegar
2 tablespoons sesame oil (optional)
2 tablespoons sugar
White pepper to taste

Approx
Per Serving:
Cal 401
Prot 23 g
Carbo 24 g
T Fat 24 g
22% Calories
from Fat
Chol 52 mg
Fiber 6 g
Sod 129 mg

Shred the cabbage finely and place in a large bowl. Add the crushed ramen noodles, cilantro and green onions. Shred the chicken and add to the salad. Mix the vegetable oil, vinegar, sesame oil, sugar, white pepper and ramen noodle seasoning in a bowl. Pour about half the dressing over the salad and toss to mix. Chill the salad and dressing, tightly covered, for several hours to overnight. Add the remaining dressing and toss well just before serving. Serve at room temperature.

Nutritional information does not include ramen noodle seasoning packet.

Karen Morikawa
Parent, Evan 2006 and Megan 2008

Chinese Chicken Salad

This salad is adored by our faculty when served at Teacher Appreciation luncheons!

Yield: variable

Maifun noodles (rice sticks)
Peanut or corn oil for frying
2 (or more) chicken breasts, roasted
Snow peas
Scallions, chopped
Cilantro, chopped (optional)

Iceberg or other mild lettuce, torn
Walnuts or roasted peanuts, chopped
Sesame seeds, toasted
Oriental Dressing

Nutritional information for this recipe is not available.

Break up the noodles. Fry the noodles in very small batches in the oil in a large saucepan until the noodles are puffed and white and rise to the surface. Drain on paper towels and reserve. Shred the chicken. Remove stems and strings from the snow peas. Blanch for a few seconds in boiling water, rinse immediately under cold running water, drain well and cut into small pieces. Combine the chicken, snow peas, scallions, cilantro, lettuce, walnuts and sesame seeds in a large salad bowl. Add the desired amount of Oriental Dressing and toss to mix. Add the noodles, toss and serve immediately.

Oriental Dressing

1/4 cup sugar
1 1/2 teaspoons dry mustard
1/4 cup soy sauce
1/4 cup rice vinegar
1/2 cup vegetable oil

1/4 teaspoon Worcestershire sauce
1/8 teaspoon sesame oil
1 tablespoon Dijon mustard (optional)
Mayonnaise to taste (optional)

Mix the sugar and dry mustard in a small bowl. Add the soy sauce, vinegar, vegetable oil, Worcestershire sauce and sesame oil and whisk until well blended. Add Dijon mustard and mayonnaise if a creamier and slightly more tangy dressing is desired.

Joan Mann Chesner
Parent, Jonathan 2002
President, Parents' Association, 1997 to 1998

Chicken Chutney Salad

Yield:
4 servings

1 (8-ounce) can pineapple chunks
2 cups chopped cooked chicken
1/2 cup sliced green onions
1 cup sliced celery
Chutney Dressing
1/2 cup sliced almonds (optional)

Approx
Per Serving:
Cal 295
Prot 19 g
Carbo 28 g
T Fat 13 g
38% Calories
from Fat
Chol 62 mg
Fiber 2 g
Sod 464 mg

Drain the pineapple and slice the pineapple chunks if desired. Combine the chicken, pineapple, green onions and celery in a salad bowl. Add the Chutney Dressing and toss until well mixed. Chill, tightly covered, for several hours. Toast the almonds in a 350-degree oven for 2 minutes or until golden brown. Sprinkle over the salad just before serving.

Chutney Dressing

2/3 cup reduced-fat mayonnaise
1/2 teaspoon grated lemon peel
1/4 cup chopped chutney
2 tablespoons lemon juice
1 teaspoon sugar
1/2 teaspoon curry powder
1/4 teaspoon salt

Combine the mayonnaise, lemon peel, chutney, lemon juice, sugar, curry powder and salt in a small bowl and mix well.

Phyllis M. Crady
Wife of Ken Crady, Director, Middle School, 1990 to 1995
Director, Upper School, 1996 to 1998

Curried Chicken Salad

Yield:
20 servings

8 cups chopped cooked chicken
2 cups chopped celery
1 pound small seedless grapes
1 to 2 cups slivered almonds, toasted
1 (15-ounce) can sliced water chestnuts, drained
1 (8-ounce) can pineapple chunks, drained
Curried Dressing

Approx
Per Serving:
Cal 451
Prot 17 g
Carbo 11 g
T Fat 37 g
75% Calories
from Fat
Chol 66 mg
Fiber 3 g
Sod 303 mg

Combine the chicken, celery, grapes, almonds, water chestnuts and pineapple in a large bowl and toss lightly. Add the Curried Dressing and toss until coated. Chill for several hours to overnight.

Curried Dressing

3 cups mayonnaise
1½ teaspoons curry powder
1 teaspoon lemon juice
1 tablespoon soy sauce

Blend the mayonnaise with the curry powder, lemon juice and soy sauce in a small bowl.

Libby Keller
Music, Lower School, 1994 to present

La Jolla Country Day School received its charter in 1955 and moved to its present location in 1961. In 1964 the La Jolla Country Day School graduated its first senior class. On the campus today there are many second generation students who perpetuate and personify the academic and personal excellence which has become the hallmark of the La Jolla Country Day School.

Maifun Salad

Yield:
2 servings

2 ounces maifun noodles (rice sticks)
Vegetable oil for deep-frying
8 ounces cooked chicken, shredded
1 head lettuce, torn
2 tablespoons sesame seeds, toasted
4 green onions, chopped
1 (2-ounce) package sliced almonds
Ginger Dressing

Approx
Per Serving:
Cal 801
Prot 42 g
Carbo 38 g
T Fat 55 g
61% Calories
from Fat
Chol 85 mg
Fiber 9 g
Sod 1283 mg

Deep-fry the noodles a small portion at a time in hot oil until puffed and slightly golden. Drain well on paper towels. Combine the chicken, lettuce, sesame seeds, green onions, almonds and fried noodles in a bowl. Add the Ginger Dressing and toss lightly. Serve immediately.

Ginger Dressing

1/4 cup salad oil
1 tablespoon vinegar
1 teaspoon salt
1/2 teaspoon pepper
1 teaspoon freshly grated ginger, or to taste
Fresh lemon juice to taste

Combine the oil, vinegar, salt, pepper, ginger and lemon juice in a small bowl.

Nutritional information does not include oil for deep-frying.

Karen Morikawa
Parent, Evan 2006 and Megan 2008

Ensalada Caramba!

This marinated flank steak recipe from the kitchen of Chef Rojay is really just a fancied-up version of taco salad. It is so much better than those made with ground meat that I couldn't bring myself to give it the same name. It makes an excellent single-dish summer evening meal, preferably eaten just at sunset on the deck with your pals. The ingredients and proportions given are variable to individual preferences so consider those given as guidelines.

Yield:
6 servings

1 head butter lettuce
1/2 head romaine
1/2 head red-leaf lettuce
2 medium tomatoes
1 medium cucumber
1 avocado
1 (16-ounce) can pitted black olives

1 bunch cilantro
Marinated Flank Steak
1 1/2 cups shredded Monterey Jack cheese
1/2 cup chopped green onions
5 ounces (about) tortilla chips

Nutritional information for this recipe is not available.

Tear the lettuces into bite-size pieces. Cut the tomatoes and cucumber into chunks and spoon the avocado from the skin into chunks. Drain the olives on paper towels and chop the cilantro lightly. Combine the vegetables and the next 3 ingredients in a large salad bowl; toss lightly. Serve the tortilla chips with the salad or crush lightly and toss with the salad just before serving.

Marinated Flank Steak

1 (1 1/2- to 2 1/2-pound) flank steak
1 (16-ounce) can tomato sauce
1 (8-ounce) can stewed tomatoes
2 (7-ounce) cans medium-hot Herdez salsa casera
2 (7-ounce) jars salsa chile fresco

2/3 cup dry red wine
1/2 cup finely chopped onion
1/3 cup finely chopped cilantro
1 tablespoon freshly ground pepper
2 tablespoons crushed garlic
Salt to taste

Place the steak in a shallow dish. Mix the tomato sauce, undrained tomatoes, salsas, wine, onion, cilantro, pepper, garlic and salt in a bowl. Pour over the steak and turn to coat. Marinate, covered, in the refrigerator for 2 to 24 hours. Drain the steak and cook by the method you prefer to the desired degree of doneness. Cut the steak into thin slices diagonally.

Roger Weaver
Parent, Rachel 1985 and Annalisa 1988
Dean, English Department and Director, Upper School, 1971 to 1983

Grandma's Potato Mac Salad

Yield:
8 servings

3 medium unpeeled potatoes
1¹/₂ cups cooked salad macaroni,
   chilled
¹/₄ cup chopped celery
¹/₄ cup finely chopped onion
¹/₄ cup grated carrot

1 (6-ounce) can tuna, drained
¹/₂ teaspoon sugar
3 cups (or more) mayonnaise
¹/₂ cup frozen peas
6 hard-cooked eggs, cut into
   ³/₈-inch pieces

Approx
Per Serving:
Cal 799
Prot 14 g
Carbo 22 g
T Fat 72 g
82% Calories
from Fat
Chol 223 mg
Fiber 2 g
Sod 591 mg

Steam the potatoes in a steamer for 40 minutes or simmer in water in a saucepan for 30 to 40 minutes or until tender; drain. Let stand until cool. Peel and chop the potatoes into ³/₈-inch pieces. Chill in the refrigerator. Combine the macaroni, celery, onion, carrot, tuna and sugar in a bowl and mix well. Stir in the mayonnaise. Add the potatoes, peas and eggs and mix gently. Store, covered, in the refrigerator until serving time.

Karen Morikawa
Parent, Evan 2006 and Megan 2008

Asparagus Salad

Yield:
6 servings

2 envelopes unflavored gelatin
¹/₂ cup cold water
³/₄ cup sugar
1 cup cold water
¹/₂ cup vinegar
1 (15-ounce) can asparagus spears,
   drained, chopped

1 cup chopped celery
¹/₂ cup chopped pecans
2 teaspoons grated onion
2 pimentos, chopped
Juice of ¹/₂ lemon
¹/₄ teaspoon salt
6 lettuce leaves

Approx
Per Serving:
Cal 197
Prot 4 g
Carbo 33 g
T Fat 7 g
29% Calories
from Fat
Chol 0 mg
Fiber 2 g
Sod 378 mg

Soften the gelatin in ¹/₂ cup cold water. Bring the sugar, 1 cup cold water and vinegar to a boil in a saucepan, stirring frequently. Stir in the gelatin mixture. Let stand until cool. Stir in the asparagus, celery, pecans, onion, pimentos, lemon juice and salt. Spoon into a greased mold. Chill until set. Invert onto a lettuce-lined serving platter. Garnish with mayonnaise and paprika.

Virginia Bial
Fourth Grade, Lower School, 1993 to present

Broccoli Salad

This is an excellent potluck item. Leave out the bacon if desired or add just before serving.

Yield:
8 servings

Florets of 3 to 4 bunches broccoli
8 ounces bacon, crisp-fried, crumbled
1/2 cup raisins
1/2 cup sunflower kernels
1/2 red onion, finely chopped
1/2 cup nonfat mayonnaise
1/2 cup sugar
2 tablespoons cider vinegar

Approx Per Serving:
Cal 214
Prot 7 g
Carbo 28 g
T Fat 9 g
37% Calories from Fat
Chol 8 mg
Fiber 3 g
Sod 275 mg

Combine the broccoli, bacon, raisins, sunflower kernels and onion in a bowl and mix well. Mix the mayonnaise, sugar and vinegar in a bowl. Add to the broccoli mixture, stirring until coated. Chill, covered, for 3 hours to overnight. May substitute bacon bits for the crisp-fried bacon.

Nancy Nevin
Parent, Jonathan 1997 and Meredith 2000

Broccoli and Cauliflower Salad

Yield:
6 servings

Florets of 1 bunch broccoli
Florets of 1 head cauliflower
1/2 cup raisins
1/2 cup slivered almonds
10 slices crisp-fried bacon, crumbled
1 cup mayonnaise-type salad dressing
1/2 cup sugar
2 teaspoons vinegar

Approx Per Serving:
Cal 398
Prot 8 g
Carbo 41 g
T Fat 24 g
53% Calories from Fat
Chol 19 mg
Fiber 3 g
Sod 466 mg

Combine the broccoli, cauliflower, raisins, almonds and bacon in a bowl and mix well. Stir in a mixture of the salad dressing, sugar and vinegar. Chill, covered, for 1 hour or longer.

Margaret Yost
Grandmother, Stephanie 2008 and Jonathan Berger 2010

Caesar Salad

Yield:
4 servings

1 (2-ounce) can anchovies in oil
3 cloves of garlic
1/3 cup olive oil
Juice of 1 small lemon
1/4 teaspoon dry mustard
1/8 teaspoon Worcestershire sauce

1/8 teaspoon Tabasco sauce
2 heads romaine, chilled, torn into
  bite-size pieces
1 cup croutons
Grated Parmesan cheese to taste
Freshly ground pepper to taste

Approx
Per Serving:
Cal 238
Prot 7 g
Carbo 10 g
T Fat 20 g
72% Calories
from Fat
Chol 10 mg
Fiber 2 g
Sod 477 mg

Mash the anchovies in a bowl until of a pasty consistency. Crush the garlic into a large salad bowl. Add the anchovies, olive oil, lemon juice, dry mustard, Worcestershire sauce and Tabasco sauce and mix well. Add the romaine, croutons, cheese and pepper, tossing to coat. Serve immediately.

Judy Braunstein
Parent, Ali 2001

Caesar Salad Dressing

Yield:
20 tablespoons

1 (2-ounce) can flat anchovies
1 or 2 cloves of garlic
2/3 cup olive or corn oil
1 egg (optional)

3 tablespoons wine vinegar
Juice of 1 lemon
1 teaspoon Dijon mustard

Approx
Per Tablespoon:
Cal 72
Prot 1 g
Carbo <1 g
T Fat 7 g
92% Calories
from Fat
Chol 2 mg
Fiber <1 g
Sod 111 mg

Process the undrained anchovies and garlic in a food processor fitted with a steel blade until mashed. Add the olive oil, egg, wine vinegar, lemon juice and Dijon mustard. Process until blended. This recipe makes enough to dress 3 heads of romaine. Sprinkle the desired amount of freshly grated Parmesan cheese on top.

Joan Mann Chesner
Parent, Jonathan 2002
President, Parents' Association, 1997 to 1998

California Caesar Salad

Yield:
6 servings

1 1/2 heads romaine, torn into bite-size pieces
Croutons to taste (optional)
1/2 cup chopped drained marinated sun-dried tomatoes
1/4 cup freshly grated Parmesan cheese
1 avocado, chopped (optional)
6 to 8 ounces chilled cooked salad shrimp (optional)
California Caesar Dressing

Approx
Per Serving:
Cal 227
Prot 6 g
Carbo 5 g
T Fat 21 g
81% Calories
from Fat
Chol 10 mg
Fiber 2 g
Sod 396 mg

Place the lettuce in a salad bowl. Add the croutons, sun-dried tomatoes, cheese, avocado and shrimp. Drizzle with the California Caesar Dressing, tossing to coat. Serve immediately.

California Caesar Dressing

1 (2-ounce) can anchovies, drained
2 cloves of garlic
1/2 cup olive oil
1/4 cup fresh lemon juice
1/2 teaspoon Dijon mustard
1/2 teaspoon Worcestershire sauce
Coarsely ground pepper to taste

Process the anchovies and garlic in a blender until puréed. Add the olive oil, lemon juice, Dijon mustard and Worcestershire sauce, processing constantly until blended. Season with pepper. May be prepared several days in advance and stored, covered, in the refrigerator for up to 2 weeks.

Gail Finegold
Parent, Jared 1997

Janice's Wilted Cucumber Slices

Yield:
10 servings

1 cup white or cider vinegar
1/2 cup sugar
1/4 cup water

2 teaspoons salt
1 teaspoon white pepper
4 cucumbers, peeled, thinly sliced

Approx
Per Serving:
Cal 126
Prot <1 g
Carbo 31 g
T Fat <1 g
1% Calories
from Fat
Chol <1 mg
Fiber 1 g
Sod 486 mg

Bring the vinegar, sugar, water, salt and white pepper to a boil in a saucepan. Boil for 5 minutes, stirring occasionally. Remove from heat. Arrange the cucumbers in a bowl or jar. Pour the vinegar mixture over the cucumbers. Marinate, covered, in the refrigerator for 3 hours or longer. Drain just before serving. Garnish with fresh dillweed.

Amy Haimsohn, 1989

Jicama and Corn Salad

Yield:
6 servings

1 cup fresh corn kernels
1 cup chopped jicama
1 medium carrot, chopped
1/3 cup chopped red onion
6 tablespoons olive oil

2 tablespoons lime juice
2 tablespoons rice vinegar
2 tablespoons chopped fresh cilantro
1 teaspoon salt
1/4 teaspoon cayenne

Approx
Per Serving:
Cal 160
Prot 1 g
Carbo 9 g
T Fat 14 g
75% Calories
from Fat
Chol 0 mg
Fiber 2 g
Sod 397 mg

Combine the corn, jicama, carrot and red onion in a bowl and mix well. Stir in a mixture of the olive oil, lime juice, rice vinegar, cilantro, salt and cayenne. Chill, covered, for 1 hour or longer. The flavor is enhanced if the salad is chilled overnight. The vegetables should be chopped approximately the same size of the corn kernels.

Vera Osterland
Parent, Elissa 2005

Alice's Marinated Salad

This salad is just as exciting as Alice was; she ran off with her lover and is no longer teaching math. Hooray for Alice!

Yield:
10 servings

Florets of 1 bunch broccoli
1 head cauliflower, chopped
2 cups diagonally sliced carrots
12 large mushrooms, cut into halves
1 large red bell pepper, chopped
1 (6-ounce) jar marinated artichokes, drained
1/4 cup chopped fresh basil
Salad Marinade

Approx
Per Serving:
Cal 206
Prot 3 g
Carbo 10 g
T Fat 18 g
76% Calories
from Fat
Chol 0 mg
Fiber 4 g
Sod 349 mg

Combine the broccoli, cauliflower, carrots, mushrooms, red pepper, artichokes and basil in a bowl and mix well. Add the Salad Marinade, tossing to coat. Marinate, covered, in the refrigerator for 6 hours or longer, stirring occasionally.

Salad Marinade

3/4 cup vegetable oil
1/4 cup plus 2 tablespoons red wine vinegar
2 large cloves of garlic, crushed
2 teaspoons sugar
1 teaspoon salt
1 teaspoon dry mustard
1/2 teaspoon pepper
1/2 teaspoon nutmeg

Combine the oil, wine vinegar, garlic, sugar, salt, dry mustard, pepper and nutmeg in a jar with a tightfitting lid. Cover the jar and shake to mix.

Jeannie Mershon
Parent, Chelsea Wonacott-Mershon 1997

Southwestern Layered Salad

Yield:
8 servings

1 (8-ounce) package corn bread mix
1 (4-ounce) can chopped green chiles
1/4 teaspoon fajita seasoning or taco seasoning
1 cup light sour cream
1 cup low-fat mayonnaise
1 envelope ranch-style salad dressing mix
2 (16-ounce) cans pinto beans, drained, rinsed
1 cup chopped green bell pepper
2 (15-ounce) cans whole kernel corn, drained
3 large tomatoes, chopped
10 slices crisp-fried bacon, crumbled
2 cups shredded Cheddar cheese
1 cup sliced green onions

Approx
Per Serving:
Cal 581
Prot 24 g
Carbo 65 g
T Fat 27 g
40% Calories
from Fat
Chol 72 mg
Fiber 11 g
Sod 1608 mg

Prepare the corn bread mix using package directions, adding green chiles and fajita seasoning. Let stand until cool. Crumble the corn bread. Combine the sour cream, mayonnaise and dressing mix in a bowl and mix well. Layer the corn bread, beans, sour cream mixture, green pepper, corn, tomatoes, bacon, cheese and green onions 1/2 at a time in a salad bowl. Chill, covered, for 2 hours.

Charlotte Garfield
Parent, Brian 2008 and Jim 1996

Mandarin Salad

Yield:
6 servings

1/2 cup sliced almonds
3 tablespoons sugar
1/2 head iceberg lettuce, torn into bite-size pieces
1/2 head romaine, torn into bite-size pieces
1 cup chopped celery
2 green onions, chopped
1 (11-ounce) can mandarin oranges, drained
Sweet and Hot Dressing

Approx
Per Serving:
Cal 211
Prot 3 g
Carbo 23 g
T Fat 13 g
54% Calories
from Fat
Chol 0 mg
Fiber 3 g
Sod 222 mg

Combine the almonds and sugar in a saucepan. Cook over medium heat until the almonds are glazed, stirring constantly. Let stand until cool. Store in an airtight container until needed. Combine the iceberg lettuce, romaine, celery, green onions and mandarin oranges in a salad bowl and mix gently. Add the almonds, drizzle with the Sweet and Hot Dressing and toss just before serving. May substitute 1/2 bunch spinach for the iceberg lettuce or romaine.

Sweet and Hot Dressing

1/4 cup vegetable oil
2 tablespoons sugar
2 tablespoons vinegar
1 tablespoon chopped fresh parsley
1/2 teaspoon salt
1/8 teaspoon pepper
1/8 teaspoon Tabasco sauce

Combine the oil, sugar, vinegar, parsley, salt, pepper and Tabasco sauce in a jar with a tightfitting lid. Shake to blend. Chill in the refrigerator.

Elizabeth Hill
Grandmother, Andrew 2009

Nola's Tossed Salad

For variety, substitute the dried cherries with any dried fruit. Try using cranberries at Thanksgiving.

Yield:
6 servings

4 ounces pecans
1 pound butter lettuce
2 medium red-skinned pears, chopped
6 ounces dried cherries
Parmigiano-Reggiano cheese to taste
Nola's Dressing

Approx
Per Serving:
Cal 416
Prot 4 g
Carbo 33 g
T Fat 31 g
66% Calories
from Fat
Chol 0 mg
Fiber 6 g
Sod 8 mg

Spread the pecans in a single layer on a baking sheet or in an ovenproof skillet. Toast at 350 degrees for 5 minutes, stirring frequently. Tear the lettuce into a large salad bowl. Add the pecans, pears and cherries. Shave the cheese with a small knife or vegetable peeler over the salad. Drizzle with the Nola's Dressing, tossing to coat.

Nola's Dressing

1/2 cup safflower oil
1/4 cup cider vinegar
Salt and freshly ground pepper to taste

Whisk the safflower oil and vinegar in a bowl until blended. Season with salt and pepper.

Amy Haimsohn, 1989

> To make a good salad is to be a brilliant diplomatist—The problem is the same in both cases. To know exactly how much oil one must put with one's vinegar.
>
> Oscar Wilde, playwright and author (1880)

Romaine and Walnut Salad

Great do-ahead salad dressing.

Yield:
6 servings

1 head romaine, torn into bite-size pieces
2 Red Delicious apples, chopped
4 ounces Gorgonzola or bleu cheese, crumbled
1/2 cup coarsely chopped walnuts, lightly toasted
Dijon Dressing

Approx
Per Serving:
Cal 284
Prot 7 g
Carbo 10 g
T Fat 25 g
76% Calories
from Fat
Chol 17 mg
Fiber 2 g
Sod 485 mg

Combine the lettuce, apples, cheese and walnuts in a salad bowl and mix well. Add the Dijon Dressing, tossing to coat.

Dijon Dressing

1/3 cup olive oil
1/4 cup white wine vinegar
2 teaspoons Dijon mustard
2 cloves of garlic, minced
1/4 teaspoon salt
1/4 teaspoon pepper

Whisk the olive oil, wine vinegar, Dijon mustard, garlic, salt and pepper in a bowl until mixed.

Kristin Gridley
Parent, Henry 2010 and William 2012

A child's education is a joint venture between the families of students and the school. La Jolla Country Day School believes this crucial partnership must be based upon trust, mutual respect, and a willingness to communicate. The tremendous success of the students from La Jolla Country Day is a testimonial to this joint venture.

Pear Florentine Salad

Yield:
6 servings

1/3 cup chopped walnuts
1 quart fresh spinach leaves, stems removed
1 1/2 heads iceberg lettuce, torn into bite-size pieces
2 large medium-ripe Anjou pears, sliced and cut into halves or chopped
Balsamic Dressing

Approx
Per Serving:
Cal 271
Prot 3 g
Carbo 17 g
T Fat 23 g
72% Calories
from Fat
Chol 0 mg
Fiber 4 g
Sod 224 mg

Arrange the walnuts in a single layer on a baking sheet. Toast at 350 degrees for 12 minutes. Let stand until cool. Mix the spinach and lettuce in a chilled salad bowl. Add the pears. Drizzle with the Balsamic Dressing, tossing to coat. Sprinkle with the walnuts. Serve Immediately.

Balsamic Dressing

1/2 cup vegetable oil
3 tablespoons lemon juice
2 tablespoons balsamic vinegar
3/4 teaspoon grated lemon peel
1/2 teaspoon salt
1/4 teaspoon basil
1/4 teaspoon tarragon
1/4 teaspoon sugar
1/8 teaspoon nutmeg
1/8 teaspoon pepper

Combine the oil, lemon juice, balsamic vinegar, lemon peel, salt, basil, tarragon, sugar, nutmeg and pepper in a jar with a tightfitting lid. Cover the jar and shake until mixed. Chill slightly.

Rita Gittes
Parent, Robert 1999

Spinach Salad

Yield:
8 servings

2 pounds fresh spinach, torn into bite-size pieces
1 (15-ounce) can French-style green beans, drained
1 (11-ounce) can mandarin oranges, drained
8 slices crisp-fried bacon, crumbled
2 hard-cooked eggs, chopped
Spinach Salad Dressing

Approx
Per Serving:
Cal 287
Prot 8 g
Carbo 13 g
T Fat 23 g
71% Calories
from Fat
Chol 58 mg
Fiber 4 g
Sod 754 mg

Mix the spinach, green beans, mandarin oranges, bacon and eggs in a salad bowl. Drizzle with the Spinach Salad Dressing, tossing to coat. Serve immediately.

Spinach Salad Dressing

2/3 cup salad oil
1/4 cup wine vinegar
2 tablespoons chablis
2 teaspoons soy sauce
1 teaspoon sugar
1 teaspoon dry mustard
1 teaspoon ground pepper
1/4 to 1 teaspoon curry powder
1/2 teaspoon salt
1/2 teaspoon garlic salt

Combine the salad oil, wine vinegar, wine, soy sauce, sugar, dry mustard, pepper, curry powder, salt and garlic salt in a jar with a tightfitting lid. Cover the jar and shake to mix. Chill slightly.

Ferne McCuen
Spanish, Upper School, 1980 to present

Sumi Salad

Yield:
10 servings

1/4 cup sliced almonds, toasted
1/4 cup sesame seeds, toasted
2 (3-ounce) packages ramen
   noodles, broken
1 head red cabbage, finely chopped
4 green onions, finely sliced
2 cups salad oil

3/4 cup sugar
2/3 cup cider vinegar
1 small white onion, chopped
2 to 3 tablespoons poppy seeds
2 teaspoons dry mustard
Salt to taste

Approx
Per Serving:
Cal 606
Prot 5 g
Carbo 34 g
T Fat 52 g
75% Calories
from Fat
Chol 0 mg
Fiber 3 g
Sod 69 mg

Toss the almonds, sesame seeds and ramen noodles in a bowl. Spoon into a container with a tightfitting lid. Mix the cabbage and green onions in a salad bowl. Whisk the remaining ingredients in a bowl until mixed. Add to the cabbage mixture, tossing to coat. Chill, covered, for several hours. Add the almond mixture just before serving and toss lightly. Serve immediately.

Nutritional information does not include ramen noodle seasoning packet.

Joan Faue-Durrant
Parent, Lara 2004

Potato Salad

Yield:
12 servings

8 to 10 medium unpeeled potatoes
1 1/2 cups chopped celery
1 1/2 cups chopped onions
2 dill pickles, chopped
8 to 10 hard-cooked eggs, chopped

3 cups mayonnaise
2 teaspoons (or more) prepared
   mustard
Salt and pepper to taste

Approx
Per Serving:
Cal 588
Prot 8 g
Carbo 29 g
T Fat 49 g
75% Calories
from Fat
Chol 217 mg
Fiber 3 g
Sod 523 mg

Combine the potatoes with enough water to cover in a saucepan. Cook just until tender; drain. Let stand until warm. Cut into chunks. Combine the warm potatoes, celery, onions and dill pickles in a bowl and mix well. Stir in the eggs. Spoon the mayonnaise on top of the potato mixture; top with the mustard. Stir until mixed. Season with salt and pepper. Chill, covered, until serving time.

Bonnie Robbins
Grandmother, Michael McKenna 2008

Garden Pasta Salad

Outstanding pasta recipe...gets even better the next day!

Yield:
8 servings

4 medium tomatoes, peeled, seeded, chopped
1 medium cucumber, peeled, seeded, chopped
1 small red or green bell pepper, chopped
1 slice red onion, separated into rings
1/4 cup fresh snipped parsley
Fresh Herb Dressing
8 ounces spaghetti
4 ounces feta cheese, crumbled

Approx
Per Serving:
Cal 241
Prot 7 g
Carbo 29 g
T Fat 11 g
39% Calories
from Fat
Chol 13 mg
Fiber 3 g
Sod 458 mg

Combine the tomatoes, cucumber, red pepper and red onion in a bowl and mix gently. Stir in the parsley. Add the Fresh Herb Dressing, tossing to coat. Chill, covered, for several hours to overnight. Cook the spaghetti using package directions; drain. Spoon into a pasta bowl. Top with the chilled tomato mixture. Sprinkle with the cheese.

Fresh Herb Dressing

1/4 cup salad oil
3 tablespoons dry white wine
2 tablespoons lemon juice
1 tablespoon sugar
1 teaspoon basil
1 teaspoon salt
1/4 teaspoon freshly ground pepper
1/8 to 1/4 teaspoon Tabasco sauce

Combine the salad oil, white wine, lemon juice, sugar, basil, salt, pepper and Tabasco sauce in a jar with a tightfitting lid. Cover and shake to mix.

Micki Mighdoll
Director, Student Support Services, 1989 to present

Tangy Pasta Salad

Great low-fat summer salad. Serve with grilled chicken, beef or pork.

Yield:
12 servings

1 (16-ounce) can artichoke quarters
1 (15-ounce) jar roasted red peppers
1/4 cup balsamic vinegar
Juice of 1 lemon
1 jalapeño, seeded, chopped
1 (3-ounce) package sun-dried tomatoes, chopped
12 ounces angel hair pasta
1/2 (4-ounce) can chopped black olives
1/2 cup chopped fresh basil
Salt and pepper to taste

Approx
Per Serving:
Cal 133
Prot 6 g
Carbo 25 g
T Fat 1 g
8% Calories
from Fat
Chol 0 mg
Fiber 2 g
Sod 478 mg

Drain the artichokes, reserving the liquid. Chop the artichokes. Reserve several of the red peppers and chop. Process the remaining red peppers, reserved artichoke liquid, balsamic vinegar, lemon juice and jalapeño in a food processor until puréed. Stir in the artichokes and sun-dried tomatoes. Cook the pasta using package directions until al dente. Drain and rinse with cold water. Combine the pasta and purée in a bowl and mix well. Stir in the reserved red peppers, black olives, basil, salt and pepper. Chill, covered, for several hours before serving.

Susan Taylor
History, Middle School, 1986 to present

La Jolla Country Day School is a coeducational, nonsectarian, college preparatory school located on 24 acres of beautiful tree lined campus. The stunning school setting is a perfect sequel to the surrounding city of San Diego, affectionately known as America's Finest City. San Diego is home to such world-renowned attractions as the San Diego Zoo, Balboa Park, the Salk Institute of Biological Research, the Old Globe Theater and La Jolla Playhouse, and Scripps Institute of Oceanography.

Wild Rice Salad

Yield:
12 servings

2 cups currants
4 carrots
5 ribs celery
1 each red and yellow bell pepper
1 medium red onion
1 shallot
2/3 cup chopped fresh parsley

1 pound wild rice, cooked
16 ounces pecans, chopped, toasted
1/4 to 1/2 cup olive oil
1/4 to 1/2 cup vegetable oil
1/4 to 1/3 cup balsamic vinegar
1 1/2 teaspoons (or less) pepper
Salt to taste

Approx
Per Serving:
Cal 585
Prot 10 g
Carbo 44 g
T Fat 44 g
65% Calories
from Fat
Chol 0 mg
Fiber 8 g
Sod 31 mg

Combine the currants with enough hot water to cover in a bowl. Let stand until plump; drain. Mince the carrots, celery, red pepper, yellow pepper, onion and shallot separately in a food processor until the pieces are approximately the size of rice grains. Drain if the vegetables appear watery. Combine the currants, vegetables, parsley, rice and pecans in a bowl and mix well. Whisk the olive oil, vegetable oil, balsamic vinegar, pepper and salt in a bowl. Pour over the rice mixture and mix well.

Jackie and Barry Seidman
Parents, David 1996 and Steven 2001

Curry Dressing for Spinach

Yield:
10 (2-tablespoon)
servings

2/3 cup olive oil
1/4 cup wine vinegar
2 tablespoons white wine
2 tablespoons sugar
2 teaspoons soy sauce

1 teaspoon dry mustard
1 teaspoon pepper
1/2 teaspoon salt
1/4 teaspoon curry powder

Approx
Per Serving:
Cal 143
Prot <1 g
Carbo 3 g
T Fat 15 g
91% Calories
from Fat
Chol 0 mg
Fiber <1 g
Sod 205 mg

Combine the olive oil, wine vinegar, white wine, sugar, soy sauce, dry mustard, pepper, salt and curry powder in a jar. Cover with a tightfitting lid, shaking to blend. Serve over torn fresh spinach. Garnish with chopped hard-cooked eggs, bacon bits and toasted pine nuts.

Marla Griswold
Grandmother, Claire 2007 and Ben Kaufman 2009

Anita's Zesty Spinach Salad Dressing

Yield:
16 (2-tablespoon) servings

1 cup salad oil
1/2 cup sugar
1/3 cup catsup
1/4 cup vinegar

1 onion, finely grated
Juice of 1/2 lemon
1 tablespoon Worcestershire sauce
1/2 teaspoon salt

Approx Per Serving:
Cal 155
Prot <1 g
Carbo 9 g
T Fat 14 g
78% Calories from Fat
Chol 0 mg
Fiber <1 g
Sod 144 mg

Combine the salad oil, sugar, catsup, vinegar, onion, lemon juice, Worcestershire sauce and salt in a jar. Cover with a tightfitting lid and shake to mix. Serve over fresh spinach. Garnish with hard-cooked eggs, bacon, mushrooms and almonds.

Virginia Erickson
French and Spanish, Middle School, 1980 to present

Avocado Soup

Yield:
3 servings

1 1/2 tablespoons onion soup mix
1 tablespoon sherry
1 chicken bouillon cube
2 tablespoons boiling water
2 medium ripe avocados, chopped

2 cups milk
1/3 cup chopped onion
2 tablespoons lemon juice
Salt and pepper to taste
1/2 cup croutons

Approx Per Serving:
Cal 367
Prot 10 g
Carbo 27 g
T Fat 27 g
62% Calories from Fat
Chol 23 mg
Fiber 8 g
Sod 961 mg

Combine the soup mix, sherry, bouillon cube and boiling water in a bowl, stirring until blended. Process the soup mixture, avocados, milk, half the onion, lemon juice, salt and pepper in a food processor for 1 minute. Chill, covered, for 2 hours. Stir in the remaining onion. Ladle into soup bowls. Top with croutons. May substitute 1 cup heated chicken broth for the chicken bouillon cube, decreasing the milk to 1 cup.

Meiling Hager
Secretary, Lower School, 1991 to present

Gazpacho

Yield:
8 servings

6 large ripe tomatoes, coarsely
   chopped
1 English cucumber, coarsely
   chopped
1/2 each red, yellow and green bell
   pepper, coarsely chopped
1 medium onion, coarsely chopped
3 cloves of garlic

1/2 cup red wine vinegar
1/2 cup olive oil
1 (32-ounce) can vegetable juice
   cocktail
Salt and freshly ground pepper
   to taste
Cumin to taste

Approx
Per Serving:
Cal 192
Prot 3 g
Carbo 16 g
T Fat 14 g
64% Calories
from Fat
Chol 0 mg
Fiber 3 g
Sod 321 mg

Reserve 1/3 of the tomatoes, cucumber and bell peppers. Process the
remaining tomatoes, remaining cucumber, remaining bell peppers, onion
and garlic in a food processor fitted with a steel blade until puréed. Add the
wine vinegar and olive oil. Process until blended. Pour into a large bowl.
Stir in the reserved tomatoes, reserved cucumber, reserved bell peppers,
vegetable juice cocktail, salt, pepper and cumin. Chill, covered, for 4 hours
or longer. Ladle into soup bowls. Garnish with sour cream. May store in the
refrigerator for up to 5 days. May substitute any combination of red, yellow
and green bell peppers, but include at least 2 varieties.

Lisa Braun-Glazer
Parent, Julia 2001

Hot or Cold Carrot Soup

Yield:
4 servings

1/2 red onion, chopped
2 tablespoons crushed fresh
   gingerroot
1 clove of garlic, minced

2 tablespoons butter
2 cups chicken or vegetable stock
3 or 4 carrots, peeled, thinly sliced
Salt and pepper to taste

Approx
Per Serving:
Cal 125
Prot 6 g
Carbo 10 g
T Fat 7 g
50% Calories
from Fat
Chol 17 mg
Fiber 2 g
Sod 795 mg

Sauté the onion, gingerroot and garlic in the butter in a saucepan until the
onion is tender. Add the chicken stock, carrots, salt and pepper. Simmer
until the carrots are tender. Pour into a food processor and process until
puréed. Return to the saucepan to heat to serving temperature if serving
warm; pour into a pitcher or bowl to chill until serving time if served cold.

Joel Salberg
Supervisor, Custodial Service, 1982 to present

Peach, Plum and Cranberry Soup

Yield:
12 servings

5 quarts cranberry juice
2 1/2 cups sugar
3/4 cup plus 3 tablespoons
   cornstarch
5 teaspoons cinnamon

5/8 teaspoon ground cloves
20 peaches or nectarines, thinly
   sliced
20 plums, sliced
5 lemons, thinly sliced

Approx
Per Serving:
Cal 580
Prot 2 g
Carbo 147 g
T Fat 1 g
2% Calories
from Fat
Chol 0 mg
Fiber 7 g
Sod 10 mg

Combine the cranberry juice, sugar, cornstarch, cinnamon and cloves in a stockpot and mix well. Bring to a boil, stirring constantly. Boil for 1 minute; reduce heat. Stir in the peaches, plums and lemons. Simmer, covered, for 10 minutes or until the fruit is tender, stirring occasionally. Chill, covered, in the refrigerator. Ladle into soup bowls.

Shelley Ackerberg-Patton
Parent, Sanders 2001 and Charlie 2004
Cookbook Editor

Navy Bean and Pasta Soup

Yield:
8 servings

1 pound dried navy beans
10 cups warm water
1 ham bone with meat or 2 ham
   hocks
2 medium onions, chopped
1 1/2 cups shredded potato
1 1/2 cups chopped celery

1/2 cup chopped celery leaves
1 (8-ounce) can tomatoes, drained
1 (6-ounce) can tomato paste
2 teaspoons salt
1/2 teaspoon pepper
16 ounces salad macaroni, cooked,
   drained

Approx
Per Serving:
Cal 518
Prot 25 g
Carbo 95 g
T Fat 5 g
8% Calories
from Fat
Chol 14 mg
Fiber 13 g
Sod 861 mg

Rinse and sort the navy beans. Combine the beans and warm water in a stockpot. Let stand for 8 to 10 hours. Add the ham bone, onions, potato, celery, celery leaves, tomatoes, tomato paste, salt and pepper and mix well. Bring to a boil; reduce heat. Simmer for 3 hours or until the beans are tender, stirring occasionally. Remove the ham bone and chop any ham attached to the bone. Return the ham to the stockpot. Stir in the pasta. Ladle into soup bowls.

Jackie and Barry Seidman
Parents, David 1996 and Steven 2001

Navy Bean Soup

This fat-free soup is served in the United States Senate Dining Room.

Yield:
6 servings

8 ounces dried navy beans
5 cups chicken stock
2 potatoes, cooked, chopped
1 cup chopped onion

1 cup chopped celery with leaves
2 cloves of garlic, crushed
1 sprig of fresh parsley, or
   1 teaspoon parsley flakes

Approx
Per Serving:
Cal 191
Prot 10 g
Carbo 37 g
T Fat 1 g
5% Calories
from Fat
Chol 1 mg
Fiber 7 g
Sod 594 mg

Rinse and sort the navy beans. Combine the beans with enough water to cover in a stockpot. Stir in the chicken stock, potatoes, onion, celery, garlic and parsley. Bring to a boil; reduce heat. Simmer for 2 hours or until the beans are tender, stirring occasionally. Ladle into soup bowls.

Helen Hauer
Grandmother, Dylan Brown 2003

Slow-Cooked Chili

Serve with rice or over a baked potato and don't forget the corn bread. Cut the fat grams by substituting ground turkey.

Yield:
6 servings

16 ounces ground veal
16 ounces lean ground beef
2 (16-ounce) cans red kidney beans,
   drained
2 (15-ounce) cans stewed tomatoes
1 medium onion, chopped

1 green bell pepper, chopped
1 teaspoon chopped garlic
3 tablespoons chili powder
1 teaspoon cumin
1 teaspoon pepper
Salt to taste

Approx
Per Serving:
Cal 485
Prot 41 g
Carbo 48 g
T Fat 15 g
28% Calories
from Fat
Chol 100 mg
Fiber 17 g
Sod 434 mg

Brown the ground veal and ground beef in a skillet, stirring until crumbly; drain. Layer the kidney beans, tomatoes, ground veal, ground beef and remaining ingredients in a slow cooker in the order listed. Cook, covered, on Low for 10 to 12 hours, stirring occasionally.

Michele Cass
Former Assistant to the Headmaster, 1986 to 1991

Cream of Chestnut Soup

This is a very rich cream soup. Excellent served during the winter holiday season.

Yield:
6 servings

1 medium onion, chopped
3 tablespoons butter
1 pound fresh chestnuts, shelled
1 large carrot, chopped
2¼ cups rich chicken broth
¾ cup light cream
¼ cup dry sherry
Salt and pepper to taste

Approx
Per Serving:
Cal 293
Prot 4 g
Carbo 32 g
T Fat 16 g
50% Calories
from Fat
Chol 49 mg
Fiber 6 g
Sod 368 mg

Sauté the onion in the butter in a heavy saucepan until light brown. Stir in the chestnuts, carrot and broth. Simmer for 20 minutes or until the chestnuts are tender, stirring occasionally. Process the chestnut mixture in small batches in a food processor until puréed. Combine the purée with the cream and sherry in a saucepan and mix well. Simmer just until heated through, stirring frequently; do not boil. Season with salt and pepper. Ladle into soup bowls. Garnish each serving with lightly salted whipped cream, paprika and a sprig of fresh parsley. Pass a cruet of sherry for those who desire extra flavoring. To shell chestnuts, slit convex sides with a knife. Bake the chestnuts in an oiled pan at 450 degrees for 5 to 6 minutes. Cool slightly. Remove the shells and skins. May substitute an 8- to 10-ounce jar of vacuum-packed chestnuts if fresh chestnuts are not available.

Nancy James
Parent, Jonathan 2004

Eggplant Soup

Serve with a green salad, garlic toast and fresh fruit for a hearty meal.

Yield:
16 servings

8 cups water
5 tablespoons beef stock base
1$^{1}/_{2}$ pounds ground round
2 onions, finely chopped
1 tablespoon olive oil
1 tablespoon margarine
3 cups finely chopped carrots
3 cups finely chopped celery
2 eggplant, peeled, cut into $^{1}/_{2}$-inch slices, cut into $^{1}/_{2}$-inch pieces
3 cloves of garlic, minced
1 (46-ounce) can chopped tomatoes
1 teaspoon pepper
1 teaspoon nutmeg
1 cup noodles or macaroni
8 ounces Cheddar cheese, shredded
$^{1}/_{2}$ cup chopped fresh parsley

Approx
Per Serving:
Cal 236
Prot 16 g
Carbo 15 g
T Fat 13 g
49% Calories
from Fat
Chol 48 mg
Fiber 4 g
Sod 1095 mg

Combine the water and beef stock base in a stockpot and mix well. Brown the ground round in a skillet, stirring until crumbly; drain. Stir into the stock mixture. Sauté the onions in a mixture of the olive oil and margarine in a skillet until tender. Add to the stock mixture. Stir in the carrots, celery, eggplant and garlic. Add the undrained tomatoes, pepper and nutmeg and mix well. Bring to a boil; reduce heat. Simmer, covered, for 1 hour or until of the desired consistency, stirring occasionally. Add the noodles. Cook for 15 minutes or until the noodles are tender, stirring occasionally. Ladle into soup bowls. Sprinkle with the cheese and parsley.

Frances Frace
Grandmother, Christopher 2007

Lentil Soup

Healthy and delicious. Serve with a tossed green salad.

Yield:
10 servings

2 cups lentils
10 cups water
5 carrots, sliced
4 onions, chopped

3 ribs celery, sliced
15 cloves of garlic, minced
Salt to taste

Approx
Per Serving:
Cal 157
Prot 10 g
Carbo 30 g
T Fat 1 g
3% Calories
from Fat
Chol 0 mg
Fiber 11 g
Sod 27 mg

Sort and rinse the lentils. Combine the lentils, water, carrots, onions, celery, garlic and salt in a stockpot. Bring to a boil; reduce heat. Simmer for 2 to 3 hours or until the lentils are tender, stirring occasionally. Ladle into soup bowls.

Judy Braunstein
Parent, Ali 2001

Low-Fat Lentil Soup

Yield:
8 servings

1 cup dried lentils
2 quarts water
1¹/2 cups chopped onions
1¹/2 cups chopped carrots
1¹/2 cups chopped potatoes
1 cup chopped tomato

³/4 cup sliced mushrooms
¹/2 cup brown rice
4 vegetable bouillon cubes
1 teaspoon cumin, or to taste
Salt and pepper to taste

Approx
Per Serving:
Cal 166
Prot 8 g
Carbo 33 g
T Fat 1 g
4% Calories
from Fat
Chol <1 mg
Fiber 8 g
Sod 29 mg

Sort and rinse the lentils. Combine the lentils, water, onions, carrots, potatoes, tomato, mushrooms, rice, bouillon, cumin, salt and pepper in a stockpot and mix well. Bring to a boil; reduce heat to low. Cook, covered, for 1¹/2 hours, stirring occasionally. Ladle into soup bowls.

Michele Zousmer
Parent, Alexandra 2002 and Maxwell 2005

Lentil and Barley Soup

Serve with crusty bread for a filling winter lunch or dinner.

Yield:
12 servings

1 cup lentils
1/2 to 1 cup barley
12 cups water
1 cup chopped carrot

1/2 cup chopped onion
Salt and pepper to taste
Garlic powder to taste

Approx
Per Serving:
Cal 114
Prot 6 g
Carbo 23 g
T Fat <1 g
3% Calories
from Fat
Chol 0 mg
Fiber 7 g
Sod 6 mg

Sort and rinse the lentils. Pour the barley into a stockpot. Add water to a depth of 1 inch. Let stand for 30 minutes; drain. Stir in the lentils and 12 cups water. Cook, covered, over low heat for 30 to 60 minutes, stirring occasionally. Mix in the carrot and onion. Cook for 1 hour longer, stirring occasionally. Season with salt, pepper and garlic powder. Ladle into soup bowls. Additional cooking time will produce a thicker soup. Add more barley if a thicker soup is desired and less barley for a thinner soup.

Helane Fronek
Parent, Jeffery 2006 and Lisa 2009

Sunday Opera Soup

Yield:
10 servings

1 1/2 cups lentils
8 cups chicken broth
1 (28-ounce) can chopped tomatoes
1 large potato, chopped
2 bunches red Swiss chard, chopped
1 large onion, chopped

1 bunch cilantro, chopped
3 cloves of garlic, crushed
2 to 3 tablespoons olive oil
3 to 4 tablespoons fresh lemon juice
1/2 teaspoon cumin
Pepper to taste

Approx
Per Serving:
Cal 196
Prot 12 g
Carbo 25 g
T Fat 6 g
25% Calories
from Fat
Chol 0 mg
Fiber 9 g
Sod 757 mg

Sort and rinse the lentils. Mix the lentils and chicken broth in a stockpot. Bring to a boil; reduce heat. Stir in the undrained tomatoes and potato. Simmer for 20 minutes, stirring occasionally. Add the chard and mix well. Simmer for 20 minutes or until the lentils are tender, stirring occasionally. Sauté the onion, cilantro and garlic in the olive oil in a skillet. Add to the stockpot. Bring to a boil. Boil for 5 minutes, stirring occasionally. Stir in the lemon juice, cumin and pepper. Ladle into soup bowls.

Sharon Horan
Kindergarten, Lower School, 1971 to present

Soups

Pumpkin Bean Soup

Yield:
8 servings

3 (16-ounce) cans black beans, drained
1 cup chopped drained tomatoes
1¼ cups chopped red or yellow onions
½ cup minced green onions
4 cloves of garlic, minced
1 tablespoon plus 2 teaspoons cumin
1 teaspoon salt
½ teaspoon pepper
¼ cup unsalted butter
4 cups beef broth
1 (16-ounce) can pumpkin purée
½ cup dry sherry
8 ounces Canadian bacon, chopped
3 tablespoons wine vinegar
Salt and pepper to taste

Approx
Per Serving:
Cal 302
Prot 18 g
Carbo 38 g
T Fat 8 g
24% Calories
from Fat
Chol 26 mg
Fiber 15 g
Sod 1663 mg

Process the beans and tomatoes in a food processor until puréed. Sauté the onions, green onions, garlic, cumin, salt and pepper in the butter in a stockpot over medium heat until the onions are tender and light brown. Stir in the bean mixture. Add the broth, pumpkin and sherry and mix well. Simmer for 25 minutes or until the soup coats the back of a spoon, stirring occasionally. Add the bacon and wine vinegar just before serving. Simmer just until heated through. Season with salt and pepper. Ladle into soup bowls. Garnish with sour cream and toasted pumpkin seeds.

Charlotte Garfield
Parent, Brian 2008 and Jim 1996

The original inhabitants of the San Diego area were approximately thirty nomadic hunting and gathering clans of Native Americans. They inhabited the area known today as Old Town and were referred to as San Dieguenos.

Soupe au Pistou

Adapted from a traditional Provençal recipe given to me by my neighbor, Christine Farget of Cavaillon, France.

Yield:
10 servings

1/4 cup olive oil
4 leeks, trimmed, minced
4 large carrots, peeled, cut into 1/2-inch slices
2 ribs celery, trimmed, cut diagonally into 1/2-inch slices
6 cloves of garlic, minced
2 large potatoes, peeled, cut into 1/2-inch pieces
3 cups fresh shell beans (red or white haricots)

12 cups water
1 (16-ounce) can stewed chopped tomatoes
Salt and pepper to taste
8 ounces haricots verts, trimmed, cut into 1-inch pieces
16 ounces zucchini, cut into 1/3-inch pieces
5 ounces small pasta
Le Pistou

Approx
Per Serving:
Cal 508
Prot 21 g
Carbo 75 g
T Fat 16 g
27% Calories from Fat
Chol 4 mg
Fiber 21 g
Sod 466 mg

Heat the olive oil in a large stockpot over medium-high heat. Add the leeks, carrots, celery and garlic. Sauté for 5 to 7 minutes. Add the potatoes and shell beans and mix well. Stir in the water and undrained tomatoes. Season with salt and pepper. Bring to a boil; reduce heat. Simmer for 45 minutes, stirring occasionally. Add the haricots verts, zucchini and pasta. Simmer for 15 to 20 minutes or until the vegetables and pasta are tender, stirring occasionally. Ladle into soup bowls. Stir a heaping tablespoon of Le Pistou into each serving. Pass the remaining pistou with the soup. May substitute two 19-ounce cans drained cannellini beans for the fresh shell beans and add with the haricots verts, zucchini and pasta.

Le Pistou

2 cups fresh basil
1/3 to 1/2 cup olive oil
1/2 cup freshly grated Parmesan cheese

1 teaspoon salt
3 cloves of garlic

Process the basil, olive oil, cheese, salt and garlic in a food processor until puréed.

Deborah Ritchken
Parent, Zoe 2003 and Zachery 2008

Vegetarian Tortilla Soup

Yield:
2 servings

5 corn tortillas
Vegetable oil for frying
1 medium white onion, chopped
1 tablespoon vegetable oil
2 cloves of garlic, minced
1½ teaspoons chili powder
1 teaspoon cumin
¼ teaspoon oregano
¼ teaspoon crushed red pepper (optional)
1 bay leaf
4 cups vegetable stock
1 (6-ounce) can tomato sauce
1 teaspoon salt
½ teaspoon sugar
¼ teaspoon ground black pepper
2 large green, red or yellow bell peppers, chopped
Juice of 1 lime
½ cup fresh or frozen corn kernels
¼ cup shredded Cheddar cheese
¼ cup shredded Monterey Jack cheese

Approx
Per Serving:
Cal 475
Prot 16 g
Carbo 65 g
T Fat 20 g
35% Calories
from Fat
Chol 27 mg
Fiber 10 g
Sod 2522 mg

Cut the tortillas into strips 3 inches long. Fry in oil in a skillet for 1 minute or until golden brown; drain. Sauté the onion in 1 tablespoon oil in a stockpot for 5 minutes or until tender. Stir in the garlic, chili powder, cumin, oregano, crushed red pepper and bay leaf. Sauté for 1 minute. Add the stock, tomato sauce, salt, sugar and black pepper. Bring to a boil; reduce heat. Simmer, covered, for 10 minutes, stirring occasionally. Stir in the green peppers and lime juice. Simmer for 5 to 10 minutes, stirring occasionally. Add the corn and ¾ of the tortilla strips. Simmer for 5 minutes longer, stirring occasionally. Discard the bay leaf. Ladle into soup bowls. Top each serving with 2 tablespoons Cheddar cheese and 2 tablespoons Monterey Jack cheese. Sprinkle with the remaining tortilla strips. Garnish with sour cream, chopped avocado, lime slices and/or chopped fresh cilantro. To save fat grams use nonfat cheeses and sauté the onion in nonstick cooking spray.

Nutritional information does not include oil for frying.

Amy Haimsohn, 1989

Meatball Soup

Yield:
6 servings

1 cup dried lentils
1 (50-ounce) can chicken broth
2 cups water
1 pound ground round
1/2 cup seasoned bread crumbs
1 egg
7 green onions, chopped
6 medium button mushrooms, chopped
1 medium tomato, chopped
2 carrots, sliced
1 green bell pepper, chopped
2 ribs celery, chopped
1/4 cup chopped fresh parsley
1 teaspoon mild curry powder
1 sprig of Italian parsley, chopped
1 sprig of oregano, chopped
1 sprig of basil, chopped
Salt and pepper to taste

Approx
Per Serving:
Cal 415
Prot 38 g
Carbo 33 g
T Fat 15 g
32% Calories
from Fat
Chol 92 mg
Fiber 10 g
Sod 1827 mg

Sort and rinse the lentils. Bring the broth and water to a boil in a stockpot. Combine the ground round, bread crumbs and egg in a bowl and mix well. Shape into 1-inch balls. Drop the meatballs into the boiling broth mixture. Add the green onions, mushrooms, tomato, carrots, green pepper, celery, chopped parsley, curry powder, Italian parsley, oregano, basil, salt and pepper. Stir in the lentils. Cook over medium heat for 1 hour or until the vegetables and lentils are tender, stirring occasionally. Ladle into soup bowls.

Suzanne Berol
Parent, David 1991

Clam Chowder

Yield:
6 servings

1 quart clams
2 (1-ounce) slices salt pork, chopped
3 cups water
3 medium potatoes, peeled, chopped
1 medium onion, chopped
1 teaspoon thyme

1³/₄ cups milk
3 tablespoons butter
1 teaspoon salt
1/8 teaspoon pepper
1/4 cup cold water
2 tablespoons flour

Approx
Per Serving:
Cal 337
Prot 32 g
Carbo 23 g
T Fat 12 g
34% Calories
from Fat
Chol 99 mg
Fiber 1 g
Sod 641 mg

Drain the clams, reserving the liquid. Brown the pork in a large saucepan. Add the reserved clam liquid, 3 cups water, potatoes, onion and thyme. Cook for 20 minutes or just until the potatoes are tender, stirring occasionally. Stir in the clams, milk, butter, salt and pepper. Cook just until heated through, stirring occasionally; do not boil. Combine 1/4 cup water and flour in a bowl, stirring until of a pasty consistency. Stir into the chowder. Cook just until heated through, stirring occasionally. Ladle into soup bowls.

Sarah Youtkus
Music, Lower and Middle Schools, 1973 to 1994

Shrimp and Mussel Soup

Yield:
8 servings

1 large red bell pepper, chopped
1 onion, chopped
1 cup chopped celery
6 mushrooms, sliced
1/4 cup sliced almonds
4 cloves of garlic, minced
1/2 cup butter
2 pounds live mussels, rinsed

1 pound deveined peeled shrimp
4 Italian tomatoes, chopped
1/4 cup chopped fresh cilantro
1/4 cup sherry
Juice of 1/2 lemon
1 teaspoon coriander
1/8 teaspoon hot pepper sauce
Salt and pepper to taste

Approx
Per Serving:
Cal 347
Prot 32 g
Carbo 13 g
T Fat 18 g
46% Calories
from Fat
Chol 163 mg
Fiber 2 g
Sod 565 mg

Sauté the red pepper, onion, celery, mushrooms, almonds and garlic in the butter in a stockpot until the vegetables are tender. Add 8 cups water and mix well. Bring to a boil; reduce heat. Stir in the remaining ingredients. Simmer until the mussels open, stirring occasionally. Ladle into soup bowls.

Shari Mount-Essex
Parent, Taylor 2007 and Jackson 2010
English, Middle School, 1986 to present

Shrimp, Chile and Smoked Corn Bisque

Yield:
6 servings

2 ears sweet white corn, shucked
1 pound peeled fresh rock shrimp
1 Anaheim chile, finely chopped
1/2 cup coarsely chopped onion
1 teaspoon chopped fresh thyme
1/2 teaspoon finely chopped garlic
1/4 cup olive oil
2 quarts fish stock
2 cups whipping cream
1/2 cup butter
1 cup flour

Approx
Per Serving:
Cal 715
Prot 24 g
Carbo 29 g
T Fat 57 g
71% Calories
from Fat
Chol 258 mg
Fiber 2 g
Sod 1322 mg

Soak the desired amount of hickory chips in water; drain. Sprinkle the wood chips over hot coals. Arrange the corn on a grill rack. Smoke the corn with the lid down over hot coals for 15 to 20 minutes. Cut the tops of the corn kernels with a sharp knife into a bowl. Sauté the corn, shrimp, chile, onion, thyme and garlic in the olive oil in a stockpot until the shrimp are almost cooked through. Add the fish stock. Bring to a boil. Remove from heat and strain. Return the liquid to the stockpot, reserving the corn, shrimp, chile and onion. Boil for 5 to 7 minutes longer. Stir in the whipping cream. Bring to a boil, stirring occasionally. Heat the butter in a saucepan until melted. Add the flour, stirring until blended. Cook until the mixture is light brown in color, stirring constantly. Add a small amount of the hot broth and mix well. Stir the mixture into the hot broth. Boil until of the desired consistency. Return the corn, shrimp, chile and onion to the stockpot. Cook just until heated through, stirring frequently. Ladle into soup bowls. Serve immediately. Do not substitute yellow corn for the white corn in this recipe.

Shelley Ackerberg-Patton
Parent, Sanders 2001 and Charlie 2004
Cookbook Editor

New Orleans Gumbo

Yield:
8 servings

2 onions, chopped
1/2 cup butter or margarine
1/4 cup flour
2 quarts chicken stock
1 (28-ounce) can tomatoes
16 ounces fresh or frozen okra, sliced
1 cup chopped celery

1 bay leaf
1/2 teaspoon each thyme and salt
1/8 teaspoon black pepper
1/8 teaspoon cayenne
6 hard-shell crabs
24 large deveined peeled shrimp
24 oysters
2 cups cooked rice

Approx
Per Serving:
Cal 309
Prot 18 g
Carbo 29 g
T Fat 14 g
40% Calories
from Fat
Chol 114 mg
Fiber 4 g
Sod 1303 mg

Sauté the onions in the butter in a stockpot. Stir in the flour. Cook until bubbly, stirring constantly. Add the stock, undrained tomatoes, okra, celery, bay leaf, thyme, salt, black pepper, cayenne and crabs and mix well. Simmer for 1 hour, stirring occasionally. Stir in the shrimp and oysters. Simmer for 5 minutes. Discard the bay leaf. Spoon 1/4 cup of the rice into each of 8 soup bowls. Ladle the gumbo over the rice.

Kay Kennard
Grandmother, Coco Schneider 2002

Seasonal Soup

Yield:
4 servings

1 butternut or acorn squash, peeled, cut into 1/2-inch-wide strips
1 medium onion, cut into quarters
2 ribs celery, cut into 2-inch strips

2 to 4 cups rice milk or skim milk
3 tablespoons honey or maple syrup
1/2 teaspoon salt

Approx
Per Serving:
Cal 214
Prot 2 g
Carbo 49 g
T Fat 2 g
9% Calories
from Fat
Chol 0 mg
Fiber 3 g
Sod 398 mg

Steam the squash, onion and celery in a steamer until tender. Combine the vegetable mixture, rice milk, honey and salt in a food processor or blender container. Process until smooth. Vary the consistency with the amount of milk added, but do not make the soup too thin. Chill, covered, for 1 hour or reheat and serve warm. May substitute 8 ounces broccoli, 8 ounces cauliflower, fresh peeled tomatoes or your favorite vegetable for the squash. If using potatoes, omit the honey or maple syrup.

Moreen Fielden
Parent, Tim 1977
Director, Lower School, 1964 to 1990

Celery Soup with Dilled Salmon Quenelles

Yield:
4 servings

1 medium baking potato, cut into
    1-inch pieces
2 cups (1-inch pieces) celery
1/2 medium brown onion, cut into
    1-inch pieces
4 cups chicken or vegetable stock

2 cups loosely packed celery leaves
1 tablespoon chopped fresh dillweed
1/4 teaspoon thyme
1/3 cup whipping cream
1 teaspoon salt
Quenelles

Approx
Per Serving:
Cal 455
Prot 25 g
Carbo 30 g
T Fat 27 g
52% Calories
from Fat
Chol 120 mg
Fiber 8 g
Sod 1577 mg

Combine the potato, celery, onion and stock in a large saucepan. Bring to a boil. Boil for 20 minutes, stirring occasionally. Add the celery leaves, dillweed and thyme and mix well. Cook for 3 minutes or until the leaves are tender but still very green, stirring occasionally. Remove from heat. Process the vegetable mixture in a blender at high speed until smooth. Press through a medium strainer into a saucepan. Cook just until heated through, stirring frequently. Stir in the whipping cream and salt. Cool at this point if not being served immediately. Ladle into soup bowls. Add 1 or 2 Quenelles per serving. Garnish with fresh dillweed.

Quenelles

12 ounces boneless fresh salmon
3 egg whites, lightly beaten
1/2 cup whipping cream

1/4 teaspoon salt
1/8 teaspoon cayenne
1 tablespoon chopped fresh dillweed

Process the salmon in a food processor until of the consistency of a thick paste. Spoon into a bowl set over ice. Add the egg whites gradually, mixing with a rubber spatula. Add the whipping cream, stirring until smooth. Stir in the salt, cayenne and dillweed. Shape by 2 tablespoonfuls into small dumplings, using 2 tablespoons to scoop and shape the mixture. Poach the dumplings in water in a skillet for 4 minutes or until cooked through; drain. Remove to a platter; cover to keep warm.

Tim Haidinger
Parent, Kerry 1987 and Tori 1989

Entrées

It is the supreme art of the teacher to awaken joy
in creative expression and knowledge.

Albert Einstein,
physicist (1879–1955)

Entrées

Beef Brisket 75
Sweet-and-Sour Brisket 75
Company Pot Roast 76
Sauerbraten 77
Sicilian Pot Roast 78
Beefsteak Bundles 78
London Broil 79
Barbecued Beef 79
Simple Short Ribs 80
Corned Beef and Cabbage 80
Meat Loaf 81
Everyone's Favorite Meat
   Loaf 81
TuTu's Famous Meat
   Loaf 82
Tamale Beef Pie 83
Veal Marsala Scaloppine 83
Okawaho (Wolf) Stew 84
Sausage and Corn
   Casserole 84
Roasted Pork Tenderloin with
   Chipotle Sauce 85
Shao Mai 86
Barbecued Spareribs 87
Barbecued Leg of Lamb 88
Leg of Lamb 89
Ruth Ann's Marvelous
   Marinade 89
Helen Fuil's Shish Kabob 90
Lamb Shanks
   Mediterranean 91
Lamb-Filled Grape
   Leaves 92
Gran Day's Shepherd's
   Pie 93
Chicken Cacciatore 94
Chicken Chasseur 95
Ginger Chicken 96

Spicy Herbed Grilled
   Chicken 97
Hungarian Chicken 98
Curried Chicken 99
Green Chicken Curry 100
Italian Chicken 100
Lemon Chicken with
   Thyme 101
Chicken in Mustard
   Sauce 102
Chicken Pineapple with
   Macadamia Nuts 103
Persian Chicken with
   Pomegranate 104
Sesame Ginger Chicken 105
Chicken Simon and
   Garfunkle 106
Chicken and Stuffing
   Casserole 106
Chickalita 107
Hot Chicken Salad 107
Chicken Potpie 108
Sherried Chicken Livers 109
Japanese-Style Steamed
   Chicken 110
Pepper Chicken with
   Cilantro 111
Chicken Enchilada
   Casserole 112
Heart-Healthy Chicken
   Enchiladas 113
Roasted Game Hens 114
Get-Rich Turkey 115
Green Chile Casserole 115
Smoked Turkey and Black-
   Eyed Peas 116
Turkey-Stuffed Potatoes 116
Sea Bass 117

Ginger Lime Marinade for
   Fish or Chicken 117
Fish for Ken 118
Sour Cream Cilantro
   Sauce 118
Orange Roughy in Cilantro
   Sauce 119
Family Fish Favorite 119
Barbecued Salmon 120
Grilled Marinated
   Salmon 120
Salmon in Champagne
   Sauce 121
Grilled Salmon with Mustard
   Mint Sauce 122
Grilled Salmon with Anchovy
   Sauce 123
Raspberry Salmon 123
Salmon Vegetable Crest 124
Broiled Swordfish 124
Creole Crab and Rice 125
Grilled Mussels 126
Bouillabaisse 127
Louisiana Shrimp Gumbo
   with Risotto Allo
   Zafferano 128
Shrimp Fried Rice 129
Sweet and Pungent Shrimp
   with Stir-Fried
   Vegetables 130
Seafood Kabobs 131
Eggplant Burritos 132
Lightly Curried Vegetable
   Burritos 133
Vegetable Chili 134
Vegetable Tacos 135
Roasted Vegetables with
   Couscous 136

Beef Brisket

Yield:
variable

1 large beef brisket, trimmed
Onion salt to taste
Seasoned salt to taste
Pepper to taste
4 onions, sliced

Minced garlic to taste
1/4 cup butter
1 cup catsup
5 tablespoons brown sugar
2 tablespoons white vinegar

Nutritional
information for
this recipe is
not available.

Rub the brisket with a mixture of the onion salt, seasoned salt and pepper. Place in a Dutch oven. Sauté the onions and garlic in the butter in a skillet until the onions are tender. Stir in the catsup, brown sugar and vinegar. Cook over medium heat for 30 minutes or until thickened, stirring frequently. Pour over the brisket. Bake at 325 degrees for 1 hour; cover. Bake for 1 to 2 hours longer or until the brisket is fork tender. Remove to a serving platter and slice on the bias. May add beef broth during the baking process for added moisture.

Carolyn Ackerberg
Grandmother, Sanders 2001, Charlie 2004 and Amy Patton

Sweet-and-Sour Brisket

Yield:
10 servings

1 (6-pound) beef brisket, trimmed
2 onions, chopped
1 clove of garlic, minced
1 cup catsup
3/4 cup packed brown sugar

1/2 cup vinegar
1 tablespoon Worcestershire sauce
1 tablespoon salt
1 teaspoon instant coffee granules
Freshly ground pepper to taste

Approx
Per Serving:
Cal 614
Prot 48 g
Carbo 26 g
T Fat 35 g
51% Calories
from Fat
Chol 165 mg
Fiber 1 g
Sod 1127 mg

Brown the brisket on all sides in a large ovenproof skillet. Remove the brisket to a platter, reserving the pan drippings. Brown the onions and garlic in the reserved pan drippings, stirring frequently. Stir in the catsup, brown sugar, vinegar, Worcestershire sauce, salt, coffee granules and pepper. Return the brisket to the skillet. Bake, covered, at 325 degrees for 2 to 3 hours or until the brisket is tender.

Barbara Weinberg
Parent, Lindsay 1999 and Kevin 2001

Company Pot Roast

Great as leftovers...just reheat the roast in gravy and serve over freshly cooked noodles.

Yield:
8 servings

1 (4- to 5-pound) chuck roast
1/3 cup flour
1 teaspoon salt
1/2 teaspoon pepper
1/4 teaspoon thyme
3 tablespoons shortening
2 medium onions, sliced
1 clove of garlic, minced
1 (16-ounce) can chopped tomatoes
1 (3-ounce) jar button mushrooms
12 black olives, cut into halves
Salt and pepper to taste
4 cups hot cooked egg noodles

Approx
Per Serving:
Cal 609
Prot 70 g
Carbo 29 g
T Fat 22 g
33% Calories
from Fat
Chol 224 mg
Fiber 2 g
Sod 592 mg

Coat the roast on all sides in a mixture of the flour, 1 teaspoon salt, 1/2 teaspoon pepper and thyme. Brown the roast in the shortening in a heavy skillet. Remove the roast to a platter, reserving the pan drippings. Sauté the onions and garlic in the reserved pan drippings until tender. Return the roast to the skillet. Add the undrained tomatoes, undrained mushrooms, black olives, salt and pepper to taste. Simmer, covered, for 2 to 3 hours or until of the desired degree of doneness. Slice the roast and serve over the hot cooked noodles.

Rachel E. Petrella
Secretary, Upper School, 1993 to 1997

One looks back with appreciation to the brilliant teachers, but with gratitude to those who touched our human feelings.

Carl Jung (1875–1961)

Sauerbraten

A great Octoberfest entrée! Serve with red cabbage and boiled potatoes.

Yield:
6 servings

1 medium onion, chopped
1 cup raisins
1 cup cider vinegar
$1/2$ cup wine vinegar
$1/2$ cup red wine
3 tablespoons brown sugar
2 bay leaves
$1/2$ teaspoon whole cloves
$1/2$ teaspoon dry mustard (optional)
Salt and pepper to taste
1 (4- to 5-pound) beef rump roast
$1/4$ cup flour

Approx
Per Serving:
Cal 606
Prot 71 g
Carbo 34 g
T Fat 18 g
27% Calories
from Fat
Chol 189 mg
Fiber 1 g
Sod 168 mg

Combine the onion, raisins, cider vinegar, wine vinegar, red wine, brown sugar, bay leaves, cloves, dry mustard, salt and pepper in a large nonreactive bowl and mix well. Add the roast, turning to coat. Marinate, covered, in the refrigerator for 2 to 3 days, turning occasionally. Drain, reserving the marinade. Pat the roast with a paper towel. Coat with the flour. Brown the roast on all sides in a nonstick skillet. Add the reserved marinade and a small amount of water to the skillet. Cook, covered, over medium-low heat for $2^1/2$ hours or until the roast is of the desired degree of doneness. Discard the bay leaves. May thicken pan juices with a small amount of flour or cornstarch for a delicious gravy.

Gertrude Nebeling
Great-Aunt, Meghan 2001 and Kathleen Sullivan 2004

Sicilian Pot Roast

Yield:
6 servings

1 (1½-pound) beef pot roast
6 to 8 tablespoons olive oil
1 (6-ounce) can pitted green
   Spanish olives
1 (6-ounce) can pitted black olives
3 dried red chiles

½ (3-ounce) jar capers
Garlic salt to taste
Pepper to taste
7 ounces mostaccioli, cooked,
   drained
Grated Parmesan cheese to taste

Approx
Per Serving:
Cal 656
Prot 25 g
Carbo 27 g
T Fat 50 g
68% Calories
from Fat
Chol 74 mg
Fiber 2 g
Sod 1136 mg

Brown the roast on all sides in the olive oil in a Dutch oven. Drain the olives, reserving the liquid. Add the olives, chiles, capers, garlic salt and pepper to the Dutch oven. Bake at 375 degrees for 2 hours or until of the desired degree of doneness, adding a small amount of the reserved olive liquid if necessary. Remove the roast with a slotted spoon to a serving platter and slice. Spoon the pasta into a serving bowl. Discard the chiles and pour the sauce over the pasta. Sprinkle generously with Parmesan cheese. Serve with the roast.

Joan Diener
String Instructor, Music Department, 1990 to present

Beefsteak Bundles

Yield:
4 servings

3 cups cooked rice
2 envelopes onion soup mix
1 pound (½-inch-thick) round steak,
   cut into 1x3-inch strips

½ cup evaporated milk
4 teaspoons butter or margarine

Approx
Per Serving:
Cal 461
Prot 37 g
Carbo 47 g
T Fat 13 g
25% Calories
from Fat
Chol 92 mg
Fiber 3 g
Sod 1855 mg

Cut four 12x18-inch sheets of foil. Place ¾ cup of the rice in the center of each sheet. Sprinkle with a heaping tablespoon of the soup mix. Layer with the steak. Drizzle each serving with 2 tablespoons evaporated milk. Top with a heaping tablespoon of the soup mix and 1 teaspoon butter. Seal the bundles by bringing together the short sides of each sheet and folding twice. Fold the ends to seal tightly. Place the bundles on a baking sheet. Bake at 350 degrees for 1 hour. Serve in the foil bundle.

Genean Dunn
Parent, Chris 1998

London Broil

Yield:
6 servings

2¹/₂ to 3 pounds flank steaks or
  London broil
Meat tenderizer to taste
¹/₂ cup canola oil
¹/₄ cup wine vinegar
¹/₄ cup light corn syrup

5 tablespoons A.1. steak sauce
¹/₄ cup catsup
3 tablespoons Worcestershire sauce
2¹/₂ tablespoons soy sauce
2 tablespoons Heinz 57 steak sauce
1 teaspoon onion flakes

Approx
Per Serving:
Cal 602
Prot 48 g
Carbo 19 g
T Fat 36 g
55% Calories
from Fat
Chol 117 mg
Fiber <1 g
Sod 1236 mg

Sprinkle both sides of the flank steaks with meat tenderizer. Place the steaks in a large sealable plastic bag. Process the remaining ingredients in a blender until smooth. Pour over the steaks; seal tightly. Marinate in the refrigerator overnight or for up to 48 hours, turning the bag occasionally. Drain, reserving the marinade. Grill the steaks over hot coals until of the desired degree of doneness. Reheat the marinade and serve with the steaks.

Ellen Person
Parent, Jeff 2000

Barbecued Beef

Barbecuing is an art just made for outdoor entertaining but there are some essentials. First is a stationary brick or a portable metal pit. Use dry live oak wood cut into suitable size pieces or charcoal. For a group of 25 people, use about 4 armsful of wood or enough charcoal for a 3- to 4-inch-deep layer. The fire should be started far enough in advance of the cooking time to insure a good bed of coals without any flame. Use an open grill rack or rods over the coals. Be sure to grease the grill or rods well to prevent sticking before placing the food over the coals.

Allow 1 pound of beef per person if the group includes both men and women or 1¹/₄ to 1¹/₂ pounds per person for an all-men group. Preferred cuts include rib steaks, sirloins or T-bones. All steaks should be cut 2 inches or thicker. Sear the steaks close to the heat for 3 minutes, raise the grill and cook slowly for about 20 minutes; turn the steaks over and repeat. Do not pierce the steaks with a fork to prevent juices from escaping. Cut the steaks across the grain into ³/₄-inch slices.

Marian Duncan
Parent, Brandon 2000 and Kenyon 2002

Simple Short Ribs

Yield:
4 servings

2 pounds beef short ribs
1 (12-ounce) bottle chili sauce

1 (12-ounce) bottle beer
1 envelope onion soup mix

Approx
Per Serving:
Cal 525
Prot 36 g
Carbo 29 g
T Fat 27 g
46% Calories
from Fat
Chol 109 mg
Fiber 2 g
Sod 2099 mg

Brown the ribs in a Dutch oven. Add a mixture of the chili sauce, beer and soup mix. Bake, covered, at 350 degrees for 1 1/2 to 2 hours or until the ribs are tender, stirring occasionally. May add broth if needed.

Anne M. Brickley
Great-Aunt, Meghan 2001 and Kathleen Sullivan 2004

Corned Beef and Cabbage

Yield:
4 servings

1 (5-pound) corned beef
Pepper to taste
4 large potatoes, peeled, sliced
2 large onions, sliced
2 large carrots, sliced

2 bay leaves
Salt to taste
1 large head cabbage, cut into
  quarters

Approx
Per Serving:
Cal 1157
Prot 71 g
Carbo 74 g
T Fat 65 g
50% Calories
from Fat
Chol 328 mg
Fiber 15 g
Sod 3877 mg

Combine the corned beef with enough water to cover in a nonreactive bowl. Let stand in the refrigerator overnight; drain. Combine the corned beef with enough cold water to cover in a stockpot. Add the pepper. Bring to a boil; skim the surface. Add the potatoes, onions, carrots, bay leaves and salt. Simmer, covered, for 1 1/2 hours, stirring occasionally. Add the cabbage. Cook, covered, for 30 minutes. Discard the bay leaves. Transfer the corned beef to a serving platter. Arrange the vegetables around the outer edge of the platter. Serve with mashed potatoes.

Marlene Gelber
Grandmother, Grace Royer 2007

Meat Loaf

Yield:
6 servings

2 eggs
1/4 cup Heinz 57 steak sauce
1/2 teaspoon seasoned salt
1/4 teaspoon onion powder

2 pounds ground beef (15% fat or less)
2 slices Hawaiian sweet egg bread

Approx
Per Serving:
Cal 270
Prot 36 g
Carbo 4 g
T Fat 12 g
40% Calories
from Fat
Chol 131 mg
Fiber 0 g
Sod 414 mg

Beat the eggs, steak sauce, seasoned salt and onion powder in a mixer bowl until blended. Add the ground beef and mix well. Moisten the bread slices 1 at a time with water; squeeze out the excess moisture. Trim and discard the crusts. Add the remaining bread to the ground beef mixture and mix well. Shape into a loaf in a 1 1/2-quart glass loaf pan. Bake at 350 degrees for 1 1/2 hours.

Roxy Ackerberg
Grandmother, Sanders 2001, Charlie 2004 and Amy Patton

Everyone's Favorite Meat Loaf

I know, I know, meat loaf as a favorite dish? Yeah, right! I have served this recipe to guests and have actually received calls the next day asking for the recipe!

Yield:
10 servings

3/4 cup skim milk
2 eggs, lightly beaten
1/2 cup fine dry bread crumbs
1/4 cup finely chopped onion
2 tablespoons chopped fresh parsley
1 tablespoon Worcestershire sauce

1 teaspoon salt
1/2 teaspoon ground sage
1/2 teaspoon dry mustard
1/2 teaspoon pepper
1 clove of garlic, crushed
1 1/2 pounds ground sirloin

Approx
Per Serving:
Cal 799
Prot 80 g
Carbo 94 g
T Fat 11 g
12% Calories
from Fat
Chol 121 mg
Fiber <1 g
Sod 1288 mg

Combine the skim milk, eggs, bread crumbs, onion, parsley, Worcestershire sauce, salt, sage, dry mustard, pepper and garlic in a bowl and mix well. Let stand for 10 minutes. Mix in the ground sirloin. Divide into 10 equal parts. Shape into loaves and place in a baking pan. Bake at 350 degrees for 20 to 25 minutes or until cooked through.

Kathleen E. Allenbach
Parent, Diana 2001, Allen 2004 and Lauren 2005

TuTu's Famous Meat Loaf

The secret is in the exact brand items and S-L-O-W baking. Easy for the grandchildren to prepare.

Yield:
4 servings

1 pound ground turkey or beef (15% fat or less)
1 Maui or brown onion, chopped
1 egg, lightly beaten
1 (15-ounce) can Campbell's vegetarian vegetable soup
1 cup crushed Ritz low-sodium crackers
Salt and pepper to taste
1 (4-ounce) can low-sodium Hunt's tomato sauce
1/4 cup packed brown sugar
1 teaspoon dry mustard

Approx
Per Serving:
Cal 438
Prot 27 g
Carbo 42 g
T Fat 18 g
37% Calories
from Fat
Chol 135 mg
Fiber 3 g
Sod 803 mg

Combine the turkey, onion, egg, soup, crackers, salt and pepper in a bowl and mix well. Spread in a 9x9-inch baking pan or dish. Bake at 325 degrees for 1 hour; drain. Simmer a mixture of the tomato sauce, brown sugar and dry mustard in a saucepan for 5 minutes, stirring occasionally. Spread over the meat loaf. Bake for 30 minutes longer. Let stand for 5 minutes before slicing. Double the recipe to serve 8.

Nanci (TuTu) Lewis
Grandmother, Katy 2003, Kelly 2005 and Kenna Foltz 2008

La Jolla Country Day School expects each student to grow in character and integrity, and holds every student accountable for personal conduct. By providing an environment in which students can feel secure and self-assured, Country Day assists students to experiment with a variety of leadership and collaborative styles while they grow in understanding, candor, kindness, helpfulness, acceptance, and their sense of their own worth and potential.

Entrées

Tamale Beef Pie

Yield:
6 servings

2 pounds ground beef
1 large green bell pepper, chopped
1 medium onion, chopped
1 (16-ounce) can tomatoes
1 (8-ounce) can tomato sauce
1 to 2 tablespoons chili powder

1 clove of garlic, crushed
1 cup shredded Monterey Jack
   cheese
1/2 cup sliced black olives
1 (6-ounce) package corn bread mix

Approx
Per Serving:
Cal 579
Prot 41 g
Carbo 31 g
T Fat 32 g
50% Calories
from Fat
Chol 125 mg
Fiber 5 g
Sod 971 mg

Brown the ground beef with the green pepper and onion in a skillet, stirring until the ground beef is crumbly; drain. Stir in the undrained tomatoes, tomato sauce, chili powder and garlic. Cook over low heat for 25 to 30 minutes, stirring occasionally. Stir in the cheese and olives. Spoon into a round 2 1/2-quart baking dish; smooth the top with a knife. Prepare the corn bread mix using package directions. Spread over the prepared layer. Bake at 425 degrees for 15 to 20 minutes or until the corn bread topping is cooked through.

Susan Small
Parent, Allison 1990

Veal Marsala Scaloppine

Yield:
6 servings

2 pounds thin veal cutlets
1/3 cup flour
1 clove of garlic, minced
1/3 cup butter or margarine

6 mushrooms, sliced
1/2 cup chicken broth
1/2 cup marsala

Approx
Per Serving:
Cal 489
Prot 38 g
Carbo 8 g
T Fat 31 g
57% Calories
from Fat
Chol 167 mg
Fiber <1 g
Sod 265 mg

Coat the cutlets with the flour. Sauté the veal and garlic in the butter in a skillet until light brown. Transfer the veal to a platter with a slotted spoon, reserving the pan drippings. Sauté the mushrooms in the reserved pan drippings. Remove the mushrooms with a slotted spoon to the platter, reserving the pan drippings. Add the broth and wine to the reserved pan drippings, stirring until blended. Return the veal and mushrooms to the skillet. Cook over high heat for 1 minute, stirring occasionally. Serve immediately over hot cooked rice or pasta.

Renata Saven
Parent, Erin 2006 and Adam 2008

Okawaho (Wolf) Stew

Yield:
8 servings

2¹/₂ pounds venison, elk, antelope or buffalo, cut into 1-inch pieces
¹/₂ cup flour
4 medium white or red potatoes, cut into ¹/₄-inch pieces
2 leeks, cut into ¹/₄-inch slices
4 to 10 green onions, sliced
2 cups thinly sliced tiny carrots

15 to 20 boiling onions
4 cups water
1 cup red wine, burgundy or cabernet sauvignon
¹/₄ cup maple syrup
Salt and pepper to taste
Herbs of choice to taste (sage and rosemary)

Approx
Per Serving:
Cal 419
Prot 35 g
Carbo 42 g
T Fat 10 g
22% Calories from Fat
Chol 114 mg
Fiber 5 g
Sod 401 mg

Coat the venison with the flour. Cook in a nonstick skillet until brown on all sides. Combine the venison, potatoes, leeks, green onions, carrots, onions, water, red wine, maple syrup, salt, pepper and herbs in an 8-quart heavy saucepan. Bring to a simmer. Simmer for 4 to 5 hours, stirring every 30 minutes. Let stand, covered, in the refrigerator for 2 to 3 days to allow the flavors to marry. Reheat before serving. May substitute a well-marbled beef pot roast for the venison.

Elynor and Charles Renshaw
Parents, Lisa 1976 and Mark 1980

Sausage and Corn Casserole

Yield:
6 servings

1 pound bulk pork sausage
1 (17-ounce) can cream-style corn
1 cup soft bread crumbs
4 eggs, beaten

¹/₄ teaspoon pepper
¹/₃ cup cracker crumbs
2 tablespoons chopped fresh parsley

Approx
Per Serving:
Cal 291
Prot 14 g
Carbo 23 g
T Fat 17 g
50% Calories from Fat
Chol 174 mg
Fiber 2 g
Sod 869 mg

Brown the sausage in a large skillet, stirring until crumbly; drain well. Combine the cooked sausage, corn, bread crumbs, eggs and pepper in a bowl and mix well. Spoon into an 8-inch baking dish. Sprinkle with the cracker crumbs. Bake at 350 degrees for 45 minutes. Sprinkle with the parsley.

Charlotte Garfield
Parent, Brian 2008 and Jim 1996

Roasted Pork Tenderloin with Chipotle Sauce

Yield:
6 servings

2 tablespoons chili powder
1 tablespoon coarsely ground pepper
2 teaspoons kosher salt
2 (12- to 16-ounce) pork tenderloins
1 to 2 teaspoons vegetable oil
Chipotle Sauce

Approx
Per Serving:
Cal 265
Prot 33 g
Carbo 16 g
T Fat 8 g
26% Calories
from Fat
Chol 90 mg
Fiber 1 g
Sod 765 mg

Combine the chili powder, pepper and kosher salt in a small bowl and mix well. Pat the spice mixture over the tenderloins. Brown the tenderloins on all sides in the oil in a heavy ovenproof skillet. Bake at 400 degrees for 20 to 30 minutes or until a meat thermometer registers 160 degrees. Let stand for 5 to 10 minutes. Transfer to a serving platter and slice. Serve with the Chipotle Sauce.

Chipotle Sauce

2 cups canned unsweetened pineapple juice
1/2 cup cider vinegar
1 to 3 tablespoons chopped seeded chipotles in adobo sauce
2 tablespoons lime juice
2 teaspoons oregano

Combine the pineapple juice, vinegar and chiles in a saucepan. Bring to a boil; reduce heat. Simmer for 45 minutes or until the mixture is reduced by 1/2, stirring occasionally. Remove from heat. Stir in the lime juice and oregano. Process the chile mixture in a blender or food processor until smooth. Chipotles are very hot so add accordingly.

Ellen Simms
Dean of Students and English, Middle School, 1973 to present
Billy Simms
Chairman, Science Department, 1972 to present

Shao Mai

6 black mushrooms
2 cups hot water
1 pound lean ground pork loin
1 (8-ounce) can water chestnuts, drained, finely chopped
2 tablespoons cornstarch
2 small eggs, beaten
2 teaspoons sesame oil
2 teaspoons salt
1 teaspoon dry sherry or rice wine
1/2 teaspoon sugar
1/4 teaspoon pepper
30 dumpling skins or won ton skins, cut into circles
Ginger Dipping Sauce

Approx
Per Serving:
Cal 68
Prot 5 g
Carbo 7 g
T Fat 2 g
32% Calories
from Fat
Chol 21 mg
Fiber <1 g
Sod 562 mg

Soak the mushrooms in the hot water in a bowl for 30 minutes or until the mushrooms are soft; drain. Discard the stems and finely chop the mushrooms. Combine the mushrooms, ground pork and water chestnuts in a bowl and mix well. Mix the cornstarch, eggs, sesame oil, salt, sherry, sugar and pepper in a bowl. Add to the ground pork mixture and mix well. Spoon about 1 teaspoon of the pork mixture in the center of each dumpling skin circle. Pinch the side together to form a tulip-shaped cup. Place the cups in a bamboo steamer lined with cheesecloth. Steam over high heat for 8 minutes. Serve with the Ginger Dipping Sauce.

Ginger Dipping Sauce

1/2 cup soy sauce
2 tablespoons vinegar, or to taste
1/4 teaspoon finely minced gingerroot

Mix the soy sauce, vinegar and gingerroot in a bowl.

Jackie Seidman
Parent, David 1996 and Steven 2001

Barbecued Spareribs

Yield:
20 servings

2 cups vegetable oil
2 cups melted butter
2 cups dry red wine
1/4 cup vinegar
2 tablespoons sugar
1 tablespoon prepared mustard
1 teaspoon poultry seasoning
2 cloves of garlic, minced
Salt and pepper to taste
1/2 cup catsup
1/4 cup Worcestershire sauce
20 pounds pork spareribs

Approx
Per Serving:
Cal 1236
Prot 63 g
Carbo 4 g
T Fat 105 g
77% Calories
from Fat
Chol 308 mg
Fiber <1 g
Sod 503 mg

Combine the oil, butter, red wine, vinegar, sugar, prepared mustard, poultry seasoning, garlic, salt and pepper in a saucepan and mix well. Simmer over low heat for 1 hour or until of the desired consistency, stirring occasionally. Stir in the catsup and Worcestershire sauce just before grilling the spareribs. Grill the spareribs over medium to high heat for 1 hour or until cooked through, turning and basting with the sauce frequently.

Marian Duncan
Parent, Brandon 2000 and Kenyon 2002

Barbecued Leg of Lamb

Yield:
8 servings

1 (6- to 7-pound) leg of lamb, boned, butterflied
3/4 cup canola oil
1/2 cup chopped onion
1/4 cup wine vinegar
2 teaspoons Dijon mustard
2 teaspoons salt
2 teaspoons freshly ground pepper
1/2 teaspoon oregano
1/2 teaspoon basil
1 bay leaf, crushed
1 clove of garlic, crushed

Approx
Per Serving:
Cal 641
Prot 49 g
Carbo 1 g
T Fat 47 g
68% Calories
from Fat
Chol 172 mg
Fiber <1 g
Sod 739 mg

Place the lamb in a large sealable plastic bag. Process the canola oil, onion, vinegar, Dijon mustard, salt, pepper, oregano, basil, bay leaf and garlic in a blender until blended. Pour over the lamb and seal tightly. Marinate in the refrigerator overnight or for up to 24 hours, turning occasionally. Grill the lamb over hot coals until of the desired degree of doneness.

Ellen Person
Parent, Jeff 2000

Leg of Lamb

Yield:
6 servings

1 (7-pound) leg of lamb
Garlic powder to taste
Salt and black pepper to taste

Red pepper to taste
1/2 cup vegetable oil
1 (12-ounce) can beer

Approx
Per Serving:
Cal 786
Prot 65 g
Carbo 2 g
T Fat 54 g
63% Calories
from Fat
Chol 229 mg
Fiber <1 g
Sod 169 mg

Pat the lamb on all sides with garlic powder, salt, black pepper and red pepper. Brush with the oil. Place the lamb in a baking pan. Broil for 10 to 15 minutes or until brown on both sides, turning several times. Pour the beer over the lamb and cover with foil. Bake at 375 to 400 degrees for 2 to 3 hours or until of the desired degree of doneness. Serve with the pan drippings and European-style roasted potatoes.

Silvana Michan
Parent, Natalie 2003

Ruth Ann's Marvelous Marinade

Yield:
1 recipe
(1/2 cup)

1/4 cup olive oil
2 tablespoons anchovy paste
1 tablespoon minced fresh garlic
Coarsely ground pepper to taste

Onion salt to taste
Chopped fresh parsley leaves
  to taste

Approx
Per Recipe:
Cal 589
Prot 10 g
Carbo 11 g
T Fat 59 g
86% Calories
from Fat
Chol 0 mg
Fiber <1 g
Sod 2 mg

Combine the olive oil, anchovy paste, garlic, pepper, onion salt and parsley in a bowl and mix well. Pour over the meat of your choice. Marinate in the refrigerator for 2 hours or longer. Grill or bake as desired.

Shelley Ackerberg-Patton
Parent, Sanders 2001 and Charlie 2004
Cookbook Editor

Helen Fuil's Shish Kabob

Yield:
10 servings

1/2 cup sherry
1 medium onion, sliced, separated into rings
2 tablespoons vegetable oil
1 tablespoon salt
1 teaspoon oregano
1 teaspoon rosemary
1/2 teaspoon pepper
1 (5- to 6-pound) leg of lamb, cut into 1-inch pieces
20 cherry tomatoes
20 pearl onions
3 green bell peppers, cut into chunks
20 small mushrooms

Approx
Per Serving:
Cal 382
Prot 36 g
Carbo 9 g
T Fat 21 g
51% Calories
from Fat
Chol 118 mg
Fiber 2 g
Sod 859 mg

Combine the sherry, sliced onion, oil, salt, oregano, rosemary and pepper in a nonreactive bowl and mix well. Add the lamb, stirring to coat. Marinate, covered, in the refrigerator overnight, stirring occasionally. Thread the lamb, cherry tomatoes, pearl onions, green peppers and mushrooms alternately on skewers. Broil or grill over hot coals for 10 to 15 minutes or until the lamb is of the desired degree of doneness, turning once or twice.

Pam Kurz
Parent, Daniel 2000

Mrs. Balmer stated in 1955 that the new La Jolla Country Day School "will be neither a servant of tradition nor a slave to an unproved theory but will use both the old and the new—if they help educate the child. It will not be interested in that kind of teacher who boasts a long line of degrees but no spark of enthusiasm with which to kindle the fires of learning. It will consider the child as a human being rather than as a statistic." The fine students and outstanding faculty are a testimonial of success to Mrs. Balmer's philosophy.

Entrées

Lamb Shanks Mediterranean

Yield:
2 servings

4 meaty lamb shanks
1 tablespoon lemon juice
Salt and pepper to taste
2 tablespoons olive oil
1 tablespoon lemon juice
1 clove of garlic, minced
$1/2$ teaspoon oregano
1 onion, cut into quarters
1 cup hot beef bouillon
1 (10-ounce) package frozen artichoke hearts
$1/4$ cup water
1 tablespoon cornstarch

Approx
Per Serving:
Cal 711
Prot 66 g
Carbo 22 g
T Fat 40 g
51% Calories
from Fat
Chol 204 mg
Fiber 7 g
Sod 795 mg

Rub the shanks, uncracked, with 1 tablespoon lemon juice. Sprinkle with salt and pepper. Sauté the shanks in the olive oil in a skillet until brown on all sides. Spoon the shanks and pan drippings into a baking dish. Drizzle with 1 tablespoon lemon juice. Sprinkle with the garlic and oregano. Add the onion. Bake, covered, at 300 degrees for $2^1/2$ hours. Add the bouillon and artichokes. Increase the oven temperature to 350 degrees. Bake, covered, for 20 to 30 minutes or until the artichokes are tender. Transfer the shanks and artichokes with a slotted spoon to a heated platter; cover to keep warm. Stir a mixture of the water and cornstarch into the pan drippings. Cook until of a sauce consistency, stirring constantly. Serve the sauce with the lamb shanks.

Luis Arellano
Building Technician, 1987 to present

Lamb-Filled Grape Leaves

Yield:
4 servings

1 (16-ounce) jar grape leaves, drained
1 pound ground lamb
1 cup uncooked rice
1/2 onion, grated
1 tablespoon allspice, or to taste
Salt and pepper to taste
Chicken broth

Approx
Per Serving:
Cal 380
Prot 25 g
Carbo 50 g
T Fat 15 g
31% Calories
from Fat
Chol 75 mg
Fiber 5 g
Sod 1565 mg

Rinse the grape leaves in warm water. Drain, remove and discard the stems. Cover the bottom of a saucepan with 2 of the largest leaves. Combine the ground lamb, rice, onion, allspice, salt and pepper in a bowl and mix well. Place 1 grape leaf vein side up on a flat surface; overlap the bottom half. Shape a small amount of the lamb mixture into a roll approximately the size of your small finger. Place the roll on the grape leaf. Roll up tightly, tucking in the corners as you roll. Arrange a layer of the rolls in the prepared pan. Arrange a second layer perpendicular to the first layer. Place a plate on top of the grape leaf rolls. Fill the pan with boiling chicken broth to the level of the plate rim. Bring the broth back to a boil and reduce the heat. Simmer for 40 minutes, adding small amounts of additional broth as necessary to maintain broth level. Remove the lamb-filled leaves from the broth.

Nutritional information does not include chicken broth.

Diana Larson
Music, Band and Technical Theater, Middle School, 1994 to 1998

Gran Day's Shepherd's Pie

*"Season as one goes along, singing merrily the while and eat hearty,"
says Gran Day.*

Yield:
8 servings

1 yellow onion, chopped
1 tablespoon butter
1½ to 2 pounds ground lamb
2 tablespoons Worcestershire sauce
2 carrots, cooked, chopped
5 potatoes, peeled, cooked
¼ cup milk
2 tablespoons butter
½ cup shredded Cheddar cheese
1 beef bouillon cube
1 cup hot water

**Approx
Per Serving:**
Cal 397
Prot 24 g
Carbo 25 g
T Fat 22 g
51% Calories
from Fat
Chol 95 mg
Fiber 2 g
Sod 315 mg

Sauté the onion in 1 tablespoon butter in a skillet until tender. Add the ground lamb and Worcestershire sauce. Cook until the ground lamb is crumbly and brown, stirring constantly. Transfer the lamb mixture with a slotted spoon to a baking dish, reserving the pan drippings. Sauté the carrots in the reserved pan drippings. Sprinkle over the lamb mixture. Beat the potatoes with the milk and 2 tablespoons butter in a mixer bowl until smooth. Add the cheese and mix well. Spread over the prepared layers. Dissolve the bouillon in the hot water and mix well. Pour over the top. Bake at 375 degrees for 40 minutes.

Kathleen Healy Day
Parent, Graham 2006 and Ian 2009

Chicken Cacciatore

Yield:
6 servings

1 (4-pound) chicken, cut up
1/4 to 1/2 cup olive oil
1 medium red onion, sliced
2 cloves of garlic, minced
1 green bell pepper, cut into strips
1 1/2 pounds mushrooms
1/4 cup capers (optional)
1 (28-ounce) can tomatoes, mashed
1/3 cup sauterne
Salt and pepper to taste
1/3 cup grated Parmesan cheese

Approx
Per Serving:
Cal 471
Prot 40 g
Carbo 13 g
T Fat 29 g
55% Calories
from Fat
Chol 100 mg
Fiber 3 g
Sod 479 mg

Brown the chicken on all sides in the olive oil in a skillet. Transfer the chicken with a slotted spoon to an 8x11-inch baking pan, reserving the pan drippings. Brown the onion and garlic in the reserved pan drippings. Sprinkle over the chicken. Sauté the green pepper in the reserved pan drippings until light brown. Arrange over the onion. Sauté the mushrooms in the reserved pan drippings until light brown. Spoon over the prepared layers. Sprinkle with the capers. Pour the tomatoes over the top. Drizzle with the wine. Sprinkle with salt and pepper. Bake, covered, at 375 degrees for 1 hour or until the chicken is cooked through. Sprinkle with the cheese. Bake until brown. Serve with potatoes and vegetables of your choice or over hot cooked noodles, spaghetti or macaroni.

Jo Higgins
Grandmother, Kimberly 2008

Part of the secret of success in life is to eat what you like
and let the food fight it out inside.

Mark Twain (1835–1910)

Chicken Chasseur

Yield:
4 servings

2 pounds chicken pieces
1/2 to 3/4 cup flour
Salt and pepper to taste
2 tablespoons butter
1 tablespoon vegetable oil
1/2 cup chopped scallions
2 tablespoons minced onion
1 (or more) clove of garlic, chopped
4 ounces mushrooms, sliced
1 tablespoon chopped fresh parsley
1/2 teaspoon thyme
1/2 cup white wine
3/4 cup chicken broth
1/2 cup chopped seeded tomato

Approx
Per Serving:
Cal 376
Prot 29 g
Carbo 23 g
T Fat 16 g
39% Calories
from Fat
Chol 87 mg
Fiber 2 g
Sod 283 mg

Coat the chicken in the flour. Sprinkle with salt and pepper. Sauté the chicken in a mixture of the butter and oil in a skillet until brown on all sides. Transfer the chicken with a slotted spoon to a platter, reserving the pan drippings. Sauté the scallions, onion and garlic in the reserved pan drippings until the onion is tender. Add the mushrooms, parsley, thyme, salt and pepper. Sauté for 5 minutes. Stir in the white wine. Cook until the liquid is reduced by 1/2, stirring frequently. Return the chicken to the skillet. Add the broth and tomato. Bring to a boil; reduce heat. Simmer, covered, for 20 minutes, stirring occasionally; remove the cover. Cook for 10 minutes longer, stirring occasionally.

Nancy Ullman
Parent, Lindsay 2005 and Max 2008

Ginger Chicken

Yield:
4 servings

1 cup soy sauce
1/2 cup sugar
2 to 3 cloves of garlic, mashed, chopped
2 thin slices fresh gingerroot
1 1/2 cups cracker crumbs
1/2 cup flour
1 teaspoon salt
1/4 teaspoon pepper
2 eggs, lightly beaten
2 tablespoons water
1 (2- to 2 1/2-pound) chicken, boned, skinned, cut into bite-size pieces
Vegetable oil for frying

Approx
Per Serving:
Cal 574
Prot 43 g
Carbo 65 g
T Fat 14 g
23% Calories
from Fat
Chol 196 mg
Fiber 1 g
Sod 6376 mg

Combine the soy sauce, sugar, garlic and gingerroot in a bowl and mix well. Let stand for several minutes to allow the flavors to marry. Mix the cracker crumbs, flour, salt and pepper in a bowl. Combine the eggs and water in a bowl and mix well. Dip the chicken in the egg mixture and coat with the cracker crumb mixture. Fry the chicken in oil in a skillet until cooked through; drain. Dip the chicken in the soy sauce mixture. Serve immediately. May substitute boneless skinless chicken breasts, thighs or drumettes for the whole chicken.

Nutritional information does not include oil for frying.

Karen Morikawa
Parent, Evan 2006 and Megan 2008

Spicy Herbed Grilled Chicken

Yield:
8 servings

1/2 cup firmly packed fresh basil
1/2 cup chopped fresh parsley
1/4 cup balsamic vinegar
1/4 cup extra-virgin olive oil
2 tablespoons Dijon mustard
2 tablespoons chopped fresh rosemary
2 tablespoons chopped fresh thyme
3/4 teaspoon salt
1/4 teaspoon red pepper flakes
2 (3 1/2-pound) chickens, cut up

Approx
Per Serving:
Cal 354
Prot 42 g
Carbo 2 g
T Fat 18 g
48% Calories
from Fat
Chol 126 mg
Fiber <1 g
Sod 443 mg

Combine the basil, parsley, vinegar, olive oil, Dijon mustard, rosemary, thyme, salt and red pepper flakes in a food processor container fitted with a metal blade. Pulse until of the consistency of a coarse paste. Place the chicken on a nonreactive platter. Rub the chicken on all sides with the paste. Marinate, covered, in the refrigerator for 4 hours or up to 24 hours. Prepare a fire in a kettle-type charcoal grill. When the coals are hot and turning white, leave them in a pile in the center of the grill or if you used enough coals, divide into 2 piles, one on each side of the grill. Arrange the chicken skin side down around the cooler portions of the grill, not directly over the coals. Grill the chicken for 45 minutes or until cooked through, turning occasionally. Serve with additional balsamic vinegar.

Rebecca Wood, 1970

There is no subject so old that something new cannot be said about it.

Dostoyevsky, **A Diary of a Writer** (1876)

Hungarian Chicken

This delicious recipe is from my mother, Sigrid Fischer, who is the proud grandmother of my children as well as three more LJCDS students, the Geffens: Brian 2003, Michelle 2005 and Nikki 2009.

Yield:
8 servings

5 pounds chicken pieces
Peri-peri to taste
Basil to taste
Paprika to taste
Salt and pepper to taste
Italian seasoning to taste
3 pounds mushrooms, sliced
1 pound onions, sliced
15 ounces catsup
3 cups (or more) water

Approx
Per Serving:
Cal 317
Prot 37 g
Carbo 25 g
T Fat 8 g
23% Calories
from Fat
Chol 90 mg
Fiber 4 g
Sod 722 mg

Arrange the chicken on a large baking sheet. Bake at 375 degrees for 20 minutes. Transfer the chicken to a large baking pan. Sprinkle with peri-peri (an African variety of red chile), basil, paprika, salt, pepper and Italian seasoning. Sauté the mushrooms and onions in a nonstick skillet until tender. Spoon over the chicken. Pour the catsup and water over the top. Bake for 1 hour longer or until the chicken is cooked through. May add additional water if needed.

Susan Morris
Parent, Sammy 2006, Tommy 2008 and Jodi 2010
President, Parents' Association, 1998 to 1999

Curried Chicken

Another zesty recipe from my mother, Sigrid Fischer, who is grandmother of six LJCDS students including the Geffens, Brian 2003, Michelle 2005 and Nikki 2009.

Yield:
12 servings

1 large onion, chopped,
1 (15-ounce) can chicken broth
1 (16-ounce) jar apricot jam
7 teaspoons curry powder
1/4 teaspoon paprika
1/8 teaspoon peri-peri
6 cups water or chicken broth
2 chicken bouillon cubes
1 beef bouillon cube
1 tablespoon Bisto or other thickening agent
24 boned chicken breasts, cut into 1- to 1 1/2-inch cubes

Approx
Per Serving:
Cal 680
Prot 109 g
Carbo 27 g
T Fat 13 g
18% Calories
from Fat
Chol 293 mg
Fiber 1 g
Sod 757 mg

Sauté the onion in a small amount of the canned broth in a skillet until tender. Add the remaining broth, jam, curry powder, paprika, peri-peri, water and bouillon cubes. Bring to a boil, stirring until the bouillon cubes dissolve. Reduce the heat and let the sauce simmer until reduced. Dissolve the Bisto in a small amount of cold water, stir into the sauce and cook until thickened, stirring constantly. Brown the chicken lightly on all sides in a large skillet. Arrange the chicken in a large baking dish. Spoon the sauce over the chicken. Bake, covered, at 350 degrees for 1 1/2 to 2 hours.

Susan Morris
Parent, Sammy 2006, Tommy 2008 and Jodi 2010
President, Parents' Association, 1998 to 1999

Green Chicken Curry

I stole this recipe from Kamila, an artist friend of mine, who is from Pakistan. The taste is very exotic, and it is so easy to prepare.

Yield:
8 servings

3 cups chopped fresh cilantro
9 serranos, or to taste
6 green onions with tops, chopped
3 tablespoons (or more) yogurt
1 tablespoon coarsely chopped
  gingerroot
3 tablespoons vegetable oil

2 teaspoons minced garlic
1 teaspoon cumin seeds
4 whole chicken breasts, split
1 (14-ounce) can unsweetened
  coconut milk
Salt to taste
1 teaspoon (or more) garam masala

Approx
Per Serving:
Cal 461
Prot 55 g
Carbo 3 g
T Fat 22 g
46% Calories
from Fat
Chol 147 mg
Fiber 1 g
Sod 143 mg

Process the cilantro, chiles, green onions, yogurt and gingerroot in a blender until smooth. Heat the oil in a skillet over high heat until hot. Stir in the garlic and cumin seeds. Add the chicken. Cook until the chicken is golden brown on all sides, turning frequently. Stir in the yogurt mixture, coconut milk and salt. Bring to a boil; reduce heat. Simmer, covered, for 30 minutes or until the chicken is cooked through, stirring occasionally. Sprinkle with the garam masala and mix well. Serve immediately.

Fumiko Tachibana
Japanese, Middle and Upper School, 1991 to present

Italian Chicken

Yield:
4 servings

4 boneless skinless chicken breasts
2 eggs, lightly beaten
1 cup bread crumbs

1 (16-ounce) jar spaghetti sauce
8 ounces mozzarella cheese,
  shredded

Approx
Per Serving:
Cal 711
Prot 73 g
Carbo 39 g
T Fat 28 g
36% Calories
from Fat
Chol 297 mg
Fiber 5 g
Sod 1165 mg

Dip the chicken in the eggs and coat with the bread crumbs. Cook the chicken in a nonstick skillet sprayed with nonstick cooking spray until brown on both sides and cooked through. Pour the spaghetti sauce into an 8x8-inch baking dish. Arrange the chicken in the prepared dish. Sprinkle with the cheese. Bake at 350 degrees for 10 minutes or until brown and bubbly.

Lynne Hansen
Parent, Lauren 2012
Dean of Students, Upper School, 1986 to 1998

Entrées

Lemon Chicken with Thyme

This dish is similar to Italian chicken piccata and is quite simple to prepare. It is low in calories and extremely tasty. Serve with steamed broccoli and rice.

Yield:
4 servings

3 tablespoons flour
1/2 teaspoon salt
1/4 teaspoon pepper
4 boneless skinless chicken breasts
2 tablespoons olive oil
1 medium onion, coarsely chopped
1 tablespoon margarine
1 cup chicken broth
3 tablespoons lemon juice
1/2 teaspoon thyme
2 tablespoons chopped fresh parsley (optional)

Approx
Per Serving:
Cal 413
Prot 56 g
Carbo 8 g
T Fat 16 g
36% Calories
from Fat
Chol 146 mg
Fiber 1 g
Sod 646 mg

Mix the flour, salt and pepper in a sealable plastic bag. Add the chicken, shaking to coat lightly. Remove the chicken to a plate, reserving the seasoned flour. Heat 1 tablespoon of the olive oil in a skillet over medium heat. Add the chicken. Cook for 5 minutes or until brown; turn the chicken. Add the remaining 1 tablespoon olive oil. Cook for 5 minutes longer or until brown on the remaining side; drain. Sauté the onion in the margarine in a skillet for 2 to 3 minutes or until tender. Stir in the reserved seasoned flour. Cook for 1 minute or until mixed, stirring constantly. Add the broth, 2 tablespoons of the lemon juice and thyme and mix well. Bring to a boil, stirring constantly. Return the chicken to the skillet. Cook, covered, over medium-low heat for 5 minutes or until the chicken is cooked through, stirring occasionally. Transfer the chicken to individual dinner plates. Stir the remaining 1 tablespoon lemon juice into the sauce and drizzle over the chicken. Sprinkle with the chopped parsley. Garnish with lemon wedges.

Kathleen Allenbach
Parent, Diana 2001, Allen 2004 and Lauren Kessler 2005

Chicken in Mustard Sauce

Elegant, but surprisingly easy. Serve with steamed rice and a tossed green salad for a family dinner everyone will love.

Yield:
4 servings

4 boneless skinless chicken breasts
2 tablespoons olive oil
1/2 cup white wine
1/2 cup milk
3 tablespoons Moutarde de Meaux

Approx
Per Serving:
Cal 391
Prot 55 g
Carbo 2 g
T Fat 14 g
34% Calories
from Fat
Chol 150 mg
Fiber <1 g
Sod 290 mg

Sauté the chicken in the olive oil in a skillet for 15 to 25 minutes or until brown on all sides and cooked through. Transfer the chicken to a platter with a slotted spoon, reserving the pan drippings. Cover to keep warm. Add the white wine to the reserved pan drippings and mix well. Cook over high heat until of the consistency of a glaze, stirring constantly. Stir in the milk. Bring to a boil. Cook for 3 minutes or until thickened, stirring constantly; reduce heat. Whisk in the mustard. Return the chicken to the skillet. Spoon the sauce over the chicken. Simmer for 5 minutes, stirring occasionally. Serve immediately.

Joan Mann Chesner
Parent, Jonathan 2002

Learning acquired in youth arrests the evil of old age; and if you understand that old age has wisdom for its food, you will conduct yourself in youth that your old age will not lack nourishment.

Leonardo da Vinci, **Notebooks** (c. 1500)

Entrées

Chicken Pineapple with Macadamia Nuts

Yield:
8 servings

6 tablespoons flour
2 tablespoons paprika
1 teaspoon salt
8 boneless skinless chicken breasts or large thighs
Vegetable oil for frying
1 (8-ounce) can pineapple chunks in heavy syrup
1 cup sherry
$1/4$ cup vegetable oil
2 tablespoons brown sugar
2 tablespoons soy sauce
1 teaspoon ground ginger
6 tablespoons (or more) chopped macadamia nuts, toasted
4 cups hot cooked rice

Approx
Per Serving:
Cal 568
Prot 57 g
Carbo 38 g
T Fat 17 g
28% Calories
from Fat
Chol 146 mg
Fiber 2 g
Sod 753 mg

Mix the flour, paprika and salt in a sealable plastic bag. Add the chicken and toss to coat. Cook the chicken in the oil for frying in a skillet over high heat until brown on all sides. Transfer the chicken with a slotted spoon to a 9x13-inch baking pan. Drain the pineapple, reserving the syrup. Combine the syrup, sherry, $1/4$ cup oil, brown sugar, soy sauce and ginger in a bowl and mix well. Pour over the chicken. Bake, covered with foil, at 375 degrees for 30 minutes. Sprinkle with the pineapple and macadamia nuts. Bake, covered, for 15 minutes longer or until the chicken is cooked through. Serve over the rice. May use juice-pack pineapple chunks.

Nutritional information does not include oil for frying.

Elynor and Charles Renshaw
Parents, Lisa 1976 and Mark 1980

Persian Chicken with Pomegranate

The unique flavor of this dish will make your guests think you have slaved in the kitchen all day. Pomegranate paste may be purchased at most Middle Eastern grocery stores.

Yield:
8 servings

1 large onion, chopped
1/4 cup vegetable oil
8 boneless skinless chicken breasts
1 (6-ounce) can tomato paste
1 tablespoon cinnamon
1 teaspoon salt
1 teaspoon turmeric
1/8 teaspoon pepper
1 cup water
1 (12-ounce) bottle pomegranate paste
1 1/2 cups finely ground walnuts
1/3 cup sugar
1/3 cup fresh lemon juice

Approx
Per Serving:
Cal 525
Prot 59 g
Carbo 25 g
T Fat 22 g
37% Calories
from Fat
Chol 146 mg
Fiber 3 g
Sod 588 mg

Sauté the onion in the oil in a heavy skillet over high heat until golden brown. Transfer the onion with a slotted spoon to a paper towel to drain, reserving the pan drippings. Brown the chicken in the reserved pan drippings over medium-high heat just until brown on all sides; drain. Discard the pan drippings. Add the tomato paste, cinnamon, salt, turmeric and pepper to the skillet and mix well. Stir in 1 cup water. Add the chicken. Add just enough additional water to cover the chicken. Simmer, covered, over low heat for 25 minutes, stirring occasionally. Stir in the onion, pomegranate paste, walnuts, sugar and lemon juice. Cook, covered, for 15 minutes, stirring occasionally. Serve with steamed white rice. May be prepared early in the day and stored, covered, in the refrigerator. Reheat, covered, at 350 degrees for 30 minutes.

Lisa Moallemi
Parent, Bijan 2006 and Keivan 2009

Entrées

Sesame Ginger Chicken

Yield:
4 servings

1/3 cup soy sauce
1/4 cup packed brown sugar
1/4 cup dry sherry
2 tablespoons wine vinegar
2 tablespoons vegetable oil
1 teaspoon ginger powder
1/4 teaspoon black pepper
1/4 teaspoon cayenne
4 boneless skinless chicken breasts, cut into 1/2-inch strips
2 teaspoons cornstarch
1 red bell pepper, cut into strips
1/4 cup chopped green onions
1/2 cup slivered almonds
2 tablespoons sesame seeds
2 tablespoons chopped fresh parsley

Approx
Per Serving:
Cal 568
Prot 60 g
Carbo 23 g
T Fat 24 g
39% Calories
from Fat
Chol 146 mg
Fiber 3 g
Sod 1893 mg

Combine the soy sauce, brown sugar, sherry, wine vinegar, oil, ginger powder, black pepper and cayenne in a dish and mix well. Add the chicken, tossing to coat. Marinate, covered, in the refrigerator for 1 hour or longer, stirring occasionally. Drain, reserving 1/4 cup of the marinade. Mix the reserved marinade and cornstarch in a bowl. Add the chicken, stirring to coat. Spoon into a microwave-safe dish. Cover with plastic wrap and vent 1 edge. Microwave on High for 9 minutes. Add the red pepper and green onions. Microwave for 3 minutes or until the chicken is cooked through. Sprinkle with the almonds, sesame seeds and parsley. Broil for 3 minutes or until brown. Serve with rotelle or steamed rice.

Brenda Riedler
Parent, Kiersten 2003 and Stephanie 2007
String Instruments, 1995 to 1997

Chicken Simon and Garfunkle

Yield:
6 servings

6 boneless skinless chicken breasts
6 tablespoons butter or margarine
6 (1-ounce) slices mozzarella cheese
Salt and pepper to taste
3 eggs, lightly beaten
1/2 cup milk
1/2 cup cracker crumbs

6 tablespoons melted butter or
  margarine
1/4 teaspoon parsley flakes
1/4 teaspoon sage
1/4 teaspoon rosemary
1/4 teaspoon thyme
1/2 cup white wine

Approx
Per Serving:
Cal 660
Prot 64 g
Carbo 7 g
T Fat 39 g
55% Calories
from Fat
Chol 340 mg
Fiber <1 g
Sod 601 mg

Pound the chicken between sheets of waxed paper with a meat mallet until flattened. Place 1 of the tablespoons of butter and 1 slice of the cheese on each chicken breast. Sprinkle with salt and pepper. Roll to enclose the filling and secure with wooden picks. Beat the eggs with the milk. Dip the chicken rolls in the mixture. Roll in the cracker crumbs. Arrange the chicken rolls in a single layer in a baking pan. Mix 6 tablespoons melted butter, parsley flakes, sage, rosemary and thyme in a bowl. Pour over the chicken. Bake at 350 degrees for 35 minutes. Add the white wine. Bake for 15 minutes longer or until the chicken is cooked through.

Jean Bartlett
Parent, Christopher 2003

Chicken and Stuffing Casserole

Yield:
10 servings

2 cups stuffing mix
1/2 cup margarine
10 boneless skinless chicken
  breasts, cut into narrow strips
10 (1-ounce) slices Swiss cheese

1 (6-ounce) can mushrooms,
  drained
2 (10-ounce) cans cream of
  mushroom soup
1/2 cup sherry

Approx
Per Serving:
Cal 652
Prot 67 g
Carbo 26 g
T Fat 29 g
41% Calories
from Fat
Chol 173 mg
Fiber 2 g
Sod 1312 mg

Sauté the stuffing mix in the margarine in a skillet. Layer the chicken, cheese and mushrooms in a baking pan. Spread with a mixture of the soup and sherry. Top with the stuffing mix. Bake at 325 degrees for 1 1/4 hours or until brown and bubbly. May be prepared in advance and stored, covered, in the freezer for future use. Bake just before serving.

Pat Bartlett
Parent, Benjamin 2004

Chickalita

May substitute turkey for the chicken, in which case the recipe would be titled Turkalita.

Yield:
6 servings

6 ounces Monterey Jack cheese, shredded
1 cup shredded sharp Cheddar cheese
6 boneless skinless chicken breasts, chopped
2 cups sour cream

1 (10-ounce) can cream of mushroom soup
1 cup chopped Anaheim chiles
1 medium onion, chopped
1/2 (10-ounce) can enchilada sauce
Garlic salt to taste

Approx
Per Serving:
Cal 730
Prot 69 g
Carbo 13 g
T Fat 44 g
55% Calories
from Fat
Chol 234 mg
Fiber 1 g
Sod 823 mg

Reserve 2/3 cup of the Monterey Jack cheese and 1/3 cup of the Cheddar cheese. Sauté the chicken in a nonstick skillet until light brown. Combine the remaining Monterey Jack cheese, remaining Cheddar cheese, chicken, sour cream, soup, chiles, onion, enchilada sauce and garlic salt in a bowl and mix well. Spoon into a baking pan. Sprinkle with the reserved cheese. Bake at 350 degrees for 45 minutes. Serve over rice.

JoAnn Burchfiel, 1973

Hot Chicken Salad

Yield:
8 servings

1 cup chopped celery
1 teaspoon minced onion
1 tablespoon butter
2 cups chopped cooked chicken breasts
1 cup cooked rice
3/4 cup mayonnaise

1 (10-ounce) can cream of chicken soup
1/2 cup sliced water chestnuts
1 teaspoon lemon juice
1 teaspoon salt
1 cup crushed cornflakes
1/2 cup sliced almonds

Approx
Per Serving:
Cal 384
Prot 14 g
Carbo 24 g
T Fat 26 g
61% Calories
from Fat
Chol 53 mg
Fiber 2 g
Sod 908 mg

Sauté the celery and onion in the butter in a skillet. Remove from heat. Stir in the chicken, rice, mayonnaise, soup, water chestnuts, lemon juice and salt. Spoon into a greased baking dish. Sprinkle with the cornflakes and almonds. Bake at 350 degrees for 30 minutes or until brown and bubbly.

Debra Charles
Parent, Laura 2001

Chicken Potpie

For variety, serve the chicken filling as a stew without the pastry.

Yield:
18 servings

4 pounds boneless skinless chicken breasts, cut into bite-size pieces
3 to 4 cups boiling water
3 large potatoes, peeled, chopped
1 large onion, chopped
2 ribs celery, chopped
1/4 teaspoon paprika
Salt to taste
5 to 6 carrots, sliced
2 tablespoons margarine
2 tablespoons flour
Pepper to taste
3 recipes (2-crust) pie pastry

Approx
Per Serving:
Cal 448
Prot 25 g
Carbo 36 g
T Fat 22 g
45% Calories
from Fat
Chol 56 mg
Fiber 2 g
Sod 366 mg

Combine the chicken with enough boiling water to cover in a stockpot. Add the potatoes, onion, celery, paprika and salt. Bring to a boil; reduce heat. Simmer for 30 minutes, stirring occasionally. Add the carrots. Simmer for 30 minutes longer or until the chicken is cooked through. Strain, reserving 3 cups of the chicken stock. Heat the margarine in a saucepan until melted. Stir in the flour. Add the reserved chicken stock and mix well. Cook until thickened, stirring constantly. Stir in the chicken and vegetables. Season with salt and pepper. Let stand until cool. Spoon the chicken mixture into three 9-inch pastry-lined pie plates. Top with the remaining pastry, fluting the edges and cutting vents. Bake at 475 degrees until golden brown. May add frozen corn and peas. May bake in individual tart shells.

Elaine Hinkle
Cook for the Kerper Family, Danielle 2004

Sherried Chicken Livers

Yield:
4 servings

8 ounces mushrooms, sliced
2 tablespoons chopped shallots
1¹/₂ pounds chicken livers, trimmed, separated into halves
¹/₂ to ³/₄ cup flour
¹/₃ cup butter or olive oil
2 to 4 tablespoons dry or cream sherry
¹/₂ teaspoon tarragon
¹/₄ to ¹/₃ cup half-and-half

Approx
Per Serving:
Cal 384
Prot 22 g
Carbo 22 g
T Fat 22 g
51% Calories
from Fat
Chol 488 mg
Fiber 1 g
Sod 202 mg

Sauté the mushrooms and shallots in a nonstick skillet until tender. Combine the chicken livers and flour in a sealable plastic bag and shake to coat. Shake to remove the excess flour. Heat the butter in a skillet until melted. Add the chicken livers in a single layer; do not overlap. Cook until blood rises on top; turn. Cook until brown on both sides. Stir in the sherry and tarragon. Mix in the mushrooms and shallots. Stir in the half-and-half. Cook just until heated through, stirring frequently; do not boil. Serve with hot cooked pasta or rice and steamed green beans, asparagus or broccoli.

Lisa Braun-Glazer
Parent, Julia 2001

Over the years, parents have been the heroes in helping
La Jolla Country Day School reach its many milestones. Starting in
The Balmer School years, parents have worked closely with the
school's headmasters to uphold the school's high ideals. The Parents'
Association has been the key to communication between the
school and the parents. Through fund-raising events, the Parents'
Association provides substantial financial assistance to the
school for the benefit of the students.

Japanese-Style Steamed Chicken

May be served as an entrée, side dish or as an appetizer.

Yield:
6 servings

1 pound chicken legs
2 teaspoons salt
Pepper to taste
$1/4$ cup Japanese rice wine (sake) or white wine
$1/4$ cup water
1 cup shredded cucumber
Soy sauce to taste
Mustard or horseradish to taste

Approx
Per Serving:
Cal 71
Prot 9 g
Carbo 1 g
T Fat 2 g
23% Calories
from Fat
Chol 29 mg
Fiber <1 g
Sod 805 mg

Sprinkle the chicken with the salt and pepper. Heat the wine and water in a saucepan. Add the chicken. Bring to a boil; reduce heat to medium. Steam, covered, for 10 minutes; drain. Let stand until cool. Cut the chicken into $1/4$-inch slices. Serve over the cucumber. Dip the chicken in a mixture of the soy sauce, mustard or horseradish as you eat.

Reiko Saito
Parent, Daichi 2010

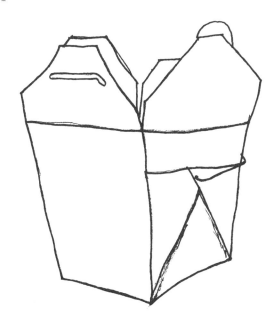

Pepper Chicken with Cilantro

Yield:
4 servings

2 medium onions, cut into quarters
3 cups cilantro leaves
10 to 15 cloves of garlic
5 to 6 green chiles
1 (1-inch piece) gingerroot
3 tablespoons vegetable oil
2 pounds boneless skinless chicken thighs, cut into bite-size pieces
4 teaspoons ground pepper

Approx
Per Serving:
Cal 394
Prot 32 g
Carbo 17 g
T Fat 23 g
51% Calories
from Fat
Chol 105 mg
Fiber 3 g
Sod 110 mg

Combine the onions, cilantro, garlic, chiles and gingerroot in a food processor container. Process until of a paste-like consistency. Heat the oil in a skillet. Stir in the cilantro paste. Cook over medium heat for 15 minutes or until all the moisture has evaporated and the paste is dark green in color, stirring occasionally. Stir in the chicken. Add the pepper and mix well. Cook for 35 minutes or until the moisture has evaporated and the oil begins to separate from the sauce, stirring occasionally; add about 1/4 cup water if the sauce becomes too dry and sticks to the bottom of the skillet. Simmer for 10 to 15 minutes longer if necessary to completely cook the chicken.

Parvine Chowfla
Parent, Anjali 2005

Chicken Enchilada Casserole

Yield:
6 servings

1 (20-ounce) can mild enchilada sauce
1 cup plain nonfat yogurt
8 corn tortillas, cut into 1-inch squares
2 cups chopped or shredded cooked chicken
1 cup shredded Monterey Jack cheese
2 tablespoons chopped canned or fresh green chiles
1 bunch green onions, chopped
1/2 cup sliced black olives

Approx
Per Serving:
Cal 395
Prot 23 g
Carbo 26 g
T Fat 23 g
51% Calories
from Fat
Chol 93 mg
Fiber 4 g
Sod 482 mg

Mix the enchilada sauce and yogurt in a bowl. Layer 1/2 of the tortillas, 1/2 of the chicken, 1/2 of the cheese, 1/2 of the chiles, 1/2 of the green onions and 1/2 of the black olives in an 8x8-inch or 9x9-inch baking dish sprayed with nonstick cooking spray. Spread with 1/2 of the enchilada sauce mixture. Layer with the remaining tortillas, remaining chicken, remaining chiles and remaining black olives. Sprinkle with half of the remaining cheese. Spread with the remaining enchilada sauce mixture. Sprinkle with the remaining cheese and remaining green onions. Bake at 350 degrees for 30 minutes. May substitute any yellow cheese for all or part of the Monterey Jack cheese.

Dorothy Trexel
Grandmother, Mandy 2010

If you think an education is expensive, try ignorance.

Attributed to Derek Bok, President, Harvard University

Heart-Healthy Chicken Enchiladas

Yield:
6 servings

1 (1³/₄-pound) chicken
1 cup mild enchilada sauce
1 cup plain nonfat yogurt
1 cup shredded low-fat Monterey Jack cheese
¹/₂ cup chopped fresh cilantro
Freshly ground pepper to taste
6 (8-inch) flour tortillas
1 (16-ounce) jar mild or medium salsa
2 cups shredded low-fat Monterey Jack cheese

Approx
Per Serving:
Cal 529
Prot 40 g
Carbo 40 g
T Fat 23 g
39% Calories
from Fat
Chol 98 mg
Fiber 4 g
Sod 1040 mg

Combine the chicken with enough cold water to cover in a stockpot. Bring to a boil; reduce heat. Poach for 1 hour or until the chicken is cooked through. Let stand in the poaching liquid until cool; drain. Chop the chicken, discarding the skin and bone. Spread ¹/₂ cup of the enchilada sauce in a shallow baking dish. Combine the chicken, yogurt, 1 cup cheese, cilantro and pepper in a bowl and mix well. Spoon some of the chicken mixture in the center of each tortilla. Roll to enclose the filling. Arrange the tortillas seam side down in the prepared baking dish. Spoon the remaining ¹/₂ cup enchilada sauce over the tortillas. Top with the salsa and sprinkle with 2 cups cheese. Bake at 350 degrees for 20 to 30 minutes or until hot and bubbly. May be frozen uncooked for future use. Bake frozen for an additional 10 minutes.

Pamela Wischkaemper
Parent, Mark 1997

Roasted Game Hens

Yield:
2 servings

1 tablespoon butter
2 Cornish game hens
Salt to taste
4 cloves of garlic, flattened with fork
3 teaspoons butter
2 tablespoons minced fresh thyme
6 small boiling onions, cut into halves
6 ounces baby carrots, peeled
8 ounces small red potatoes, cut into halves
$1/3$ cup chicken broth
2 tablespoons lemon juice
4 tablespoons minced fresh thyme
Olive oil to taste
Pepper to taste

Approx
Per Serving:
Cal 606
Prot 57 g
Carbo 46 g
T Fat 21 g
32% Calories
from Fat
Chol 264 mg
Fiber 6 g
Sod 427 mg

Brush a roasting pan with 1 tablespoon butter. Remove the giblets from the hens. Rub salt in the cavities of the hens. Place 2 of the cloves of garlic, $1^{1}/_{2}$ teaspoons of the butter and 1 tablespoon of thyme in each cavity; truss. Place the hens breast side down in the prepared roasting pan. Arrange the onions, carrots and potatoes around the hens. Pour a mixture of the chicken broth and lemon juice over the top. Sprinkle with 2 tablespoons of the thyme. Roast, covered with foil, at 400 degrees for 20 minutes. Turn the hens breast side up. Ladle the pan juices over the hens. Sprinkle with the remaining 2 tablespoons thyme. Drizzle olive oil over the hens and vegetables. Season with salt and pepper. Roast, uncovered, for 50 minutes longer or until a meat thermometer registers 175 degrees.

Mary Anne Brower
Chairman, Mathematics Department, 1984 to present

Get-Rich Turkey

I serve this dish as an alternate to the same old turkey and dressing, with mashed potatoes as a side dish.

Yield:
4 servings

1/4 cup butter
2 cloves of garlic, minced
1/2 teaspoon coarsely ground pepper
4 (4-ounce) turkey cutlets
1/4 cup crumbled bleu cheese

8 ounces mushrooms, cut into halves
1 cup chopped pecans
1/2 cup (1/2-inch) slices green onions
1/3 cup dry white wine

Approx
Per Serving:
Cal 488
Prot 34 g
Carbo 9 g
T Fat 35 g
63% Calories
from Fat
Chol 114 mg
Fiber 3 g
Sod 289 mg

Heat the butter in a 9x13-inch baking pan for 5 to 6 minutes or until melted. Stir in the garlic and pepper. Add the turkey, turning to coat. Sprinkle with the bleu cheese. Bake at 325 degrees for 50 to 60 minutes, basting occasionally. Add the remaining ingredients. Bake for 10 to 15 minutes longer or until the mushrooms are tender and a meat thermometer placed in the turkey registers 180 degrees. Slice the turkey diagonally and arrange on a serving platter. Top with the mushrooms, pecans and green onions.

Ann Blankenship
Parent, Philip Marks 2004

Green Chile Casserole

Yield:
6 servings

2 cups shredded cooked turkey or chicken
2 (10-ounce) cans cream of mushroom soup
1 (12-ounce) can evaporated milk
1/2 medium onion, chopped

1 (4-ounce) can chopped green chiles
1 (9-ounce) bag tortilla chips
2 cups shredded Monterey Jack cheese

Approx
Per Serving:
Cal 621
Prot 32 g
Carbo 42 g
T Fat 36 g
53% Calories
from Fat
Chol 79 mg
Fiber 3 g
Sod 1441 mg

Combine the first 5 ingredients in a saucepan and mix well. Cook until thickened, stirring frequently. Layer the tortilla chips, soup mixture and cheese 1/3 at a time in a 9x13-inch baking pan. Bake at 350 degrees for 30 minutes or until bubbly. Serve with salsa, guacamole and/or sour cream.

Mary Burns
Kindergarten, Lower School, 1990 to present

Smoked Turkey and Black-Eyed Peas

Yield:
6 servings

2 (16-ounce) cans black-eyed peas, drained, rinsed
1 (14-ounce) can stewed tomatoes, chopped
1 medium onion, sliced
1 1/2 teaspoons basil

1/2 teaspoon oregano
1/2 teaspoon thyme
1/2 teaspoon ground black pepper
1/4 teaspoon cayenne
3 pounds smoked turkey legs
3 cups cooked brown or white rice

Approx Per Serving:
Cal 429
Prot 43 g
Carbo 49 g
T Fat 6 g
13% Calories from Fat
Chol 134 mg
Fiber 8 g
Sod 695 mg

Combine the black-eyed peas, undrained tomatoes, onion, basil, oregano, thyme, black pepper and cayenne in a 6-quart stockpot and mix well. Add the turkey. Bring to a boil; reduce heat. Simmer, covered, for 30 minutes, stirring occasionally; remove the cover. Simmer for 30 minutes longer, stirring occasionally. Remove the turkey legs to a platter. Slice the turkey into bite-size pieces, discarding the bones. Return the turkey to the stockpot. Serve over the rice.

Lee Sawyer
Supervisor, Grounds Maintenance, 1970 to present

Turkey-Stuffed Potatoes

Great meal for hungry teenagers!

Yield:
4 servings

1 pound ground turkey
1 envelope chili mix
3/4 to 1 cup water

4 large baked potatoes
1 cup shredded Cheddar cheese
1/2 cup sour cream

Approx Per Serving:
Cal 573
Prot 34 g
Carbo 50 g
T Fat 26 g
41% Calories from Fat
Chol 125 mg
Fiber 4 g
Sod 332 mg

Brown the turkey in a skillet, stirring until crumbly; drain. Stir in the chili mix and water. Simmer for 10 minutes, stirring frequently. Split the baked potatoes. Spoon 1/4 of the turkey mixture over each potato. Sprinkle each potato with 1/4 cup cheese and top with 2 tablespoons sour cream. Garnish with chopped green onions and bacon bits.

Karen Stewart
Parent, Ty 1980 to 1993 and Tara 1999
Pre-Kindergarten, 1984 to present

Sea Bass

Yield:
4 servings

4 (6-ounce) sea bass steaks
2 cups bread crumbs
Chopped garlic to taste
Chopped gingerroot to taste

1/2 cup peanut oil
1/4 cup unsalted butter, clarified
3/4 cup oyster sauce
1/4 cup Japanese rice vinegar

Approx
Per Serving:
Cal 702
Prot 34 g
Carbo 40 g
T Fat 44 g
57% Calories
from Fat
Chol 92 mg
Fiber 1 g
Sod 895 mg

Coat the bass with the bread crumbs. Sauté the garlic and gingerroot in the peanut oil in a large skillet until brown; discard the garlic. Stir the butter into the peanut oil mixture. Add the fish. Fry for 2 minutes; turn. Fry for 2 minutes longer or until the fish flakes easily; drain. Remove to a serving platter. Drizzle with a mixture of the oyster sauce and rice vinegar.

Lorraine Kaa
Parent, Michael 2002
Cultural Geography, Middle School, 1996 to present

Ginger Lime Marinade for Fish or Chicken

Yield:
3/4 cup

1 (2- to 3-inch) piece gingerroot,
  peeled
1/2 cup fresh lime juice

1 tablespoon olive oil
6 cloves of garlic, finely minced
1/2 teaspoon pepper

Approx
Per 3/4 Cup:
Cal 181
Prot 2 g
Carbo 17 g
T Fat 14 g
62% Calories
from Fat
Chol 0 mg
Fiber 1 g
Sod 5 mg

Process the gingerroot in a food processor until finely minced. Add the lime juice, olive oil, garlic and pepper. Process until mixed. Use as a marinade for fish or chicken. Marinate overnight in the refrigerator for the best flavor.

Betsy McCallum
Parent, Jason 2010 and Kaitlin 2012
Mathematics, Middle School, 1994 to present

Fish for Ken

Yield:
2 servings

1 small onion, chopped
1 to 2 cloves of garlic, minced
1 tablespoon olive oil
1 (15-ounce) can diced tomatoes, or
   2 cups chopped Roma tomatoes

$1/2$ cup dry white wine or dry
   vermouth
$1/4$ teaspoon thyme
12 ounces sea bass
Juice of $1/2$ lemon

Approx
Per Serving:
Cal 305
Prot 30 g
Carbo 15 g
T Fat 10 g
29% Calories
from Fat
Chol 61 mg
Fiber 3 g
Sod 419 mg

Sauté the onion and garlic in the olive oil in a skillet; do not brown. Stir in the undrained tomatoes, white wine and thyme. Simmer, covered, for 20 minutes, stirring frequently. Add the bass, spooning the sauce over the fish. Cook for 10 to 15 minutes or until the fish flakes easily. Drizzle with lemon juice. Serve immediately. May be baked, covered, in a 350-degree oven. Substitute halibut, cod or orange roughy for the sea bass for variety.

Phyllis M. Crady
Wife of Ken Crady, Director, Middle School, 1990 to 1996
Director, Upper School, 1996 to 1998

Sour Cream Cilantro Sauce

Yield:
8 servings

2 bunches cilantro
1 bunch green onions, white part
   only
$1/4$ cup chicken broth

1 large clove of garlic
$1/8$ teaspoon cumin
$1/2$ cup sour cream

Approx
Per Serving:
Cal 37
Prot 1 g
Carbo 2 g
T Fat 3 g
72% Calories
from Fat
Chol 6 mg
Fiber <1 g
Sod 35 mg

Process the cilantro, green onions, broth, garlic and cumin in a food processor until finely minced. Add the sour cream. Process until mixed. Heat in a saucepan before serving. Serve over sea bass or chicken.

Sage Valenzuela
Aunt, Julie Landa 1999

Orange Roughy in Cilantro Sauce

Yield:
3 servings

2 tablespoons olive oil
1½ pounds orange roughy or any
   whitefish
1 medium tomato, finely chopped
¼ cup white wine

2 cloves of garlic, minced
1 to 2 tablespoons finely chopped
   cilantro
Salt and pepper to taste

Approx
Per Serving:
Cal 266
Prot 35 g
Carbo 3 g
T Fat 11 g
37% Calories
from Fat
Chol 47 mg
Fiber 1 g
Sod 152 mg

Heat a large skillet until hot. Add the olive oil. Cook the fish in the hot oil for 2 to 4 minutes or until brown on both sides. Transfer the fish to a platter, reserving the pan drippings. Cover to keep warm. Stir the tomato, white wine, garlic, cilantro, salt and pepper into the reserved pan drippings. Cook over high heat until reduced, stirring constantly. Return the fish to the skillet. Cook for 1 minute. Place the fish on a serving platter; drizzle with the sauce.

Nancy Ullman
Parent, Lindsay 2005 and Max 2008

Family Fish Favorite

Yield:
2 servings

½ cup medium salsa
10½ ounces red snapper
Salt and pepper to taste

4 ounces Monterey Jack cheese,
   thinly sliced or shredded

Approx
Per Serving:
Cal 326
Prot 35 g
Carbo 4 g
T Fat 19 g
52% Calories
from Fat
Chol 87 mg
Fiber 1 g
Sod 516 mg

Spoon 2 to 3 tablespoons of the salsa liquid into a 9x13-inch baking pan. Arrange the fish over the liquid. Sprinkle with salt and pepper. Bake at 350 degrees for 10 minutes. Spoon the salsa over the fish. Bake for 10 minutes. Arrange the cheese over the top. Bake for 10 minutes longer or until the fish flakes easily. Serve with additional salsa if desired. May substitute halibut or sea bass for the red snapper.

Cherry Lee
Parent, Christie Gerry 1980
Art, Fine Arts Department, 1970 to 1995

Barbecued Salmon

Yield:
6 servings

¹/₂ cup butter or margarine
1 tablespoon soy sauce
1 tablespoon Dijon mustard
1 tablespoon Worcestershire sauce

Crushed garlic or garlic powder to taste
3 pounds salmon fillets

Approx
Per Serving:
Cal 480
Prot 43 g
Carbo 1 g
T Fat 33 g
63% Calories
from Fat
Chol 177 mg
Fiber <1 g
Sod 570 mg

Combine the butter, soy sauce, Dijon mustard, Worcestershire sauce and garlic in a skillet. Cook until the butter melts, stirring occasionally. Add the salmon. Cook 10 minutes per inch of thickness or until the fish flakes easily, spooning the sauce over the salmon occasionally.

Susie Olson
Director of Community Service, 1997 to present
English, Middle School, 1987 to 1997

Grilled Marinated Salmon

Yield:
6 servings

¹/₄ cup sugar
2 tablespoons kosher salt
2 tablespoons grated orange peel

1 teaspoon pepper
6 (6-ounce) salmon fillets

Approx
Per Serving:
Cal 287
Prot 32 g
Carbo 9 g
T Fat 13 g
42% Calories
from Fat
Chol 102 mg
Fiber <1 g
Sod 1997 mg

Combine the sugar, salt, orange peel and pepper in a bowl and mix well. Spread over both sides of the salmon. Arrange the salmon in a single layer in a nonreactive dish. Marinate, covered, in the refrigerator for 4 hours. Grill over hot coals until the salmon flakes easily.

Rama Iaco
Parent, Michael 2001 and Garrett 2004

Salmon in Champagne Sauce

Yield:
3 servings

1¹/₂ pounds salmon fillets, cut into 2-inch rectangles
Salt and pepper to taste
1 tablespoon butter
Champagne Sauce

Approx
Per Serving:
Cal 721
Prot 49 g
Carbo 9 g
T Fat 43 g
54% Calories
from Fat
Chol 353 mg
Fiber 1 g
Sod 211 mg

Sprinkle the salmon on both sides with salt and pepper. Heat the butter in a skillet until melted. Sauté the salmon in the butter for 2 minutes per side or until the salmon flakes easily. Remove to a serving platter. Drizzle with the Champagne Sauce.

Champagne Sauce

2 or 3 shallots, minced
1 tablespoon butter
8 ounces mushrooms
2 cups Champagne
¹/₂ cup whipping cream
2 egg yolks, lightly beaten

Sauté the shallots in the butter in a skillet. Add the mushrooms and mix well. Sauté until the mushrooms are tender. Remove to a bowl. Bring the Champagne to a boil in the skillet. Boil until reduced by ¹/₂. Whisk in a mixture of the whipping cream and egg yolks. Cook over low heat until thickened, stirring constantly. Stir in the shallot mixture. Cook just until heated through, stirring constantly.

Pam Madigan
Parent, Taylor 2012
Mathematics, Middle School, 1991 to present

Grilled Salmon with Mustard Mint Sauce

Yield:
4 servings

4 (6-ounce) salmon fillets
2 tablespoons olive oil
Minced garlic to taste
Salt and pepper to taste
Mustard Mint Sauce

Approx
Per Serving:
Cal 687
Prot 33 g
Carbo 2 g
T Fat 60 g
80% Calories
from Fat
Chol 102 mg
Fiber 1 g
Sod 168 mg

Brush the salmon on both sides with a mixture of the olive oil and garlic. Sprinkle with salt and pepper. Grill over hot coals until the salmon flakes easily. Transfer the salmon to a serving platter. Drizzle with the Mustard Mint Sauce just before serving.

Mustard Mint Sauce

1/4 cup packed mint leaves
3 tablespoons white wine vinegar
1 1/2 tablespoons coarse grain mustard
3/4 cup olive oil

Combine the mint, wine vinegar and mustard in a food processor fitted with a steel blade. Process until blended. Add the olive oil in a fine stream, processing constantly until smooth.

Rebecca Wood, 1970

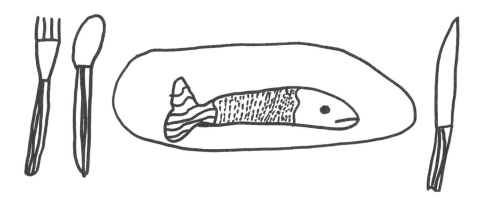

Grilled Salmon with Anchovy Sauce

Yield:
2 servings

1 slice white bread
1/4 cup vinegar
1/2 cup chopped fresh parsley
3 tablespoons olive oil
1 1/2 tablespoons capers

2 cloves of garlic
1/2 teaspoon anchovy paste
1/8 teaspoon sugar
2 (6-ounce) salmon fillets

Approx
Per Serving:
Cal 497
Prot 35 g
Carbo 13 g
T Fat 34 g
62% Calories
from Fat
Chol 103 mg
Fiber 1 g
Sod 405 mg

Soak the bread in the vinegar in a bowl until soft. Process the bread mixture, parsley, olive oil, capers, garlic, anchovy paste and sugar in a blender until puréed. Grill the salmon over hot coals until the salmon flakes easily. Serve the salmon hot or cold with the sauce. Garnish with fresh parsley.

Ruthi Warburg
Parent, Jeremy 2004

Raspberry Salmon

Yield:
4 servings

1 (2- to 2 1/2-pound) salmon fillet
1 (16-ounce) jar raspberry jam
1 (750-milliliter) bottle inexpensive
  white wine

Green peppercorns to taste

Approx
Per Serving:
Cal 823
Prot 54 g
Carbo 75 g
T Fat 22 g
23% Calories
from Fat
Chol 170 mg
Fiber 1 g
Sod 184 mg

Spread the salmon on both sides with 3/4 of the jam. Place in baking dish. Pour the wine over the salmon. Sprinkle with the peppercorns. Marinate, covered, in the refrigerator for 2 to 4 hours or longer. Pour off the majority of the wine. Spread the fillets with the remaining jam. Bake at 350 degrees for 30 minutes or until the salmon flakes easily.

Ronni Zeidman
Parent, Jared 2004

Salmon Vegetable Crest

Yield:
2 servings

2 (6-ounce) salmon steaks
3 tablespoons lemon or lime juice
1/4 cup grated carrot
1/4 cup chopped tomato

2 tablespoons chopped green onions
1 tablespoon chopped fresh parsley
1/8 teaspoon salt
1/8 teaspoon pepper

Approx
Per Serving:
Cal 272
Prot 33 g
Carbo 5 g
T Fat 13 g
44% Calories
from Fat
Chol 102 mg
Fiber 1 g
Sod 232 mg

Arrange the steaks in a baking dish sprayed with nonstick cooking spray. Drizzle with the lemon juice. Marinate, covered, in the refrigerator for the desired amount of time. Combine the carrot, tomato, green onions, parsley, salt and pepper in a bowl and mix well. Mound the vegetable mixture over the steaks. Bake at 400 degrees for 14 to 20 minutes or until the salmon flakes easily. Garnish with lemon or lime wedges.

Lerena Kreiss
Parent, Loren 1999 and Nick 2001

Broiled Swordfish

Yield:
5 servings

2 1/4 pounds swordfish, cut into
    1-inch-thick pieces
1/4 cup orange juice
1/4 cup soy sauce
3 tablespoons tomato paste
2 tablespoons lemon juice

2 tablespoons chopped fresh parsley
1 teaspoon minced garlic
1 teaspoon oregano
1/2 teaspoon salt
Freshly ground pepper to taste
1 to 2 teaspoons butter, softened

Approx
Per Serving:
Cal 208
Prot 29 g
Carbo 5 g
T Fat 7 g
32% Calories
from Fat
Chol 59 mg
Fiber 1 g
Sod 1504 mg

Arrange the swordfish in a single layer on a foil-lined baking sheet. Mix the orange juice, soy sauce and next 7 ingredients in a bowl. Brush all sides of the swordfish with some of the marinade. Marinate, covered, in the refrigerator for 4 hours. Preheat the broiler for 10 minutes. Brush a foil-lined baking sheet with the butter. Arrange the swordfish in a single layer on the baking sheet. Brush heavily with the marinade. Broil 3 inches from the heat source for 5 minutes; turn. Brush the swordfish with the remaining marinade. Broil for 3 to 5 minutes or until the fish is firm but not hard to the touch; do not overcook. Transfer the swordfish to a serving platter. Drizzle with the pan juices. Garnish with parsley sprigs and lemon slices. Serve with brown and wild rice, glazed baby carrots and tartar sauce.

Rita Gittes
Parent, Robert 1999

Creole Crab and Rice

Yield:
4 servings

2 cups water
2 cups uncooked rice
1 tablespoon vegetable oil or butter
1 teaspoon salt
2 (6-ounce) cans Dungeness crab or lump crab meat
2 tablespoons olive oil or butter
1 cup water
1 small red bell pepper, chopped
1 small onion, sliced
Juice of 1 lemon
Thyme to taste
Parsley flakes to taste
Salt to taste

Approx
Per Serving:
Cal 528
Prot 25 g
Carbo 78 g
T Fat 12 g
21% Calories
from Fat
Chol 76 mg
Fiber 2 g
Sod 870 mg

Bring 2 cups water to a boil in a saucepan. Add the rice, vegetable oil and 1 teaspoon salt and mix well. Cook, covered, over low heat for 20 to 30 minutes or until the rice is tender and the water has been absorbed. Remove from heat. Let stand, covered, until ready to serve. Sauté the crab meat in the olive oil in a skillet for 5 minutes. Stir in 1 cup water, red pepper, onion, lemon juice, thyme, parsley flakes and salt to taste. Cook for 30 minutes, stirring occasionally. Serve with the hot rice.

Denyse Pierre-Pierre
Grandmother, Michelle 1999

Grilled Mussels

Yield:
4 servings

8 pounds mussels in shells, scrubbed
1 to 2 cups butter
6 cloves of garlic, minced
Rosemary, thyme, oregano, basil, dillweed and parsley flakes to taste
2 cups seasoned bread crumbs

Approx
Per Serving:
Cal 1737
Prot 106 g
Carbo 74 g
T Fat 112 g
58% Calories
from Fat
Chol 477 mg
Fiber 3 g
Sod 4023 mg

Fill a steamer with water just to the bottom of the steamer rack. Bring to a boil. Add the mussels to the steamer rack. Steam, covered, for 5 to 10 minutes or until the shells open. Open the shells, discarding the empty half. Arrange the remaining halves open side up in a baking pan. Heat the butter, garlic, rosemary, thyme, oregano, basil, dillweed and parsley in a saucepan until the butter melts, stirring occasionally. Baste each mussel with some of the butter mixture using a baster. Sprinkle with the bread crumbs. Broil for 3 to 5 minutes or until light brown. Don't use utensils; pick up 2 mussels and use each one to scrape the mussel out of the other. That's the fun part.

Chick Pyle
Parent, Katie 1991 and Greg 1993
Board of Trustees, 1989 to 1992

La Jolla Country Day School is committed to integrating character education and core ethical values into the programs for all students. The Six Pillars of Character—Trustworthiness, Respect, Responsibility, Fairness, Caring, Citizenship—form the cornerstone of the relationships at La Jolla Country Day School.

Bouillabaisse

Yield:
15 servings

1 pound white fish, cut into chunks
1 (7-ounce) can chopped clams
1 (32-ounce) bottle clam juice
Salt and pepper to taste
3 large onions, chopped
2 bunches green onions, chopped
4 ribs celery, finely chopped
4 carrots, thinly sliced
1 green bell pepper, thinly sliced
1 tablespoon salt
1 tablespoon pepper
$1/2$ teaspoon saffron powder
3 cloves of garlic, crushed
Juice of 2 lemons

$1/2$ cup olive oil
2 (15-ounce) cans tomato sauce
$1/2$ cup finely chopped parsley
2 (11-ounce) cans tomato purée
4 large potatoes, coarsely chopped
2 envelopes onion soup mix
2 pounds peeled shrimp
2 pounds lobster tails, cut into
  chunks
2 pounds large scallops
2 pounds bass or cod, cut into
  chunks
8 ounces crab meat

Approx
Per Serving:
Cal 436
Prot 49 g
Carbo 29 g
T Fat 14 g
29% Calories
from Fat
Chol 189 mg
Fiber 5 g
Sod 2246 mg

Combine 1 pound white fish, clams, clam juice and salt and pepper to taste with a minimum amount of water in a large saucepan. Cook for 30 minutes, stirring occasionally. Remove from heat. Sauté the onions, green onions, celery, carrots, green pepper, 1 tablespoon salt, 1 tablespoon pepper, saffron, garlic and lemon juice in the olive oil in a large skillet until the vegetables are light brown. Stir in 1 can of the tomato sauce. Simmer for 30 minutes, stirring occasionally. Combine the fish mixture, sautéed vegetables, remaining can of tomato sauce, parsley, tomato purée, potatoes and soup mix in a stockpot and mix well. Bring to a boil. Stir in the shrimp, lobster, scallops, bass and crab meat. Bring to a boil, stirring gently. Boil for 5 minutes, stirring occasionally. Ladle into soup bowls. Serve with crusty sour dough French bread or garlic toast. Do not add the seafood until just before serving.

Dr. Daniel and Lauren Salomon
Parents, Rennie 1997 and Marc 2000

Louisiana Shrimp Gumbo with Risotto Allo Zafferano

The risotto recipe is from the Lorenzade Medici Cooking School located in Tuscany.

Yield:
8 servings

6 tablespoons vegetable oil
6 tablespoons flour
2$\frac{1}{2}$ pounds shrimp, peeled, deveined
1 large onion, thinly sliced
6 ribs celery, sliced
$\frac{1}{2}$ small head garlic, sliced
8 ounces Polish sausage, sliced
1 (28-ounce) can whole tomatoes, chopped
$\frac{3}{4}$ tomato can hot water
2 tablespoons Kitchen Bouquet
1 teaspoon salt
$\frac{1}{2}$ teaspoon pepper
1 (16-ounce) package frozen sliced okra, thawed
2 tablespoons Creole seasoning
Tabasco sauce to taste
Risotto Allo Zafferano (page 129)

Approx
Per Serving:
Cal 692
Prot 38 g
Carbo 74 g
T Fat 23 g
32% Calories
from Fat
Chol 203 mg
Fiber 3 g
Sod 3177 mg

Heat the oil in a heavy stockpot. Stir in the flour. Cook for 10 to 12 minutes or until the roux is brown, stirring constantly; do not burn. Add the shrimp, stirring to coat. Stir in the onion, celery, garlic and sausage. Cook for 10 minutes, stirring occasionally. Add the undrained tomatoes and hot water and mix well. Stir in the Kitchen Bouquet, salt and pepper. Bring to a boil; reduce heat. Simmer for 1 hour, stirring occasionally. Add the okra, Creole seasoning and Tabasco sauce and mix well. Simmer for 30 minutes, stirring occasionally. Let stand for 1 hour before serving. Ladle over the Risotto Allo Zafferano in soup bowls.

Risotto Allo Zafferano

8 cups chicken or beef broth
1/2 teaspoon saffron
2 tablespoons chicken or beef broth
1/2 small white onion, finely chopped
2 tablespoons unsalted butter

6 cups Italian arborio rice
1 cup grated Parmesan cheese
2 tablespoons unsalted butter
Salt and freshly ground pepper
  to taste

Bring 8 cups broth to a boil in a saucepan; reduce heat. Cover and maintain on a low boil. Dissolve the saffron in 2 tablespoons of the broth in a bowl and mix well. Sauté the onion in 2 tablespoons butter in a saucepan over medium heat until tender. Add the rice, stirring to coat. Cook for several minutes, stirring constantly. Add just enough boiling broth to cover, stirring constantly. Add the remaining broth 1 cup at a time, stirring constantly. The rice should always be covered by a veil of broth. Stir in the saffron mixture. Cook for 15 minutes. Stir in the cheese, 2 tablespoons butter, salt and pepper. Remove from heat. Let stand, covered, for 2 minutes. The risotto should have the consistency of a creamy porridge.

Joyce Browning-Summers
Parent, Tyson 1999

Shrimp Fried Rice

Yield:
6 servings

3 tablespoons vegetable oil
3 eggs, beaten
4 cups cold cooked rice
1 onion, chopped
1 pound peeled small fresh shrimp

1/2 cup sliced fresh mushrooms
1/4 cup sliced water chestnuts
1/2 cup watercress
2 tablespoons soy sauce
1/2 teaspoon sugar

Approx
Per Serving:
Cal 306
Prot 18 g
Carbo 34 g
T Fat 10 g
31% Calories
from Fat
Chol 214 mg
Fiber 1 g
Sod 597 mg

Heat 1 tablespoon of the oil in a large skillet. Pour the beaten eggs into the skillet. Cook until firm on both sides. Remove the eggs and cut into shreds. Add the remaining 2 tablespoons oil to the skillet. Add the rice and onion and cook until light brown, stirring frequently. Add the shrimp. Cook until the shrimp turn pink, stirring constantly. Add the mushrooms, water chestnuts, watercress, soy sauce, sugar and shredded egg. Stir-fry for 5 to 8 minutes or until heated through.

Barbara Trigueros
Parent, Amber 2001

Sweet and Pungent Shrimp with Stir-Fried Vegetables

Try this recipe substituting chicken cut into bite-size pieces for the shrimp. I usually double the sauce recipe.

Yield:
6 servings

1 pound peeled and deveined fresh shrimp
1/2 egg white, beaten
1 cup cornstarch
1/2 teaspoon salt

3 to 4 cups light clear sesame oil for deep-frying
Sweet and Pungent Sauce
Stir-Fried Vegetables (page 131)

Approx
Per Serving:
Cal 303
Prot 15 g
Carbo 58 g
T Fat 2 g
6% Calories
from Fat
Chol 108 mg
Fiber 6 g
Sod 677 mg

Rinse the shrimp and pat dry. Place the shrimp in a large bowl. Add the egg white and mix well. Mix 1 1/2 tablespoons of the cornstarch with the salt. Sprinkle over the shrimp and stir until well coated. Refrigerate for 30 minutes or longer. Remove the shrimp to a work surface and dust with the remaining cornstarch; the shrimp should be dry to the touch. Heat the oil for deep-frying to 350 to 375 degrees in a large wok. Fry several of the shrimp at a time in the hot oil for 1 1/2 to 2 minutes or until crisp, separating carefully with chopsticks. Remove from the oil with a slotted spoon to drain on paper towels. Toss the shrimp with 1/2 cup of the Sweet and Pungent Sauce. Turn onto a serving platter. Sprinkle with chopped green onions. Serve with the Stir-Fried Vegetables and remaining sauce.

Sweet and Pungent Sauce

4 1/2 tablespoons sugar
4 1/2 tablespoons catsup
1/4 cup vinegar
1/2 teaspoon salt
1 tablespoon sherry
1/2 teaspoon cornstarch
1 teaspoon vegetable oil

2 large cloves of garlic, minced
3 to 4 teaspoons minced fresh gingerroot
1 tablespoon chopped green onions
1 teaspoon grated lemon zest
1 teaspoon grated orange zest

Blend the sugar, catsup, vinegar and salt in a bowl and set aside. Blend the sherry and cornstarch in a bowl and set aside. Heat the oil in a wok. Add the garlic, gingerroot, green onions, lemon and orange zests. Stir-fry for 30 seconds. Stir in the catsup mixture and the cornstarch mixture. Cook until slightly thickened, stirring constantly.

Stir-Fried Vegetables

8 ounces Chinese pea pods
Florets of 1 bunch broccoli
1 red bell pepper, cut into 1-inch
   pieces
1 large onion, cut into 1-inch pieces

1 (7-ounce) can water chestnuts,
   drained
2 carrots, sliced 1/4 inch thick
1 (16-ounce) can pineapple chunks,
   drained

Stir-fry the vegetables and pineapple in a large wok until the vegetables are tender-crisp. Place in a bowl and keep warm.

Nutritional information does not include oil for deep-frying.

Cameron Volker, 1972
Parent, John 2010

Seafood Kabobs

Yield:
6 servings

1 cantalope
1 honeydew melon
8 ounces scallops
12 ounces uncooked peeled shrimp with tails
1/4 cup lemon juice
2 tablespoons melted butter
1/4 cup Brie cheese with skin removed
1/4 cup light cream

Approx
Per Serving:
Cal 254
Prot 15 g
Carbo 29 g
T Fat 10 g
34% Calories
from Fat
Chol 114 mg
Fiber 2 g
Sod 280 mg

Use a melon baller to scoop out 30 melon balls from each melon. Thread the melon balls, scallops and shrimp onto six 8-inch skewers. Blend the lemon juice and butter in a small bowl. Place the skewers on a rack in a broiler pan. Broil for 10 minutes or until the scallops and shrimp are opaque, turning and basting with the lemon juice mixture occasionally. Melt the cheese in a small saucepan. Whisk in the cream gradually. Drizzle the mixture over the kabobs. Broil until golden brown. Serve over hot cooked rice. Two pounds of firm fish such as shark or swordfish is a tasty alternative to the scallops and shrimp.

Diane de Sequera
Science, Middle School, 1991 to present

Eggplant Burritos

Yield:
6 servings

1 (1½-pound) eggplant, cut into 1x3-inch strips
2 tablespoons olive oil
2 cups red bell pepper strips
2 tablespoons chopped jalapeño
1 cup sliced red onion
1 teaspoon oregano
1 teaspoon chili powder
2 cloves of garlic, minced
2 cups tomato juice or vegetable juice cocktail
1 cup water
1 tablespoon lime juice
¼ teaspoon salt
6 (10-inch) flour tortillas
1½ cups shredded nonfat Monterey Jack cheese
6 tablespoons sour cream or yogurt

Approx
Per Serving:
Cal 406
Prot 17 g
Carbo 56 g
T Fat 13 g
29% Calories
from Fat
Chol 9 mg
Fiber 6 g
Sod 968 mg

Sauté the eggplant in the olive oil in a large skillet until almost tender. Add the red pepper strips, jalapeño, onion, oregano, chili powder and garlic. Sauté until vegetables are tender. Add the tomato juice and water. Simmer until the mixture is almost dry. Remove from heat. Mix in the lime juice and salt. Arrange the tortillas on a baking sheet. Divide the vegetable mixture among the tortillas. Top with the cheese. Fold the tortilla sides over to enclose the filling and turn seam side down on the baking sheet. Bake at 350 degrees for 5 to 10 minutes or until the tortillas are golden brown. Top with the sour cream.

Kathryn Woods
Parent, Kaitlin and Megan 2012
Director of College Counseling, 1987 to present

Lightly Curried Vegetable Burritos

Kids have a knack for eating these. They know just what to do with a messy, sauce-oozing burrito—pick it up and eat it. Do not put it down until it's all gone—that's the secret.

Yield:
8 servings

1/2 green bell pepper, chopped
1/2 red bell pepper, chopped
1 medium red onion, chopped
4 cloves of garlic, finely minced
1 teaspoon curry powder
1 tablespoon sesame oil (not toasted) or canola oil
4 cups chopped mixed vegetables such as broccoli, zucchini, cauliflower, carrots, or steamed potatoes, or 1-inch pieces asparagus tips and green beans
4 cups shredded red leaf or butter lettuce
8 (10-inch) whole wheat flour tortillas
8 teaspoons crumbled feta cheese, rinsed

Approx
Per Serving:
Cal 116
Prot 4 g
Carbo 24 g
T Fat 3 g
20% Calories
from Fat
Chol 3 mg
Fiber 3 g
Sod 210 mg

Sauté the bell peppers, onion, garlic and curry powder in the sesame oil in a large skillet for 5 minutes. Add your choice of vegetables and shredded lettuce. Cook, covered, over low heat for 10 minutes. Warm the tortillas until pliable by placing in a nonstick skillet or wrapping in moist paper towels and microwaving on High for 30 to 60 seconds. Spoon about 1/2 cup of the vegetables down the center of a warm tortilla, sprinkle with 1 teaspoon feta cheese, fold the sides of the tortilla over the filling and roll up from the bottom toward the top. Repeat the process with the remaining vegetables, tortillas and cheese. Serve immediately.

Nutritional information does not include vegetables.

Lesa Heebner
Friend, Sanders 2001, Charlie 2004 and Amy Patton

Vegetable Chili

Yield:
8 servings

3 large cloves of garlic, minced
1 teaspoon chili powder
1/2 teaspoon ground cumin
1/2 teaspoon dry mustard
1/4 teaspoon celery seeds
1/4 teaspoon freshly ground pepper
1 tablespoon canola oil
1 (16-ounce) can tomatoes
12 ounces fresh green beans, cut
  into 1-inch pieces

1 1/2 cups 1/4-inch carrot slices
1 1/2 cups 1/2-inch diagonally sliced
  celery
1 cup chopped onion
2 cups mixed red and green bell
  pepper strips
1 2/3 cups cooked kidney beans, or
  1 (16-ounce) can
1 cup cooked garbanzo beans
Cucumber Yogurt Sauce

Approx
Per Serving:
Cal 197
Prot 9 g
Carbo 29 g
T Fat 6 g
26% Calories
from Fat
Chol 6 mg
Fiber 8 g
Sod 143 mg

Sauté the garlic, chili powder, cumin, dry mustard, celery seeds and pepper in the canola oil in a large deep skillet or Dutch oven over low heat for 1 to 2 minutes. Drain the tomatoes, reserving the juice. Add 1/2 cup of the reserved juice, green beans, carrots and celery to the skillet and mix well. Cook, covered, for 10 minutes. Add the onion and pepper strips. Cook, covered, for 10 minutes. Add the drained tomatoes, remaining tomato juice, and the kidney and garbanzo beans with their liquid. Cook for 10 minutes longer. Serve topped with the Cucumber Yogurt Sauce.

Cucumber Yogurt Sauce

1 1/2 cups plain yogurt
1 tablespoon olive oil
2 teaspoons apple cider vinegar
1 cup finely chopped unpeeled
  cucumber
1 teaspoon finely minced garlic

2 tablespoons finely snipped fresh
  dill, or 2 teaspoons dried dillweed
Salt to taste
1/4 cup crumbled feta cheese
  (optional)

Combine the yogurt, olive oil and vinegar in a small bowl and blend well. Add the cucumber, garlic, dill, salt and feta cheese and mix well. Chill, covered, until serving time. Sauce may also be served as a dip for fresh vegetables or pita bread.

Cameron Volker, 1972
Parent, John 2010

Vegetable Tacos

As a vegetarian meal these are delicious but you could also add 12 ounces of pork, beef, turkey or chicken to the sautéed vegetables and sauté until cooked through.

Yield:
12 tacos

2 tomatoes, chopped
4 carrots, grated
8 green onions with tops, chopped
1 onion, chopped
4 small or 2 large zucchini, grated
2 sunburst or crookneck squash, grated
1 clove of garlic, pressed
1 tablespoon canola oil
1 tablespoon apple cider vinegar
$1/2$ teaspoon ground cumin
$1/8$ teaspoon salt
$1/8$ teaspoon freshly ground pepper
$1/2$ cup canola oil
12 corn tortillas
Feta cheese to taste, crumbled
Homemade Mexican Salsa (page 15)

Approx
Per Taco:
Cal 101
Prot 3 g
Carbo 19 g
T Fat 2 g
17% Calories
from Fat
Chol 0 mg
Fiber 4 g
Sod 80 mg

Sauté the tomatoes, carrots, green onions, onion, zucchini, squash and garlic in 1 tablespoon oil in a large skillet or saucepan over medium heat for 25 minutes. Add the vinegar, cumin, salt and pepper. Cook for 5 to 10 minutes, stirring occasionally. Heat $1/2$ cup canola oil in a medium saucepan. Fry each tortilla in the hot oil for several seconds on each side to soften. Place the tortillas between paper towels. Spoon the vegetable mixture onto the tortillas, sprinkle with cheese and fold the tortillas over to enclose the filling. Serve immediately with Homemade Mexican Salsa.

Nutritional information does not include oil for frying tortillas.

Cameron Volker, 1972
Parent, John 2010

Roasted Vegetables with Couscous

Yield:
6 servings

2 medium zucchini, cut into 1-inch slices
1 large red bell pepper, cut into 1-inch pieces
1 large yellow bell pepper, cut into 1-inch pieces
1 medium red onion, cut into 8 wedges
8 ounces fresh whole mushrooms
2 cloves of garlic, crushed
1 tablespoon extra-virgin olive oil
2 tablespoons minced fresh basil
2 tablespoons balsamic vinegar
$1/4$ teaspoon salt
4 to 5 ounces chèvre
3 cups cooked couscous

Approx
Per Serving:
Cal 216
Prot 10 g
Carbo 28 g
T Fat 8 g
31% Calories
from Fat
Chol 11 mg
Fiber 3 g
Sod 193 mg

Combine the zucchini, bell peppers, onion and mushrooms in a roasting pan. Combine the garlic, olive oil, minced basil, vinegar and salt in a small bowl and mix well. Drizzle over the vegetables and toss to coat. Roast at 425 degrees for 35 minutes or until the vegetables are tender. Spoon into a serving bowl. Top with the chèvre. Garnish with basil leaves and serve with the couscous.

Jackie and Barry Seidman
Parents, David 1996 and Steven 2001

Pasta and Pizza

The undeveloped piece of property with the greatest
potential is still between the ears.

Anonymous

Pasta and Pizza

Lasagna

Yield:
6 servings

8 ounces uncooked lasagna noodles
1 tablespoon salt
1 teaspoon olive oil
Lasagna Sauce
8 ounces mozzarella cheese, sliced
1 cup cream-style cottage cheese
1/2 cup grated Parmesan cheese

Approx
Per Serving:
Cal 529
Prot 38 g
Carbo 41 g
T Fat 24 g
40% Calories
from Fat
Chol 95 mg
Fiber 3 g
Sod 1509 mg

Cook the noodles according to the package directions in a large pot of boiling water to which the salt and olive oil have been added. Drain, rinse with cold water and drain well. Arrange half the noodles in a lightly greased 8x12-inch baking dish. Add layers of 1/3 of the Lasagna Sauce and half the mozzarella and cottage cheeses. Add layers of half the remaining sauce, all the remaining mozzarella and cottage cheeses, remaining sauce and the Parmesan cheese. Bake at 350 degrees for 25 to 30 minutes. Let stand for 15 minutes before cutting into squares.

Lasagna Sauce

1 pound ground beef
1 (29-ounce) can tomatoes
1 (8-ounce) can tomato sauce
2 cloves of garlic, minced
1 envelope spaghetti sauce mix
Salt to taste

Brown the ground beef in a large skillet, stirring frequently until crumbly; drain well. Add the tomatoes, tomato sauce, garlic and spaghetti sauce mix and mix well. Simmer, covered, for 40 minutes, stirring occasionally. Add salt to taste.

Eileen Huffman
Parent, Peter 1997

More

Yield:
8 servings

8 ounces uncooked rigatoni
8 ounces fresh green beans
4 ounces carrots, sliced
1 green bell pepper, sliced
1 pound ground beef
1 (3-ounce) can pitted black olives
1 (16-ounce) can cream-style corn

1 medium onion, chopped
4 ounces fresh mushrooms, sliced
Minced fresh garlic to taste
1 (28-ounce) can stewed tomatoes
Tabasco sauce to taste
Lemon pepper to taste
12 ounces Cheddar cheese, shredded

Approx
Per Serving:
Cal 515
Prot 30 g
Carbo 46 g
T Fat 24 g
42% Calories
from Fat
Chol 85 mg
Fiber 5 g
Sod 765 mg

Cook the rigatoni al dente using the package directions. Drain the pasta, rinse, drain well and set aside. Steam the green beans, carrots and green pepper until tender-crisp and set aside. Brown the ground beef in a skillet, stirring frequently until crumbly; drain well. Combine the rigatoni, ground beef, steamed vegetables, olives, corn, onion, mushrooms, garlic and tomatoes in a large bowl and mix gently. Add the Tabasco sauce, lemon pepper and about 2 cups of the shredded cheese and mix gently. Spoon into a greased baking dish. Sprinkle the remaining cheese over the top. Bake at 350 degrees for 1 hour.

Vicki McGhee
Parent, Paris 2009

Spaghetti Sauce

Yield:
10 cups

2 pounds lean ground beef
1 large green bell pepper, chopped
1 large onion, chopped
1 (6-ounce) can chopped
   mushrooms

2 (15-ounce) cans tomato sauce
1 (16-ounce) can stewed tomatoes
1 (12-ounce) can tomato paste
1 teaspoon garlic powder
1 tablespoon dried oregano

Approx
Per Cup:
Cal 281
Prot 23 g
Carbo 19 g
T Fat 13 g
41% Calories
from Fat
Chol 65 mg
Fiber 4 g
Sod 993 mg

Brown the ground beef in a large stockpot, stirring frequently until crumbly; drain well. Add the green pepper, onion, mushrooms, tomato sauce, stewed tomatoes, tomato paste, garlic powder and oregano and mix well. Simmer, covered, for 2 hours, stirring occasionally. Serve over hot cooked spaghetti.

Chan Pike
Parent, Mary Smedes 1998, Daniel 1999 and Eliza 2002

Norwegian Spaghetti Sauce

Yield:
4 cups

1 pound lean ground beef
1 medium onion, chopped
1 teaspoon vegetable oil
1 (46-ounce) can tomato juice

1 teaspoon (or more) garlic powder
1/2 cup butter
Salt to taste

Approx
Per Cup:
Cal 526
Prot 28 g
Carbo 16 g
T Fat 40 g
67% Calories
from Fat
Chol 143 mg
Fiber 2 g
Sod 1479 mg

Brown the ground beef with the onion in the oil in a large skillet, stirring frequently until crumbly; drain well. Add the tomato juice, garlic powder, butter and salt and mix well. Simmer, uncovered, for several hours or until very thick, stirring occasionally and adding additional garlic if desired. Serve over hot cooked pasta of your choice.

Linda Saavedra
Parent, Jaclyn 1998 and Britni 2000
Kindergarten Teaching Assistant, 1993 to present

Stuffed Shells

Yield:
8 servings

2 eggs
2 cups cottage cheese
2 cups shredded Cheddar cheese
2 cups shredded mozzarella cheese
1/2 teaspoon salt
1/8 teaspoon pepper
2 teaspoons dried parsley

2 (10-ounce) packages frozen
   chopped spinach, thawed
4 cups homemade or commercial
   spaghetti sauce
12 ounces uncooked large pasta
   shells, cooked, drained
1/4 cup grated Parmesan cheese

Approx
Per Serving:
Cal 605
Prot 32 g
Carbo 60 g
T Fat 27 g
40% Calories
from Fat
Chol 115 mg
Fiber 8 g
Sod 1384 mg

Beat the eggs lightly in a large bowl. Add the next 6 ingredients and mix well. Drain the spinach and squeeze dry. Add to the egg mixture and mix well. Spread a portion of the spaghetti sauce in a 9x13-inch baking pan. Stuff the pasta shells with the spinach mixture. Arrange the stuffed pasta shells in the pan. Spoon the remaining spaghetti sauce over the pasta and sprinkle with Parmesan cheese. Bake at 350 degrees for 30 to 40 minutes.

Nutritional information does not include spaghetti sauce.

Pat Konkle
Parent, Scott 1997

Best Spaghetti Sauce Ever

I would like to dedicate this recipe to my mom, who though far away is always close at heart.

For an easy 15-minute dinner, keep some of the sauce in the freezer to partially thaw in the microwave, then simmer in a saucepan over medium heat while boiling water for pasta and making a salad.

Yield:
8 servings

1 large onion, chopped
4 or 5 cloves of garlic, cut into
   halves lengthwise
3 tablespoons vegetable oil
1 (12-ounce) can tomato paste
1 (15-ounce) can tomato sauce
1 tablespoon dried oregano

1 tablespoon dried parsley
1 tablespoon dried basil
1 bay leaf
1 teaspoon salt
$1/8$ teaspoon pepper
1 tablespoon sugar
Meatballs

Approx
Per Serving:
Cal 226
Prot 17 g
Carbo 20 g
T Fat 10 g
38% Calories
from Fat
Chol 49 mg
Fiber 3 g
Sod 1090 mg

Sauté the onion and garlic in the oil in a Dutch oven over high heat for 3 to 4 minutes or until the onion becomes clear. Add the tomato paste and tomato sauce. Fill each can with water and add to the mixture. Stir in the oregano, parsley, basil, bay leaf, salt, pepper and sugar and mix well. Bring to a simmer, cover and simmer for $1^1/2$ hours, stirring occasionally. Add the Meatballs and mix gently. Simmer, uncovered, for 1 hour, stirring occasionally. Discard the bay leaf. Serve the meatballs and sauce over your favorite hot cooked pasta.

Meatballs

1 pound extra-lean ground beef
1 small onion, finely chopped
1 egg

$1/4$ teaspoon salt
$1/8$ teaspoon pepper
$1/4$ cup bread crumbs

Combine the ground beef, onion, egg, salt, pepper and bread crumbs in a bowl and mix well by hand. Shape into small meatballs. Brown on all sides in a large skillet and drain on paper towels.

Lisa Moallemi
Parent, Bijan 2006 and Keivan 2009

Tagarina

Yield:
8 servings

1 pound ground beef
1 large onion, chopped
1 clove of garlic, minced
2 (8-ounce) cans tomato sauce
1 (29-ounce) can tomatoes
8 ounces uncooked noodles
1 (16-ounce) can cream-style corn
4 ounces Velveeta cheese, sliced

Approx
Per Serving:
Cal 351
Prot 22 g
Carbo 39 g
T Fat 13 g
32% Calories
from Fat
Chol 75 mg
Fiber 4 g
Sod 893 mg

Brown the ground beef with onion and garlic in a large skillet, stirring frequently until crumbly; drain. Add the tomato sauce and tomatoes and mix well. Sprinkle the uncooked noodles on top; do not stir. Bring the mixture to a boil, reduce heat and cover. Simmer for 10 to 15 minutes or until the noodles are tender. Add the corn and mix gently. Pour into a greased casserole. Top with the cheese slices. Bake at 375 degrees for 25 minutes or until the cheese is melted and the casserole is heated through. Serve with a spinach salad.

Cathy Ellison
Parent, Jennifer 2003 and Elizabeth 2008
Physical Education, 1987 to present

Baked Ziti

Use your own favorite spaghetti sauce with meat but, if it is freshly made, cool it with a few ice cubes. All the ingredients should be cool when combined to avoid souring the ricotta.

Yield:
12 servings

2 pounds uncooked ziti
3 pounds whole milk ricotta cheese
2 eggs
1/2 cup grated Romano cheese
4 cups spaghetti sauce, cooled
3 pounds mozzarella cheese, shredded

Approx
Per Serving:
Cal 790
Prot 45 g
Carbo 55 g
T Fat 43 g
49% Calories
from Fat
Chol 186 mg
Fiber 2 g
Sod 581 mg

Cook the ziti according to the package directions, drain, rinse with cold water and drain well. Mix the ricotta cheese with the eggs in a large bowl. Add the Romano cheese, about half the cooled sauce, cooled ziti and about 3/4 of the mozzarella cheese and mix gently. Spread a small amount of the remaining sauce in the bottom of two 9x12-inch aluminum baking pans. Divide the ziti mixture between the baking pans, add the remaining sauce and sprinkle with the remaining mozzarella cheese. Bake at 350 degrees for 1 to 1 1/2 hours or until heated through.

Nutritional information does not include spaghetti sauce.

Dorothy Stanziano
Grandparent, Stephanie 2011

Penne with Spicy Sauce

Yield:
4 servings

3 or 4 cloves of garlic, finely chopped
3 tablespoons extra-virgin olive oil
1 pound hot pork or turkey sausage
1 (28-ounce) can crushed tomatoes with purée
1/4 to 1/2 teaspoon red pepper flakes
1 pound fresh penne
12 to 15 fresh basil leaves, torn into 1/2-inch pieces
3 tablespoons grated Pecorino Romano cheese

Approx
Per Serving:
Cal 757
Prot 29 g
Carbo 90 g
T Fat 32 g
38% Calories
from Fat
Chol 53 mg
Fiber 7 g
Sod 1070 mg

Sauté the garlic in the olive oil in a large skillet over medium-high heat until sizzling. Remove the casing from the sausage or cut into large pieces and add to the skillet. Cook the sausage until brown. Add the tomatoes and pepper flakes. Reduce the heat. Simmer for 30 minutes, stirring occasionally. Cook the penne according to package directions, drain and set aside. Add the basil and cheese to the sauce. Simmer for 2 minutes. Add the pasta to the sauce, mix gently and serve immediately.

Carole Kerr
Parent, Hillary E. 1997
First Grade Teaching Assistant, 1986

La Jolla Country Day School strives to provide its students with opportunities to develop those character traits which allow them to be successful participants in their future endeavors. The educational program, and community service requirements, encourage our students to be responsible, aware, informed, tolerant, flexible, creative, appreciative of differences, capable of collaboration, and imbued with a sense of personal integrity.

Pasta with White Beans and Spinach

Make this pasta as a hearty vegetarian entrée or add some reduced-fat smoked sausage with the beans to satisfy the meat eaters.

Yield:
4 servings

4 medium cloves of garlic, minced
Pinch of red hot pepper flakes
2 teaspoons olive oil
2 (14-ounce) cans Italian tomatoes
1/4 teaspoon salt
1/4 teaspoon pepper
1 teaspoon crushed dried basil
1 teaspoon crushed dried oregano
1 (15-ounce) can small white beans
1 (12-ounce) package fresh spinach, rinsed, chopped
12 ounces uncooked corkscrew pasta, cooked

Approx
Per Serving:
Cal 502
Prot 22 g
Carbo 93 g
T Fat 4 g
8% Calories
from Fat
Chol 0 mg
Fiber 12 g
Sod 582 mg

Sauté the garlic and pepper flakes in the olive oil in a large skillet. Add the tomatoes, salt, pepper, basil and oregano and mix well. Simmer for 5 minutes. Drain and rinse the beans. Add to the skillet and simmer for 5 minutes. Add the spinach. Cook just until the spinach wilts, stirring frequently. Stir in the pasta gently. Serve immediately topped with Parmesan cheese.

Susan Taylor
History, Middle School, 1986 to present

No man is lonely while eating spaghetti;
it requires so much attention.

Christopher Morley, American novelist

Pasta

Chicken Lasagna with Vegetables

Yield:
6 servings

Approx
Per Serving:
Cal 504
Prot 34 g
Carbo 41 g
T Fat 21 g
38% Calories
from Fat
Chol 75 mg
Fiber 4 g
Sod 1343 mg

8 ounces uncooked lasagna noodles
Mushroom Sauce

Chicken Filling
Tomato Sauce

Cook the lasagna noodles according to the package directions, drain, rinse and drain well. Cover the bottom of a 9x13-inch baking dish with Mushroom Sauce. Alternate layers of noodles, Chicken Filling and Mushroom Sauce. Spread the Tomato Sauce over the top. Bake at 400 degrees for 30 minutes or until heated through. Let stand for 10 minutes before cutting into portions.

Mushroom Sauce

2 (10-ounce) cans cream of
    mushroom soup
1 tablespoon instant dried onion

1 cup chicken broth
1/2 cup dry wine
Salt and pepper to taste

Combine the soup, dried onion, broth, wine and salt and pepper in a medium saucepan. Bring to a boil, stirring constantly and remove from the heat.

Chicken Filling

1 (10-ounce) package frozen
    chopped broccoli or spinach,
    thawed, well drained

3 cups chopped cooked chicken
1 cup shredded mozzarella cheese
1/2 cup grated Parmesan cheese

Combine the broccoli, chicken, mozzarella and Parmesan cheeses in a large bowl and mix well.

Tomato Sauce

1 cup favorite marinara sauce or
    spaghetti sauce

1/4 teaspoon grated dried orange
    peel

Mix the sauce with the dried orange peel in a small bowl.

Kay Foltz
Parent, Katy 2003, Kelly 2005 and Kenna 2008

Noodle Casserole

Yield:
8 servings

1/2 cup sliced fresh mushrooms
1 medium onion, chopped
1 small green bell pepper, chopped
1/4 cup sliced green olives
3 tablespoons vegetable oil
1 (10-ounce) can cream of
    mushroom soup

1 cup chicken broth
Salt and pepper to taste
8 ounces uncooked kluski noodles,
    cooked
2 tablespoons grated Parmesan
    cheese

Approx
Per Serving:
Cal 220
Prot 6 g
Carbo 25 g
T Fat 11 g
43% Calories
    from Fat
Chol 29 mg
Fiber 1 g
Sod 524 mg

Sauté the mushrooms, onion, green pepper and olives in the oil in a large skillet. Add the soup, broth and salt and pepper and mix well. Simmer for several minutes. Mix in the cooked noodles gently. Spoon into a lightly greased 9x13-inch baking dish. Sprinkle with the Parmesan cheese. Bake at 325 degrees for 25 minutes or until heated through.

Lillian Hurwitz
Grandparent, Andrea 2001 and Alex Leverant 2003

Spicy Macaroni and Cheese

Add new life to the old macaroni and cheese dinner for an inexpensive, quick, spicy teacher's meal or a great camping dish.

Yield:
4 servings

2 (7-ounce) packages macaroni and
    cheese
1 teaspoon paprika

1 teaspoon cayenne
1 teaspoon black pepper

Approx
Per Serving:
Cal 590
Prot 17 g
Carbo 68 g
T Fat 27 g
42% Calories
    from Fat
Chol 18 mg
Fiber 1 g
Sod 1075 mg

Prepare the macaroni and cheese according to the package directions. Add the paprika, cayenne and black pepper and mix well.

David Johns
Computer Science, Middle School, 1991 to 1997

Linguini with Clam Sauce

Yield:
4 servings

2 (6-ounce) cans minced clams
2 (6-ounce) cans chopped clams
1 teaspoon minced garlic
1/4 cup butter
2 tablespoons flour
1/2 cup dry white wine
1/8 teaspoon dried thyme leaves
1/8 teaspoon dried red pepper flakes
1/4 cup chopped fresh parsley
1 tablespoon fresh lemon juice
Salt and black pepper to taste
1 pound uncooked linguini, cooked

Approx
Per Serving:
Cal 654
Prot 28 g
Carbo 96 g
T Fat 15 g
20% Calories
from Fat
Chol 64 mg
Fiber 9 g
Sod 443 mg

Drain the minced and chopped clams, reserving the juice. Sauté the garlic in the butter in a medium skillet over medium-high heat just until the garlic begins to brown. Remove the skillet from the heat and blend in the flour. Cook over low heat for 1 minute, stirring constantly. Stir in the reserved clam juice, wine, thyme and red pepper flakes. Bring to a simmer, stirring constantly. Simmer for 1 to 2 minutes, stirring frequently. Stir in the clams, parsley and lemon juice and heat to serving temperature. Add salt and black pepper. Serve over hot cooked linguini.

Rama Iaco
Parent, Michael 2001 and Garrett 2004

Scallop Lasagna

Yield:
8 servings

2 pounds bay scallops
1/3 cup butter
1 cup chopped green onions
1 clove of garlic, chopped
1 tablespoon chopped fresh thyme
2 tablespoons chopped fresh parsley
1/3 cup flour
1 cup chicken broth
1 cup whipping cream
1/2 cup vermouth
8 ounces uncooked lasagna noodles
8 ounces Swiss cheese, shredded

Approx
Per Serving:
Cal 479
Prot 23 g
Carbo 28 g
T Fat 29 g
55% Calories
from Fat
Chol 105 mg
Fiber 1 g
Sod 498 mg

Rinse the scallops, drain and set aside. Melt 1 tablespoon of the butter in a medium skillet over medium heat. Add the green onions and garlic. Sauté until clear. Add the thyme, parsley and scallops and sauté until the scallops are cooked through. Strain the mixture and reserve both the scallop mixture and the juices. Melt the remaining butter in a saucepan over medium heat. Add the flour and blend well. Cook until golden brown, stirring constantly. Whisk in the broth, cream and vermouth until smooth. Bring to a simmer, whisking constantly. Remove from the heat. Cook the lasagna noodles al dente according to package directions, drain, rinse and set aside. Pour the reserved scallop juices into a small pan. Cook over high heat until the juices are reduced to 2 tablespoons. Blend into the cream sauce. Layer the noodles, cream sauce, scallop mixture and cheese 1/3 at a time in a lightly greased 9x13-inch baking pan. Bake at 350 degrees for 20 minutes. Let stand for 20 minutes before cutting into portions.

Kate Bradbury, 1985

Tex-Mex Lasagna

Yield:
6 servings

1 (30-ounce) can refried beans
1 (16-ounce) jar mild chunky salsa
1 (11-ounce) can whole kernel corn, drained
1 (4-ounce) can chopped green chiles
3 cups shredded Cheddar cheese
2 cups shredded Monterey Jack cheese
1 (15-ounce) carton ricotta cheese
8 ounces uncooked lasagna noodles

Approx
Per Serving:
Cal 822
Prot 45 g
Carbo 66 g
T Fat 42 g
46% Calories
from Fat
Chol 140 mg
Fiber 10 g
Sod 1723 mg

Combine the refried beans, salsa, corn and green chiles in a large bowl and mix well. Combine the Cheddar, Monterey Jack and ricotta cheeses in a large bowl and toss to mix. Cook the lasagna noodles according to the package directions. Spread 1 cup of the bean mixture in a lightly greased 9x13-inch baking dish. Layer half the noodles, half the remaining bean mixture and 1/4 of the cheese mixture in the prepared baking dish. Top with the remaining noodles, bean mixture and cheese mixture. Bake at 350 degrees for 45 to 60 minutes or until heated through.

Mark Marcus
Staff, Business Manager, 1985 to present

Gratinéed Ziti and Spinach Parmesan

Yield:
3 servings

1 medium onion, coarsely chopped
3 medium cloves of garlic, finely chopped
2 tablespoons extra-virgin olive oil
1 (35-ounce) can peeled Italian tomatoes
1/4 teaspoon crushed red pepper
3/4 teaspoon salt
1/4 teaspoon freshly ground black pepper
1 pound fresh spinach
10 ounces uncooked ziti
Salt to taste
6 ounces part-skim mozzarella cheese, shredded
1 cup freshly grated Parmesan cheese

Approx
Per Serving:
Cal 818
Prot 48 g
Carbo 85 g
T Fat 31 g
34% Calories
from Fat
Chol 57 mg
Fiber 10 g
Sod 2226 mg

Sauté the onion and garlic in the olive oil in a large skillet over medium heat for 5 minutes or until the onion is tender. Crush the tomatoes and add the tomatoes with juice to the skillet. Add the red pepper and mix well. Cook over medium-high heat for 18 minutes or until most of the liquid has evaporated, stirring constantly. Add 3/4 teaspoon salt and pepper. Discard the spinach stems, rinse and dry the spinach leaves, chop coarsely and set aside. Cook the ziti in a large pot of boiling salted water for 9 to 11 minutes or until al dente. Drain the ziti well and return to the dry pot. Add the spinach, mozzarella cheese and 1/3 of the Parmesan cheese to the ziti. Add the tomato sauce and toss to mix. Pour the hot ziti into a shallow 14-inch oval gratin dish and sprinkle with the remaining Parmesan cheese. Broil under a preheated broiler for 1 to 2 minutes or until brown. Serve immediately.

Ruth Todd Evans, M.D.
Parent, Andrew 1996 and Suzanne 1996

Pasta

Thai Noodles and Asparagus in Peanut Sauce

Yield:
6 servings

8 ounces uncooked linguini
Peanut Sauce
5 tablespoons sesame seeds, toasted
1 pound fresh asparagus
4 scallions, slivered
1 cup shredded carrots
2 small pickling cucumbers, peeled, slivered

Approx
Per Serving:
Cal 394
Prot 15 g
Carbo 47 g
T Fat 18 g
39% Calories
from Fat
Chol 0 mg
Fiber 8 g
Sod 984 mg

Cook the linguini al dente according to the package directions, drain and place in a large bowl. Add the Peanut Sauce and 4 tablespoons of the sesame seeds and toss to mix. Steam the asparagus until tender-crisp and cut into pieces if desired. Arrange the asparagus, scallions, carrots and cucumbers over the top. Sprinkle with the remaining sesame seeds. Serve at room temperature.

Peanut Sauce

6 tablespoons chunky peanut butter
1 tablespoon red wine vinegar
1 tablespoon brown sugar
1/4 cup soy sauce
2 tablespoons Chinese chili paste
1 teaspoon sugar
2 tablespoons vegetable oil
1/2 cup vegetable stock
1 1/2 tablespoons minced gingerroot
3 green onions, minced
1 tablespoon minced garlic

Combine the peanut butter, vinegar, brown sugar and soy sauce in a small bowl and mix well. Add the chili paste, sugar and oil. Stir in the vegetable stock gradually, blending well. Mix in the gingerroot, green onions and garlic.

Debbie Lynn
Parent, Zachary 2000

Cool and Spicy Thai Linguini

Yield:
4 servings

8 ounces uncooked linguini
Tomato Lime Sauce
3 scallions, sliced into rounds
1 jalapeño, finely minced
4 tablespoons minced fresh mint
2 cups mung bean sprouts
4 tablespoons roasted peanuts, finely chopped

Approx
Per Serving:
Cal 366
Prot 14 g
Carbo 57 g
T Fat 9 g
23% Calories
from Fat
Chol 0 mg
Fiber 8 g
Sod 213 mg

Bring a large pot of water to a boil. Break the linguini into halves and add to the boiling water. Cook for 10 minutes or until al dente, drain well and place in a large bowl. Add the Tomato Lime Sauce and toss to mix. Add the scallions, jalapeño, mint and bean sprouts and toss. Sprinkle the peanuts on top and serve immediately.

Tomato Lime Sauce

4 cloves of garlic, finely minced
1 tablespoon sesame oil (not toasted) or canola oil
3 tablespoons dry sherry
1/2 cup canned tomato sauce
3 tablespoons fresh lime juice
1 teaspoon grated lime peel
1/2 teaspoon Tabasco sauce

Sauté the garlic in the sesame oil in a small skillet over medium heat for 1 minute. Add the sherry, tomato sauce, lime juice, lime peel and Tabasco sauce. Mix well and simmer for 5 minutes, stirring occasionally.

Lesa Heebner
Friend, Sanders 2001, Charlie 2004 and Amy Patton

Pasta del Vecchio

Yield:
6 servings

8 to 10 large ripe tomatoes
3 tablespoons olive oil
2 (or more) cloves of garlic, minced
12 to 16 ounces goat or feta cheese
Fresh Italian parsley to taste, finely chopped
16 ounces uncooked linguini or thin spaghetti, cooked
Freshly ground pepper to taste

Approx
Per Serving:
Cal 763
Prot 36 g
Carbo 76 g
T Fat 36 g
42% Calories
from Fat
Chol 79 mg
Fiber 9 g
Sod 291 mg

Chop the tomatoes. Sauté the tomatoes in the olive oil in a large skillet for several minutes. Add the garlic. Cook for about 10 minutes or until the liquid is reduced. Crumble the cheese. Add the cheese to the sauce and mix until smooth. Add the parsley and mix well. Ladle the sauce over the hot cooked pasta in a large bowl. Top with freshly ground pepper.

Carol R. Pratt
Parent, David 2005 and Elizabeth 2006

What sculpture is to a block of marble,
education is to the human soul.

Joseph Addison, English essayist (1711)

Triple-Treat Cheese and Mushroom Pizza

Yield:
6 servings

1 cup shredded mozzarella cheese
1/2 cup crumbled goat cheese
1/2 cup grated Pecorino Romano cheese
6 cloves of garlic, minced
1 cup sliced portobello mushrooms
6 tablespoons unsalted butter
1/2 cup sliced shiitake mushrooms
1/2 cup sliced oyster mushrooms
1 teaspoon dried oregano
Juice of 1 fresh lemon wedge
Salt and pepper to taste
1 unbaked homemade or commercial pizza crust
Extra-virgin olive oil to taste

Approx
Per Serving:
Cal 399
Prot 16 g
Carbo 26 g
T Fat 26 g
58% Calories
from Fat
Chol 65 mg
Fiber 3 g
Sod 345 mg

Combine the mozzarella, goat and Pecorino Romano cheeses in a bowl, toss to mix and set aside. Sauté the garlic and portobello mushrooms in the butter in a medium skillet for 3 to 5 minutes. Add the shiitake and oyster mushrooms and oregano. Sauté for 3 to 5 minutes longer and remove from heat. Add the lemon juice, salt and pepper and mix well. Place the pizza crust on a baking stone or baking sheet. Spread the mushroom mixture over the crust and sprinkle with the mixed cheeses. Drizzle olive oil over the top. Bake according to the pizza crust directions.

Nutritional information for this recipe does not include pizza crust.

Vina Saycocie
Director, Finance and Administration, 1982 to 1984

Thai Chicken Pizza

This pizza created by Margi Grant is especially good the next day right out of the refrigerator.

Yield:
6 servings

1 boneless skinless chicken breast
1 tablespoon peanut oil
$1/2$ teaspoon chili paste
$3/4$ cup coconut milk
$1/2$ tablespoon sugar
$1/8$ teaspoon salt
$1/4$ teaspoon chili powder
$1/4$ cup peanut butter
1 baked homemade or commercial pizza crust
4 ounces bean sprouts
$1/4$ cup peanuts
$1/4$ cup chopped cilantro
$1/2$ cup shredded mozzarella cheese

Approx
Per Serving:
Cal 352
Prot 15 g
Carbo 22 g
T Fat 24 g
59% Calories
from Fat
Chol 20 mg
Fiber 3 g
Sod 276 mg

Grill or broil the chicken breast, chop and set aside. Combine the peanut oil, chili paste, coconut milk, sugar, salt and chili powder in a small saucepan. Heat over medium heat until well blended, stirring constantly. Remove from the heat and blend in the peanut butter. Spread half the sauce over the pizza crust. Mix the chicken into the remaining sauce and spread over the pizza. Sprinkle with bean sprouts, peanuts, cilantro and cheese. Bake at 450 degrees until the cheese is melted.

Nutritional information for this recipe does not include pizza crust.

Kathleen Allenbach
Parent, Diana 2001, Allen 2004 and Lauren Kessler 2005

Margarita Pizza

Yield:
6 servings

1/4 cup frozen orange juice
concentrate, thawed
1/4 cup tequila
1/4 cup fresh lime juice
2 cloves of garlic, crushed
1 teaspoon dried oregano
1/8 teaspoon ground red pepper
Salt and black pepper to taste

2 cups cubed chicken breasts
1 tablespoon olive oil
1 unbaked homemade or
commercial pizza crust
1 cup shredded mozzarella cheese
Extra-virgin olive oil
Orange Salsa

Approx
Per Serving:
Cal 370
Prot 22 g
Carbo 27 g
T Fat 17 g
42% Calories
from Fat
Chol 54 mg
Fiber 2 g
Sod 233 mg

Combine the orange juice concentrate, tequila, lime juice, garlic, oregano, red pepper, salt and black pepper in a bowl and mix well. Add the chicken and mix to coat. Marinate, covered, in the refrigerator for 4 hours to overnight. Drain the chicken and discard the marinade. Sauté the chicken in 1 tablespoon olive oil in a medium skillet over medium heat until cooked through. Spread over the pizza crust and sprinkle with the cheese. Drizzle the desired amount of extra-virgin olive oil over the top. Bake according to the pizza crust requirements. Garnish with chopped fresh cilantro and lime wedges. Serve with the Orange Salsa.

Orange Salsa

1 whole orange
6 tablespoons finely chopped red
onion
4 tablespoons chopped fresh cilantro

2 tablespoons fresh lime juice
2 tablespoons olive oil
1/2 teaspoon dried oregano
Salt to taste

Peel and seed the orange and chop into 1/2-inch pieces. Combine the orange, red onion, cilantro, lime juice, olive oil, oregano and salt in a small bowl and mix well. Refrigerate, covered, for 2 hours or longer. Use as additional garnish or topping for pizza.

Nutritional information for this recipe does not include pizza crust.

Vina Saycocie
Director, Finance and Administration, 1982 to 1984

Side Dishes

It is time for us all to stand and cheer for the doer,
the achiever—the one who recognizes the
challenge and does something about it.

Vince Lombardi

Side Dishes

German Baked Beans

Yield:
8 servings

8 ounces ground beef or ground
   turkey
1 small onion, chopped
2 tablespoons olive oil
2 (16-ounce) cans baked beans

1/4 cup catsup
3 tablespoons brown sugar
1 cup applesauce
1 teaspoon Worcestershire sauce
Salt to taste

Approx
Per Serving:
Cal 242
Prot 12 g
Carbo 35 g
T Fat 8 g
28% Calories
from Fat
Chol 20 mg
Fiber 6 g
Sod 568 mg

Brown the ground beef with onion in the olive oil in a medium skillet, stirring frequently until the ground beef is crumbly; drain. Combine the ground beef mixture with the beans, catsup, brown sugar, applesauce, Worcestershire sauce and salt and mix well. Pour into a beanpot or casserole. Bake at 325 degrees for about 45 minutes or until heated through.

Kathy Hewitt
Parent, James 2000

Gourmet Baked Beans

Yield:
6 servings

1 cup evaporated milk
1 tablespoon cider vinegar
1/3 cup packed brown sugar
1/4 cup sifted flour
1 teaspoon dry mustard

1/2 teaspoon salt
1 tablespoon molasses
1/4 teaspoon Worcestershire sauce
2 drops of Tabasco sauce
2 (16-ounce) cans baked beans

Approx
Per Serving:
Cal 270
Prot 11 g
Carbo 53 g
T Fat 4 g
11% Calories
from Fat
Chol 7 mg
Fiber 8 g
Sod 843 mg

Blend the evaporated milk with the vinegar and set aside. Combine the brown sugar, flour, dry mustard and salt in a large bowl. Add the evaporated milk mixture gradually, blending well. Stir in the molasses, Worcestershire sauce and Tabasco sauce. Add the beans and mix well. Pour into a 1 1/2-quart casserole. Bake at 350 degrees for 35 to 40 minutes or until bubbly, stirring 3 times.

Sarah Youthus
Music, Lower and Middle Schools, 1973 to 1994

Zesty Baked Beans

Yield:
8 servings

1 (48-ounce) can pork and beans
1 cup (or more) packed brown sugar
2 tablespoons Worcestershire sauce
2 teaspoons (or more) chili powder

1/4 cup (or more) dark molasses
1/2 cup chili sauce
2 tablespoons vinegar

Approx
Per Serving:
Cal 300
Prot 9 g
Carbo 68 g
T Fat 2 g
5% Calories
from Fat
Chol 12 mg
Fiber 8 g
Sod 812 mg

Combine the beans, brown sugar, Worcestershire sauce, chili powder, molasses, chili sauce and vinegar in a large bowl and mix well. Pour into a beanpot or large baking dish. Bake, covered, at 325 to 350 degrees for 1 to 2 hours or longer if a thicker sauce is desired.

Peggy Kratzmier
Grandparent, Michael McKenna 2008

Cheese-Topped Baked Beans

Yield:
8 servings

1 pound lean ground beef
1 medium brown onion, coarsely
  chopped
2 (12-ounce) cans dark red kidney
  beans, drained

2 (8-ounce) cans tomato sauce
1 tablespoon chili powder
1 pound Monterey Jack cheese,
  shredded

Approx
Per Serving:
Cal 460
Prot 33 g
Carbo 25 g
T Fat 26 g
50% Calories
from Fat
Chol 91 mg
Fiber 9 g
Sod 691 mg

Brown the ground beef with the onion in a large skillet, stirring until the ground beef is crumbly; drain. Add the beans, tomato sauce and chili powder and mix well. Simmer for 5 minutes. Pour into a greased casserole. Top with the cheese. Bake at 350 degrees for 20 minutes.

Judy Haidinger
Parent, Kerry 1987 and Tori 1989
Director of Admissions 1989 to 1995
Trustee 1985 to 1988

Lima Beans with Cider

Amazingly, teenagers like this vegetarian dish. Double it for potlucks.

Yield:
6 servings

3 large brown onions, sliced
2 cloves of garlic, crushed
1 tablespoon butter
1 tablespoon canola oil
1 pound carrots, scraped, sliced $1/4$ inch thick
$1^{1}/_{4}$ cups vegetable broth or soup stock
2 (16-ounce) cans lima beans, drained
$2/3$ cup apple cider or dry white wine
Bouquet garni
Sea salt and freshly ground pepper to taste
1 teaspoon cornstarch or arrowroot

Approx
Per Serving:
Cal 260
Prot 10 g
Carbo 46 g
T Fat 5 g
18% Calories
from Fat
Chol 5 mg
Fiber 10 g
Sod 614 mg

Sauté the onions and garlic in a mixture of the butter and canola oil in a large skillet until light brown. Add the carrots. Sauté for 4 to 5 minutes longer. Add the broth and mix well. Stir in the beans, cider, bouquet garni, salt and pepper. Bring just to the boiling point. Pour into a lightly greased $2^{1}/_{2}$-quart casserole. Bake, covered, at 325 degrees for 1 to $1^{1}/_{2}$ hours or just until the carrots are tender. Remove $1/2$ cup of the liquid from the casserole, pour into a small saucepan and let cool. Blend the liquid with the cornstarch or arrowroot and cook until thickened, stirring constantly. Stir the mixture into the casserole. Bake, uncovered, until the liquid is thickened. Remove the bouquet garni before serving.

Laura Temmer
Third Grade and Librarian, Lower School, 1976 to 1981

Beans and Broccoli Casserole

Yield:
15 servings

1 (16-ounce) package frozen chopped broccoli
1 (16-ounce) package frozen tiny lima beans
1 (10-ounce) can cream of mushroom soup
1 cup sour cream
1 envelope onion soup mix
1 (7-ounce) can sliced water chestnuts, drained
$1/2$ cup melted margarine
3 cups crisp rice cereal

Approx
Per Serving:
Cal 190
Prot 5 g
Carbo 19 g
T Fat 11 g
52% Calories
from Fat
Chol 7 mg
Fiber 4 g
Sod 534 mg

Cook the broccoli and lima beans separately according to the package directions and drain well. Mix the broccoli and beans together and spoon into a lightly greased 3-quart casserole. Mix the soup, sour cream, soup mix and water chestnuts together in a bowl. Toss the melted margarine with the cereal. Alternate layers of the soup mixture and the cereal mixture over the vegetables, ending with the cereal mixture. Bake at 350 degrees for 30 minutes or until bubbly and golden brown.

Peggy Meehl
Wife of John, History and Government, Upper School, 1967 to 1969; 1973 to 1977
Head Varsity Coach for Boys Soccer, Cross Country and Tennis

Mrs. Schrope's Corn Casserole

Yield:
8 servings

1 (16-ounce) can whole kernel corn
1 (16-ounce) can cream-style corn
1 cup sour cream
1/2 cup melted butter
2 eggs, beaten
1 (8-ounce) package corn bread mix

Approx
Per Serving:
Cal 377
Prot 7 g
Carbo 40 g
T Fat 23 g
52% Calories
from Fat
Chol 97 mg
Fiber 4 g
Sod 746 mg

Combine the undrained whole kernel corn, cream-style corn, sour cream, butter and eggs in a large bowl and mix well. Add the corn bread mix and stir until well mixed. Pour into a soufflé dish or casserole. Bake at 350 degrees for 1 hour or until puffed and golden brown. We use this as a side dish for Rosh Hashannah and Thanksgiving but I also serve it as a family meal with a green salad.

Barbara J. Weinstein
Parent, Lauren 2003
Fine Arts, Lower School, 1995 to present

Grilled Vegetables

Yield:
4 servings

2 medium zucchini
1 red bell pepper
1 green bell pepper
1 large white onion
1 pound mushrooms
3 tablespoons soy sauce
1 1/2 tablespoons olive oil
1/2 teaspoon dried rosemary, crushed
1/2 teaspoon crushed dried oregano
1/2 teaspoon crushed dried basil
1/2 teaspoon garlic powder

Approx
Per Serving:
Cal 123
Prot 7 g
Carbo 15 g
T Fat 5 g
36% Calories
from Fat
Chol 0 mg
Fiber 4 g
Sod 992 mg

Cut the zucchini into 1-inch slices and the bell peppers into thick slices. Cut the onion and mushrooms into quarters. Place all the vegetables in a large bowl. Add the soy sauce, olive oil, rosemary, oregano, basil and garlic powder and mix gently until the vegetables are coated. Marinate for 15 minutes or longer, stirring occasionally. Pour the vegetables into a grill basket. Grill over medium-high heat for 8 to 10 minutes or until the vegetables are tender, stirring occasionally.

Nutritional information includes entire amount of marinade.

Julie Cary
Assistant Director of Development, 1993 to present

Oven-Grilled Vegetables

Yield:
6 servings

1/2 cup balsamic vinegar
1/2 cup olive oil
1 tablespoon Dijon mustard
1/2 teaspoon salt
Freshly ground pepper to taste
1 large eggplant or 3 or 4 Japanese eggplant
3 medium or 4 small zucchini
1 large red onion
6 small or 2 large portobello mushrooms
1 large red bell pepper
4 ounces goat cheese (optional)

Approx
Per Serving:
Cal 255
Prot 6 g
Carbo 21 g
T Fat 19 g
61% Calories
from Fat
Chol 0 mg
Fiber 8 g
Sod 281 mg

Combine the vinegar, olive oil, mustard, salt and pepper in a jar, shake to mix well and set aside. Slice the vegetables 3/8 to 1/2 inch thick and then cut into 3- to 4-inch-long pieces. Place the vegetables in a large bowl or 2-gallon sealable plastic bag. Add the marinade and mix until the vegetables are coated with marinade. Marinate, tightly sealed, in the refrigerator for 24 hours to 3 days, turning several times. Pour the vegetables into a large roasting pan. Place under a preheated broiler 4 inches from the heat source. Broil for 10 minutes or until brown and lightly charred. Stir the vegetables and broil for 10 to 15 minutes longer or until all the vegetables are cooked and browned; do not overcook. Serve with crumbled goat cheese as an accompaniment with grilled fish or over pasta.

Dr. Lisa Braun-Glazer
Parent, Julia 2001

Mission Statement:
The mission of La Jolla Country Day School is to prepare individuals for a lifetime of intellectual exploration, personal growth and social responsibility.

Side Dishes

Roast Curried Vegetables

Yield:
4 servings

1 Idaho potato, peeled
1 large sweet potato, peeled
3 tablespoons olive oil
4 ounces fresh green beans
1 red bell pepper
2 medium onions
6 cloves of garlic
1 (14-ounce) can plum tomatoes
2 tablespoons curry powder
2 cups broccoli florets
1 cup vegetable broth
2 teaspoons kosher salt
Freshly ground pepper to taste
2 tablespoons fresh lime juice

Approx
Per Serving:
Cal 246
Prot 6 g
Carbo 36 g
T Fat 12 g
41% Calories
from Fat
Chol 0 mg
Fiber 8 g
Sod 1387 mg

Cut the Idaho and sweet potatoes into quarters and each quarter into 4 wedges. Place the potato pieces in a 13x18-inch roasting pan. Drizzle 2 tablespoons of the olive oil over the potatoes and mix until coated. Roast at 500 degrees for 15 minutes. Snap the ends from the green beans and snap the beans into halves. Cut the red pepper into 1-inch pieces and the onions into wedges. Move the potato pieces to the sides of the roasting pan to make a clear area in the center. Place the green beans, red pepper, onions and garlic in the center. Drizzle with the remaining 1 tablespoon olive oil. Roast for 15 minutes. Drain and crush the tomatoes. Mix the curry powder with the tomatoes and pour over the vegetables, tossing to mix. Arrange the broccoli florets around the edge of the pan on top of the vegetables. Roast for 15 minutes. Remove the vegetables to a serving bowl with a slotted spoon. Place the roasting pan on the stovetop over high heat. Pour in the broth. Deglaze the roasting pan, stirring constantly. Boil until the juices are reduced by half. Stir in the salt, pepper and lime juice. Pour over the vegetables. Serve with hot cooked rice as a vegetarian main dish or serve as a side dish.

Gwen Hiatt
Parent, Keeley 2000

Freda's Baked Onions

A real delight for the palate when served with roast beef, pork, leg of lamb or Thanksgiving turkey. Make it ahead and hold or reheat.

Yield:
12 servings

4 large yellow onions
2 tablespoons melted butter
1/4 cup red raspberry vinegar
1/4 teaspoon each salt and pepper
1/4 cup packed brown sugar
1/4 cup water

Approx
Per Serving:
Cal 54
Prot 1 g
Carbo 9 g
T Fat 2 g
32% Calories
from Fat
Chol 5 mg
Fiber 1 g
Sod 71 mg

Slice the onions thinly and place in a large retangular baking dish. Combine the butter, vinegar, salt, pepper, brown sugar and water in a small bowl and mix well. Drizzle the mixture over the onions and mix gently to coat. Bake, covered, at 350 degrees for 1 hour. Stir the onions and bake for 40 minutes longer. Stir the mixture, cover and hold at a low temperature until serving time or reheat.

Rita Gittes
Parent, Robert 1999

Balsamic Roasted Spuds

Yield:
6 servings

2 pounds small new potatoes
2 tablespoons olive oil
1 tablespoon minced garlic
1 tablespoon minced shallot
1 teaspoon minced fresh thyme
1 teaspoon minced fresh rosemary
1/8 teaspoon freshly ground nutmeg
1/4 cup balsamic vinegar
Salt and pepper to taste

Approx
Per Serving:
Cal 154
Prot 4 g
Carbo 29 g
T Fat 5 g
23% Calories
from Fat
Chol 0 mg
Fiber 3 g
Sod 3 mg

Scrub the potatoes, pat dry and cut into quarters. Heat the olive oil in a 12-inch skillet over medium-high heat. Add the potatoes, garlic and shallot and toss until well mixed. Add the thyme, rosemary and nutmeg and toss to mix. Spread the potatoes in a single layer on a baking sheet. Place the baking sheet on a rack in the lower third of a 400-degree oven. Roast for 25 minutes or just until the potatoes are golden brown and tender, turning once. Drizzle with the vinegar and sprinkle with salt and pepper. Roast for 7 minutes longer or until the potatoes are sizzling. Serve immediately.

Gloria and Chris Salem
Friends of the Patton Family, Sanders 2001, Charlie 2004 and Amy

Potatoes Peruvian-Style

A typical Peruvian dish, this can be served as a first course or a side dish.

Yield:
10 servings

10 yellow or white potatoes
2 cups crumbled feta cheese
3 hard-cooked egg yolks
2 tablespoons ground hot peppers
Salt and black pepper to taste

1 cup vegetable oil
$1/2$ cup evaporated milk
Several drops of fresh lemon juice
$1/4$ cup finely chopped onion

Approx
Per Serving:
Cal 405
Prot 9 g
Carbo 25 g
T Fat 31 g
67% Calories
from Fat
Chol 92 mg
Fiber 2 g
Sod 364 mg

Boil the potatoes in water to cover until tender, drain and peel. Arrange the potatoes on a bed of lettuce on a serving platter. Mash the cheese and egg yolks in a medium bowl using a fork. Mix in the hot peppers, salt and black pepper. Add the oil in a fine stream, beating constantly until the mixture is the consistency of mayonnaise. Beat in the evaporated milk, lemon juice and onion. Spoon the sauce over the potatoes. Garnish with hard-cooked egg halves and black olives. Serve at room temperature.

Sandra N. Rovira
Parent, Diego 2000

Gourmet Potatoes

Yield:
6 servings

8 medium potatoes
1 bunch green onions, chopped
2 tablespoons butter
2 cups shredded Cheddar cheese

3 cups sour cream
$1/2$ teaspoon salt
$1/8$ teaspoon pepper

Approx
Per Serving:
Cal 566
Prot 17 g
Carbo 36 g
T Fat 41 g
63% Calories
from Fat
Chol 101 mg
Fiber 3 g
Sod 540 mg

Boil the unpeeled potatoes in water to cover for 12 minutes or until cooked through but still firm. Cool, peel and grate the potatoes. Place in a lightly greased 9x13-inch baking dish. Sauté the green onions in the butter in a large skillet until tender. Add the cheese, sour cream, salt and pepper and mix well. Cook over low heat until the cheese melts, stirring constantly. Pour the sauce over the potatoes, mixing gently with a fork. Bake at 350 degrees for 45 minutes.

Debra Charles
Parent, Laura 2001

Creamed Spinach

Yield:
6 servings

2 (10-ounce) packages frozen
  chopped spinach
2 tablespoons butter
2 tablespoons flour

1 cup 2% milk or half-and-half
1/4 teaspoon salt
1/8 teaspoon pepper
2 hard-cooked eggs, finely chopped

Approx
Per Serving:
Cal 112
Prot 7 g
Carbo 8 g
T Fat 7 g
51% Calories
from Fat
Chol 84 mg
Fiber 3 g
Sod 247 mg

Cook the spinach in the microwave according to the package directions, pour into a colander and let stand until well drained. Melt the butter in a large skillet. Add the flour and blend well. Stir in the milk gradually and cook until slightly thickened, stirring constantly. Add a small amount of additional milk if necessary to make the sauce of the desired consistency. Add the spinach and mix gently. Heat to serving temperature, stirring constantly. Sprinkle with the hard-cooked eggs just before serving.

Roxy Ackerberg
Grandparent, Patton Children, Sanders 2001, Charlie 2004 and Amy

Rice and Spinach Casserole

Yield:
10 servings

2 (16-ounce) packages frozen
  spinach, thawed
2 tablespoons butter
2 tablespoons flour
2 cups milk
1/2 cup balsamic vinegar
1/4 teaspoon nutmeg

3/4 cup grated Parmesan or asiago
  cheese
6 cups cooked white rice
Salt and pepper to taste
2 eggs, beaten
1/2 cup whole wheat bread crumbs

Approx
Per Serving:
Cal 263
Prot 12 g
Carbo 37 g
T Fat 8 g
27% Calories
from Fat
Chol 61 mg
Fiber 3 g
Sod 283 mg

Drain the spinach well and set aside. Melt the butter in a large saucepan. Add the flour and blend well. Stir in the milk gradually. Stir in the vinegar. (The mixture will appear to curdle but will smooth as it cooks.) Cook until thickened, stirring constantly. Add the nutmeg and cheese and cook over low heat until the cheese melts, stirring constantly. Remove from the heat. Add the spinach and rice and mix well. Adjust the seasonings. Mix in the eggs. Pour into a buttered 3-quart casserole. Sprinkle with the bread crumbs. Bake at 325 degrees for 40 minutes or until bubbly and light brown. Serve as a side dish or a vegetarian entrée.

Diane Demeter
Parent, Sara 2003 and Nikki 2005

Baked Squash

Serve this traditional Passover recipe year-round by substituting bread crumbs for matza meal.

Yield:
10 servings

3 pounds yellow squash or zucchini
1/2 cup matzo meal or bread crumbs
1 cup chopped onion
1/4 cup vegetable oil
1/2 teaspoon salt
1/2 teaspoon pepper
1 tablespoon sugar
2 eggs

Approx
Per Serving:
Cal 108
Prot 4 g
Carbo 10 g
T Fat 7 g
53% Calories
from Fat
Chol 43 mg
Fiber 2 g
Sod 134 mg

Rinse the squash and cut into 1-inch slices. Steam the squash until tender but do not overcook. Drain the squash and mash in a large bowl. Add the matzo meal, onion, oil, salt, pepper, sugar and eggs and mix well. Pour into a lightly oiled square or rectangular baking dish. Bake at 375 degrees for 1 hour or until light brown.

Eileen A. Schwartz
Parent, Marissa 1985

Baked Hubbard Squash

Whether it travels to potlucks or appears elegantly at dinner parties, this recipe is fantastic, flexible and never-fail.

Yield:
variable

Several large Hubbard squash
1/4 cup (about) butter
1 cup (about) sour cream
3/4 cup (about) chopped onion
1/4 cup (about) milk
Salt and pepper to taste
Paprika to taste

Nutritional
information for
this recipe is
not available.

Cut the squash lengthwise into halves and place cut side down in a baking pan. Bake at 350 degrees for 1 hour. Cool slightly, scoop the pulp into a large bowl and mash. Mix in the remaining ingredients. (Adjust the amounts as needed for the amount of squash.) Spoon into a lightly greased baking dish. Sprinkle with paprika. Bake at 400 degrees for 45 minutes.

Susan Roberts
Parent, Tesse 1994, Brad 1997 and Volker, German exchange student 1996

Italian Squash a la Neka

Yield:
6 servings

1 brown or white onion, minced
2 tablespoons olive oil
1 (8-ounce) can tomato sauce
1 to 1½ cups water
1 teaspoon salt

Pepper, garlic powder and ground
  cinnamon to taste
2 pounds squash, sliced
¼ cup (or more) grated Parmesan
  cheese

Approx
Per Serving:
Cal 98
Prot 4 g
Carbo 9 g
T Fat 6 g
51% Calories
from Fat
Chol 3 mg
Fiber 3 g
Sod 699 mg

Sauté the onion in the olive oil in a large skillet until brown. Add the tomato sauce and 1 cup of the water. Stir in the salt, pepper, garlic powder and cinnamon. Bring the mixture to a boil and stir in the squash. Reduce the heat to a simmer and cook, covered, for 45 to 60 minutes or until the squash is tender. Add the remaining ½ cup water if the sauce becomes too thick. Remove from the heat and stir in the Parmesan cheese. Spoon the squash into a serving dish. Sprinkle with additional Parmesan cheese. Neka (Nekoletta Tsioutsias) is my grandmother.

Katrina A. Beers
Aunt, Matt 2007 and Amanda Mulligan 2009

Tomato Pie

Yield:
8 servings

2 or 3 large tomatoes
2 or 3 green onions, chopped
1 baked (9-inch) pie shell
Salt, pepper and basil to taste

1 cup mayonnaise
1 cup shredded Cheddar cheese
6 slices crisp-cooked bacon,
  crumbled

Approx
Per Serving:
Cal 419
Prot 7 g
Carbo 14 g
T Fat 37 g
79% Calories
from Fat
Chol 39 mg
Fiber 1 g
Sod 442 mg

Cut the tomatoes into thick slices. Layer half the tomatoes and half the green onions in the pie shell. Sprinkle with salt, pepper and basil. Repeat the layers. Mix the mayonnaise and cheese together in a bowl. Spread the mixture over the layers, sealing to the edge of the pie shell. Sprinkle the bacon over the top. Bake at 350 degrees for 30 minutes. Let stand for 5 to 10 minutes before serving. May substitute a mixture of ½ cup mayonnaise and ½ cup sour cream for the 1 cup mayonnaise or mozzarella cheese for the Cheddar.

Mary K. and Steve Newnham
Parents, Sam 1979, Matt 1980, Kathryn 1982 and Drew 1984

Yam Casserole

Yield:
8 servings

4 cups mashed baked yams, cooled
1/3 cup butter or margarine,
   softened
2 tablespoons sugar
2 eggs, beaten
1/2 cup milk

1/3 cup chopped pecans
1/3 cup flaked coconut
1/3 cup packed brown sugar
2 tablespoons flour
2 tablespoons melted butter or
   margarine

Approx
Per Serving:
Cal 394
Prot 6 g
Carbo 56 g
T Fat 17 g
38% Calories
from Fat
Chol 84 mg
Fiber 5 g
Sod 156 mg

Combine the yams, softened butter and sugar in a bowl and mix well. Add the eggs and milk and beat until smooth. Spoon into a 2-quart casserole. Combine the pecans, coconut, brown sugar and flour in a small bowl and mix well. Add the melted butter and mix until crumbly. Sprinkle over the yam mixture. Bake at 325 degrees for 1 hour. The kids prefer that the topping be doubled and the yams be baked in a 9x13-inch baking dish for more topping per spoonful. Reduce the baking time to 45 minutes.

Teri McHugh
Parent, Kimberly 2000 and Christopher 2002

Zucchini Casserole

Yield:
6 servings

1 1/2 pounds zucchini
2 onions, chopped
2 tablespoons butter
Salt, pepper and garlic to taste

1 cup milk
2 or 3 egg yolks, beaten
1 cup shredded Cheddar cheese
Croutons or bread crumbs to taste

Approx
Per Serving:
Cal 194
Prot 9 g
Carbo 9 g
T Fat 14 g
64% Calories
from Fat
Chol 142 mg
Fiber 2 g
Sod 184 mg

Cut the zucchini into quarters. Cook the zucchini in a small amount of water in a saucepan until tender, drain and set aside. Sauté the onions in the butter in a large skillet until tender. Combine the zucchini, sautéed onions, salt, pepper and garlic in a large bowl and mix well. Add the milk and egg yolks and mix well. Spoon into a lightly greased baking dish. Sprinkle with the cheese. Top with croutons or bread crumbs. Bake at 350 degrees for 40 minutes.

Beth Wilkie Dowding
Parent, Linda 1976, Doug 1978 and Susanne Wilkie
Kindergarten and First Grade, Lower School, 1967 to 1995

Alice's Super Gnarly Stuffing for the Totally Rad at Heart

Yield: variable

1 cup white rice
1/2 cup wild rice
3/4 cup dried cherries or cranberries
1 1/4 cups chopped assorted dried fruit
1 medium onion, chopped
2 sausages (chicken apple, chicken Thai preferred or Italian)
1 packet giblets
1 (8-ounce) can water chestnuts, drained, chopped
3/4 cup drinking sherry
1/4 cup orange juice
Fresh sage to taste
Garlic to taste
Cayenne pepper to taste
Pinch of curry (for complexity, not curry flavor)
Pinch of garam masala

Nutritional information for this recipe is not available.

OK, here's what you do, step-by-step, easy-to-follow directions for the culinarily challenged. First you have to taste the sherry. Why, you ask? Well, if you don't taste the sherry, how will you know if it is any good? I usually find that I have to taste it twice before I get started, so have an extra bottle just in case. Now where was I? Oh yeah, cook the rice and wild rice together (and don't forget the water; for all of you kitchen novices, check the instructions on the package). Sauté (translation: to cook with grease) the sausages and onions 'til they are totally done (well excuuuuse me "finished," are you a cake, or what) but don't, I repeat DO NOT, eat the sausages. Alice sez it would be grossly uncool and also spoil your appetite—sheeeeesh, mothers . . . . So now chop the dried fruit small enough to elegantly stuff into your mouth after you have stuffed it into the bird, and no you can't use that piece that you dropped onto the floor, because you weren't brought up in a barn now were you? Wheeew, at this time it is imperative to taste (taste as defined by Webster, that's W. C. GroggluttonWebster, is to "ascertain the flavor of by the taking of large quantities in the mouth followed by occasional breaths of air") the sherry to make sure that it hasn't gone bad (bad sherry equals an unqualified cosmic bummer), then go yell at the kids (if you have any) to keep that racket down, and if you don't, just yell out the window. Now, in a total panic, go to the refrigerator and dig out that giblet bag, which you totally forgot and left inside the bird. Tear it open (don't use your teeth) and put the contents into the sauté pan.

Now that things have calmed down a bit, take a moment to relax. While you are relaxing, take the time to double check the accuracy of your measuring cups. I usually find that 1/4 cup is exactly the same as a mouthful, sooo, drag out that old sherry bottle and test my theory. The next step is to call for reinforcements. NEW SHIFT. Now that the stuffing ingredients are completely and totally cooked, toss it all into a big bowl and mix it together (did I remember to tell you to wash your hands first?) and stuff it into the bird. No no no, not the bowl, just the ingredients—Jeez Louise. Whatever is left over put in a covered dish and stuff into the oven. This, my esteemed colleagues, is why they call it stuffing.

Now while everything is cooking, scrape the walls and hose down the kitchen, or, better yet, get that good-for-nothing lazy bum to hose down the kitchen, and while he's at it, have him get you a drink, 'cause this has been one grueling experience, and you really deserve it.

Oh yeah, Happy Holiday.

Jack Carpenter, 1974

The direction in which education starts a man,
will determine his future life.

Plato, **The Republic,** (4th C.B.C.)

Grand Marnier Cranberry Relish

Yield:
24 servings

3 Granny Smith apples
2 slightly ripe pears
2 pounds fresh cranberries
1 cup golden raisins
2 cups sugar

1 cup freshly squeezed orange juice
1 tablespoon grated orange peel
2 teaspoons ground cinnamon
$1/4$ teaspoon ground nutmeg
$1/2$ cup Grand Marnier

Approx
Per Serving:
Cal 134
Prot 1 g
Carbo 32 g
T Fat <1 g
1% Calories
from Fat
Chol 0 mg
Fiber 3 g
Sod 1 mg

Peel, core and chop the apples and pears. Combine the apples and pears with the cranberries, raisins, sugar, orange juice, orange peel and spices in a large saucepan and mix well. Bring to a boil, stirring constantly. Reduce the heat to a simmer. Simmer for 45 minutes or until thickened to the desired consistency, stirring frequently. Remove from the heat. Stir in the Grand Marnier. Let stand until cool. Refrigerate, covered, until serving time.

Jan Ann Kahler
Parent, Christopher 2002

Homemade Sauce for Barbecue

Yield:
25 cups

12 tomatoes, peeled
6 medium onions
3 green bell peppers
2 cloves of garlic, minced

$1/4$ cup vinegar
1 teaspoon sugar
1 teaspoon salt
$1/4$ cup vegetable oil

Approx
Per Cup:
Cal 47
Prot 1 g
Carbo 6 g
T Fat 2 g
43% Calories
from Fat
Chol 0 mg
Fiber 1 g
Sod 99 mg

Mash the tomatoes and grind the onions and peppers. Combine the tomatoes, onions, peppers, garlic, vinegar, sugar, salt and oil in a large bowl and mix well. Spoon the mixture into a large jar or several smaller jars and store, covered, in the refrigerator.

Marian Duncan
Parent, Brandon 2000 and Kenyon 2002

Wine Mushroom Gravy

Try this terrific sauce for any beef dish, especially flank steak or beef tenderloin. It can be made several days ahead.

Yield:
20 tablespoons

3 green onions, chopped
1 tablespoon margarine or butter
3/4 cup dry red wine

1 (10-ounce) can beef gravy
1 (4-ounce) can mushrooms, drained

Approx
Per Tablespoon:
Cal 21
Prot 1 g
Carbo 1 g
T Fat 1 g
38% Calories
from Fat
Chol <1 mg
Fiber <1 g
Sod 107 mg

Sauté the green onions in the margarine in a medium saucepan until tender but not brown. Add the wine. Boil until the liquid is reduced by half. Add the canned gravy and mushrooms and heat to the simmering point, stirring frequently.

Gail Finegold
Parent, Jared 1997

Low-Fat Noodle Kugel

Yield:
12 servings

8 ounces uncooked egg noodles
1 egg or equivalent amount of egg substitute
1/2 cup sugar
1 teaspoon fresh lemon juice

1 cup fat-free sour cream
1 1/2 cups fat-free cottage cheese
1 teaspoon ground cinnamon
1 tablespoon cinnamon-sugar

Approx
Per Serving:
Cal 166
Prot 8 g
Carbo 32 g
T Fat 1 g
6% Calories
from Fat
Chol 38 mg
Fiber 1 g
Sod 141 mg

Cook the noodles according to the package directions and drain well. Combine the egg, sugar, lemon juice, sour cream, cottage cheese and cinnamon in a large bowl and mix well. Add the noodles and mix gently. Pour the mixture into a greased 9x13-inch baking pan. Sprinkle with the cinnamon-sugar. Bake at 350 degrees for 1 hour.

Jeannie Mershon
Parent, Chelsea Wonacott-Mershon 1997

Noodle Kugel

Yield:
12 servings

16 ounces uncooked wide noodles
3 ounces cream cheese, softened
1/2 cup butter or margarine, softened
8 ounces small curd cottage cheese
3 eggs, beaten
1 cup sugar
1 cup sour cream
Cinnamon to taste
Raisins (optional)
1/2 cup melted butter or margarine

Approx
Per Serving:
Cal 486
Prot 11 g
Carbo 45 g
T Fat 30 g
55% Calories
from Fat
Chol 161 mg
Fiber 1 g
Sod 331 mg

Cook the noodles according to the package directions, drain well and return to the saucepan. Add the cream cheese, softened butter and cottage cheese to the hot noodles. Cook over low heat until the cream cheese and butter melt, stirring gently. Beat the eggs with the sugar and add to the noodle mixture. Remove from the heat and stir in the sour cream. Add the cinnamon and raisins, mix gently and set aside. Pour the melted butter into a large rectangular baking dish and tilt to coat with the butter. Pour the noodle mixture into the dish. Bake at 350 degrees for 1 hour or until the top is brown.

Susan Herman
Parent, Jenny 2000 and Brian 2003

Variation: Nancy Nevin, Parent of Jonathan 1997 and Meredith 2000, suggests reducing the noodles to 8 ounces, omitting the cream cheese, using only 1/4 cup butter, increasing the number of eggs to 4, adjusting the amount of sugar depending on the intended use, adding dried apricots or other dried fruit to taste and pouring a cup of milk mixed with a teaspoon of vanilla over the noodle mixture in the baking dish. Cool or refrigerate before cutting into squares and serve as a side dish, brunch dish or dessert.

Potato-Filled Pierogies

Yield:
4 (5-pierogi)
servings

2 cups flour
1/2 teaspoon salt
1 egg, beaten
3/4 cup cold water
Potato Filling

Approx
Per Serving:
Cal 455
Prot 11 g
Carbo 72 g
T Fat 14 g
27% Calories
from Fat
Chol 84 mg
Fiber 4 g
Sod 1014 mg

Sift the flour and salt together. Beat the egg and water together and mix into the flour mixture gradually. Knead the mixture until the dough is smooth and elastic. Roll to 1/8-inch thickness on a floured surface. Cut into 2 1/2-inch rounds. Place a rounded teaspoonful of Potato Filling on each round, fold over and press edges to seal well. Bring several quarts of water to a boil in a large pot. Place six or seven pierogies in the boiling water. Bring the water back to a boil and cook for 6 minutes. Remove the pierogies with a slotted spoon. Repeat the process with the remaining pierogies. Serve with generous portions of melted butter and sautéed chopped onions.

Potato Filling

4 medium potatoes
1 medium onion, chopped
1/4 cup butter
1 teaspoon salt
1/4 teaspoon pepper

Peel and chop the potatoes. Cook the potatoes in boiling water to cover until tender, drain and mash. Sauté the onion in the butter in a small skillet until tender. Add the sautéed onion, salt and pepper to the mashed potatoes and mix well.

Karen Lon
Librarian, Upper School, 1992 to present

Polenta Triangles with Saffron Tomatoes

I was introduced to polenta by Bruce and Marsha Boston and was given this recipe by Ferne McCuen.

Yield:
6 (3-triangle)
servings

6 cups water
1 teaspoon salt (optional)
1$^1/4$ cups polenta or coarse-grind cornmeal
$^1/3$ cup freshly grated Parmesan cheese
2 teaspoons chopped fresh rosemary
Salt and freshly ground pepper to taste
Canola oil for frying
2 cups flour
Saffron Tomato Sauce (page 181)
$^1/2$ cup freshly grated Parmesan cheese

Approx
Per Serving:
Cal 392
Prot 14 g
Carbo 60 g
T Fat 10 g
24% Calories
from Fat
Chol 11 mg
Fiber 5 g
Sod 302 mg

Butter a 9-inch-square baking pan and set aside. Bring the water with salt to a boil in a large saucepan. Stir in the polenta gradually. Cook over medium heat for 20 to 30 minutes or until the mixture pulls from the side of the pan, stirring constantly. Stir in the cheese and rosemary. Add salt and pepper. Pour into the prepared pan and smooth the top. Refrigerate, covered, until completely cooled. Pour $^1/2$ inch canola oil into a large deep skillet. Heat to 400 degrees. Cut the polenta into nine 3-inch squares and each square into 2 triangles. Coat the triangles lightly with flour. Place several at a time in the hot oil. Fry for 4 to 6 minutes or until golden brown, turning once. Remove with a slotted spoon to drain briefly on paper towels. Arrange the triangles on a platter or individual plates. Top with the Saffron Tomato Sauce and sprinkle with the cheese. Garnish with fresh rosemary sprigs.

Saffron Tomato Sauce

1 large yellow onion, chopped
2 tablespoons olive oil
1/4 cup dry red wine
1 tablespoon balsamic vinegar
1/8 teaspoon red pepper flakes
1 tablespoon tomato paste

1/4 teaspoon dried oregano
4 cups finely chopped peeled, seeded
  Roma tomatoes
Salt and freshly ground pepper to
  taste
1 teaspoon saffron threads

Sauté the onion in the olive oil in a large skillet over medium heat for 10 minutes. Add the wine, vinegar, red pepper flakes, tomato paste, oregano, tomatoes, salt and pepper. Reduce the heat to low. Simmer for 20 minutes or until the sauce begins to thicken, stirring occasionally. Add the saffron and simmer for 5 minutes longer.

Nutritional information for this recipe does not include oil for frying.

Dara Hensley
English, Upper School, 1981 to 1986, 1989 to 1995

Favorite Rice Casserole

Yield:
6 servings

1 cup uncooked long grain rice
1 cup sliced fresh mushrooms
1/3 cup butter
1/2 cup pine nuts
1 cup raisins

1/2 cup chopped scallions or
  green onions
2 cups chicken broth
1 teaspoon salt
1/2 cup chopped fresh parsley

Approx
Per Serving:
Cal 360
Prot 8 g
Carbo 47 g
T Fat 17 g
41% Calories
from Fat
Chol 28 mg
Fiber 2 g
Sod 760 mg

Sauté the rice and mushrooms in the butter in a large skillet for 5 minutes. Stir in the pine nuts, raisins, scallions, broth and salt. Pour into an oiled baking dish. Bake, covered, at 350 degrees for 45 to 60 minutes or until the rice is tender. Let stand, covered, for 10 to 15 minutes. Fluff the rice with a fork, stir in the parsley and serve immediately.

Claudia Law-Greenberg
Parent, Jacob 2001

Mexican Chili Rice

Yield:
8 servings

1 tablespoon chili powder
2 teaspoons cumin
4 shallots, chopped
4 cloves of garlic, minced
1 (14-ounce) can beef broth
3 (16-ounce) cans diced tomatoes
1 (16-ounce) can black beans,
   rinsed

1 (16-ounce) can white beans,
   rinsed
2 teaspoons chopped jalapeños
1/2 teaspoon ground red pepper
2 cups hot cooked white rice

Approx
Per Serving:
Cal 212
Prot 11 g
Carbo 42 g
T Fat 1 g
5% Calories
from Fat
Chol 1 mg
Fiber 8 g
Sod 811 mg

Sauté the chili powder and cumin in a dry skillet for 1 to 2 minutes or until the flavor intensifies. Sauté the shallots and garlic in 1/4 of the broth in a large saucepan for 2 minutes. Add the remaining broth, undrained tomatoes, beans, jalapeños, red pepper and sautéed spices and mix well. Bring to a simmer. Simmer for 15 minutes. Add the hot cooked rice and serve immediately as a side dish or vegetarian main dish.

Mary Anne Brower
Chairman, Mathematics Department, Middle School, 1984 to present

Rice Pilaf

Yield:
4 servings

1/2 cup orzo
1 tablespoon butter
1 (4-ounce) can mushrooms,
   drained

1 (14-ounce) can fat-free, low-salt
   chicken broth
1 broth can water
1 cup uncooked white rice

Approx
Per Serving:
Cal 367
Prot 11 g
Carbo 70 g
T Fat 4 g
10% Calories
from Fat
Chol 8 mg
Fiber 2 g
Sod 186 mg

Sauté the orzo in the butter in a large saucepan until brown. Add the mushrooms and sauté for a minute or two longer. Add the chicken broth and water. Cover and bring to a boil. Stir in the rice and return to the boil. Cover and reduce the heat to a simmer. Simmer for 20 to 25 minutes or until the water is absorbed, stirring every 7 minutes.

Gail Finegold
Parent, Jared 1997

Rice and Vermicelli Pilaf

Yield:
6 servings

3/4 cup loosely packed 1-inch pieces vermicelli
2 tablespoons vegetable oil
1 cup uncooked long grain rice

2 cups chicken broth
3 tablespoons unsalted butter, chopped
Salt and pepper to taste

Approx
Per Serving:
Cal 254
Prot 5 g
Carbo 32 g
T Fat 11 g
40% Calories
from Fat
Chol 16 mg
Fiber 1 g
Sod 262 mg

Sauté the vermicelli in the oil in a 3-quart saucepan until golden brown. Add the rice. Sauté until the rice grains turn white. Stir in the broth and butter. Season with salt and pepper. Bring to a boil, mix well and cover. Reduce the heat to a simmer and cook for 20 minutes. Partially remove the cover and cook for 5 minutes longer or until the vermicelli has begun to curl. Remove from the heat and let stand for 10 minutes before serving.

Carol Spaulding
Parent, Jessica 1999

Skillet Rice Supreme

Yield:
8 servings

1 cup chopped tomatoes
1 pound fresh mushrooms, sliced
1/2 cup butter or margarine
2 cups white rice
3 cups chicken broth
1 1/2 cups sauterne

2 teaspoons salt
1/4 teaspoon pepper
1 (10-ounce) package frozen baby peas
1/4 cup grated Parmesan cheese

Approx
Per Serving:
Cal 371
Prot 11 g
Carbo 46 g
T Fat 14 g
35% Calories
from Fat
Chol 34 mg
Fiber 3 g
Sod 1373 mg

Sauté the tomatoes and mushrooms in the butter in a large skillet until tender. Add the rice and sauté until some of the rice grains are golden brown. Stir in the broth, wine, salt and pepper. Simmer, covered, for about 35 minutes or until 10 minutes before the rice is tender. Sprinkle with the frozen peas and Parmesan cheese; do not mix in. Cook, covered, until the peas are heated through. Serve immediately.

Rebecca Wood, 1970

Taiwanese Fried Rice

Yield:
8 servings

1/4 cup vegetable oil
3 eggs, beaten
1 teaspoon wine
Salt and pepper to taste
1/4 cup vegetable oil
1 large onion, thinly sliced
8 ounces Virginia ham, cut into strips
2 tablespoons light soy sauce
1 tablespoon dark soy sauce
3 cups steamed or cooked rice
3 green onion tops, finely chopped
Green peas (optional)

Approx
Per Serving:
Cal 302
Prot 12 g
Carbo 21 g
T Fat 18 g
74% Calories
from Fat
Chol 107 mg
Fiber <1 g
Sod 303 mg

Heat 1/4 cup oil in a wok. Beat the eggs with the wine, salt and pepper. Pour the egg mixture into the wok. Scramble the eggs and set aside. Heat the remaining 1/4 cup oil in the wok until very hot. Add the sliced onion. Stir-fry until transparent. Add the ham and stir-fry until light brown. Stir in the soy sauces and rice. Stir-fry for 3 minutes. Add the green onion tops and peas. Adjust the seasonings if necessary by adding light soy sauce or salt. Serve immediately.

Meiling Hager
Secretary, Lower School, 1991 to present

Bread and Brunch

The things taught in schools are not an education
but the means of an education.

Ralph Waldo Emerson

Bread and Brunch

Best-Ever Banana Bread

Yield:
12 slices

1½ cups sugar
½ cup vegetable oil
2 eggs
1 teaspoon vanilla extract
2 medium bananas, mashed

1¾ cups flour
½ teaspoon salt
5 tablespoons buttermilk
1 teaspoon baking soda
1 cup chopped walnuts (optional)

Approx
Per Slice:
Cal 276
Prot 3 g
Carbo 44 g
T Fat 10 g
33% Calories
from Fat
Chol 36 mg
Fiber 1 g
Sod 220 mg

Beat the sugar and oil in a large bowl until well blended. Add the eggs and vanilla and mix well. Blend in the bananas. Mix the flour and salt together. Blend the buttermilk and baking soda until the baking soda is dissolved. Add the flour mixture and buttermilk mixture alternately to the banana mixture, mixing well after each addition. Add the walnuts and mix well. Pour into a greased and floured 5x9-inch loaf pan. Bake at 325 degrees for 1 hour and 20 minutes or until the top is golden brown and slightly split and a wooden pick inserted in the center comes out clean. Turn onto a wire rack to cool slightly. Serve warm. Do not double the recipe.

Shani Clarke
Parent, Alexandra 2011

Banana Nut Bread

Yield:
12 slices

½ cup butter, softened
1 cup sugar
2 eggs, beaten
2 cups flour

1 teaspoon baking soda
3 large overripe bananas, whipped
½ cup walnuts or pecans

Approx
Per Slice:
Cal 287
Prot 4 g
Carbo 42 g
T Fat 12 g
37% Calories
from Fat
Chol 56 mg
Fiber 2 g
Sod 195 mg

Cream the butter and sugar in a large bowl. Add the eggs and beat well. Add a mixture of the flour and baking soda and beat until blended. Beat in the bananas. Stir in the walnuts. Pour into a lightly greased and floured 5x9-inch loaf pan or 12 greased muffin cups. Bake at 350 degrees for 1 hour for the loaf or less time for the muffins.

Sue Higgins
Parent, Hillary 2005 and Hunter 2010

Chocolate Chip Banana Bread

Yield:
12 slices

1/2 cup butter, softened
1 cup sugar
2 eggs, beaten
2 cups flour
1 teaspoon baking soda

1/2 teaspoon salt
4 medium ripe bananas, mashed
1/2 cup chopped walnuts (optional)
1/2 cup semisweet chocolate chips

Approx
Per Slice:
Cal 290
Prot 4 g
Carbo 46 g
T Fat 11 g
33% Calories
from Fat
Chol 56 mg
Fiber 2 g
Sod 292 mg

Cream the butter and sugar in a bowl until light and fluffy. Beat in the eggs. Sift the flour, baking soda and salt into the egg mixture and mix well. Add the bananas and beat until smooth. Fold in the walnuts and chocolate chips. Pour into a greased 5x9-inch loaf pan. Bake at 350 degrees for 1 hour or until a wooden pick inserted in the center comes out clean.

Izzy Leverant
Parent, Andrea 2001 and Alex 2003
President, Parents' Association, 1996 to 1997
Board of Trustees, 1998 to present

Whole Wheat Chocolate Chip Banana Bread

Yield:
12 slices

1 cup whole wheat flour
1 cup all-purpose flour
1 1/2 teaspoons baking powder
1 teaspoon baking soda
1/2 teaspoon cinnamon
1/8 teaspoon salt (optional)

4 medium ripe bananas, mashed
1/4 cup melted butter
2 eggs, beaten
1 teaspoon vanilla extract
1/2 cup semisweet chocolate chips

Approx
Per Slice:
Cal 188
Prot 4 g
Carbo 29 g
T Fat 7 g
33% Calories
from Fat
Chol 46 mg
Fiber 3 g
Sod 217 mg

Mix the flours, baking powder, baking soda, cinnamon and salt together. Blend the bananas and melted butter in a medium bowl. Let stand until slightly cooled. Add the eggs and vanilla and mix well. Fold the flour mixture into the banana mixture gradually. Stir in the chocolate chips; do not overmix. Pour into a buttered and floured 5x9-inch loaf pan. Bake at 350 degrees for 1 hour or until a wooden pick inserted in the center comes out clean. Cool on a wire rack.

Marissa Schwartz-Brooks, 1985

Extra-Quick Banana Bread

Yield:
12 slices

2¹⁄₃ cups baking mix
1 cup sugar
¹⁄₃ cup vegetable oil

3 eggs
¹⁄₂ teaspoon vanilla extract
2 bananas, mashed

Approx
Per Slice:
Cal 250
Prot 3 g
Carbo 36 g
T Fat 11 g
39% Calories
from Fat
Chol 53 mg
Fiber 1 g
Sod 310 mg

Combine the baking mix, sugar, oil, eggs and vanilla in a medium bowl and mix until smooth. Add the bananas and mix well. Pour into a greased 5x9-inch loaf pan. Bake at 350 degrees for 55 to 65 minutes or until golden brown and a wooden pick inserted in the center comes out clean. Cool on a wire rack for 1 hour. May add the desired amount of raisins and chopped walnuts for added flavor.

Debbie Valentine
Physical Education, 1986 to present

Father's Beer Bread

For cooks who like to get in and out of the kitchen fast, here's a wonderful recipe. It is so simple that the ingredients can be mixed, put in the oven and the utensils cleaned within ten minutes. The bread smells wonderful baking, has a crusty top and a tender texture inside. It only rises 3½ to 4½ inches so it won't do for sandwiches but is delicious freshly sliced or toasted. The beer gives it an unusual slightly salty taste, with each brand of beer yielding a slightly different flavor.

Yield:
12 slices

3 cups self-rising flour
3 tablespoons sugar

1 (12-ounce) can beer

Approx
Per Slice:
Cal 134
Prot 3 g
Carbo 27 g
T Fat <1 g
2% Calories
from Fat
Chol 0 mg
Fiber 1 g
Sod 398 mg

Combine the flour, sugar and beer in a large bowl and mix well. Pour the batter into a greased 5x9-inch loaf pan. Moisten fingers and smooth the top of the batter. Bake at 325 degrees for 40 to 60 minutes or until golden brown and a wooden pick inserted in the center comes out clean. Brush the top with melted butter. Cool on a wire rack before slicing.

Susan M. Huggin
Parent, Betsy McCallum, Mathematics, Middle School
Grandparent, Jason 2011 and Kaitlin McCallum 2012

Cranberry Nut Bread

Yield:
12 slices

2 cups sifted flour
1½ teaspoons baking powder
1 teaspoon salt
½ teaspoon baking soda
¼ cup shortening
1 cup sugar

1 teaspoon grated orange peel
¾ cup orange juice
1 egg, well beaten
1 cup coarsely chopped fresh
  cranberries or dried cranberries
½ cup chopped walnuts

Approx
Per Slice:
Cal 222
Prot 3 g
Carbo 35 g
T Fat 8 g
32% Calories
from Fat
Chol 18 mg
Fiber 1 g
Sod 314 mg

Sift the flour, baking powder, salt and baking soda into a medium bowl. Cut in the shortening until crumbly. Mix in the sugar. Combine the orange peel, orange juice and egg. Add to the dry ingredients and mix just until moistened. Fold in the cranberries and walnuts. Spoon into a greased 5x9-inch loaf pan. Bake at 350 degrees for 55 to 60 minutes or until golden brown and a wooden pick inserted in the center comes out clean.

Gail Finegold
Parent, Jared 1997

Grandmother's Famous Cranberry Bread

Yield:
16 slices

2 cups sifted flour
1 cup sugar
1½ teaspoons baking powder
1 teaspoon salt
½ teaspoon baking soda
¼ cup butter or margarine

1 egg, beaten
1 teaspoon grated orange peel
¾ cup orange juice
1 cup light raisins
2 cups fresh cranberries

Approx
Per Slice:
Cal 170
Prot 2 g
Carbo 34 g
T Fat 3 g
18% Calories
from Fat
Chol 21 mg
Fiber 1 g
Sod 265 mg

Sift the flour, sugar, baking powder, salt and baking soda into a large bowl. Cut in the butter until crumbly. Add the egg, orange peel and orange juice all at once and mix just until moistened. Fold in the raisins and cranberries. Spoon into a greased 5x9-inch loaf pan. Bake at 350 degrees for 1 hour and 10 minutes or until a wooden pick inserted in the center comes out clean. Remove from the pan to a wire rack to cool.

Ellen Simms
Dean of Students, Middle School, 1995 to present and English, Middle School, 1973 to 1995
Billy Simms
Chairman, Science Department, 1972 to present

Czech Christmas Cake (Vánočka)

Yield:
16 slices

1 envelope dry yeast
1/4 cup warm water
4 cups flour
1/2 cup sugar
1 teaspoon salt
1/4 teaspoon mace or nutmeg
1/2 cup butter
1 egg, slightly beaten
1 cup warm milk
1 teaspoon vanilla extract
1 tablespoon lemon peel
1/4 cup slivered almonds or walnuts
1/2 to 1 cup seedless raisins
1/3 cup chopped citron
1 egg, beaten
2 tablespoons milk

Approx
Per Slice:
Cal 265
Prot 6 g
Carbo 43 g
T Fat 8 g
28% Calories
from Fat
Chol 44 mg
Fiber 2 g
Sod 236 mg

Dissolve the yeast in 1/4 cup warm water. Combine the flour, sugar, salt and mace in a large bowl. Cut in the butter until crumbly. Beat 1 egg with the warm milk and mix with the dissolved yeast. Mix in the vanilla and lemon peel. Mound the flour mixture on a work surface and make a depression in the center. Add the milk mixture to the flour mixture gradually, kneading to make a smooth dough. Knead on the lightly floured surface for 10 minutes or until smooth and elastic. Shape the dough into a ball. Place in a greased bowl, turning to coat the surface. Let rise, covered with a clean towel, in a warm place until doubled in bulk. Place the dough on the lightly floured surface and knead in the almonds, raisins and citron. Divide the dough into 9 equal portions. Shape each portion into a 20-inch-long strip. Place 4 strips together and twist. Place the twist on a greased baking sheet. Twist 3 of the remaining strips together and place on top the 4-strip twist, twisting and shaping to secure the layers. Twist the remaining 2 strips together and place on top the twisted layers. Secure the layers together with wooden picks if necessary. Let rise until doubled in bulk. Beat 1 egg with 2 tablespoons milk. Brush over the twists. Bake at 350 degrees for 45 minutes or until golden brown. Let stand overnight before cutting. Do not substitute margarine for butter in this recipe.

Linda Moyer
Staff, Assistant to the Headmaster, 1990 to present

Date and Nut Bread

Yield:
12 slices

1 cup boiling water
1 cup chopped dates
1 teaspoon baking soda
1/4 cup butter, softened
1 cup sugar
2 eggs

1 teaspoon vanilla extract
2 cups flour
1 teaspoon baking powder
1/8 teaspoon salt
1 cup chopped walnuts

Approx
Per Slice:
Cal 292
Prot 5 g
Carbo 45 g
T Fat 11 g
33% Calories
from Fat
Chol 46 mg
Fiber 2 g
Sod 221 mg

Pour the boiling water over the the dates in a bowl. Add baking soda; set aside. Cream the butter and sugar in a large bowl until light and fluffy. Beat in the eggs and vanilla. Sift the flour, baking powder and salt into the egg mixture and mix well. Fold in the dates and walnuts. Spoon into a 5x9-inch loaf pan sprayed with nonstick cooking spray. Bake at 350 degrees for 55 to 60 minutes or until golden brown and a wooden pick inserted in the center comes out clean. Cool in the pan on a wire rack for 15 minutes. Remove to the wire rack to cool completely. Serve plain or with cream cheese.

Gail Finegold
Parent, Jared 1997

Lemon Bread

Yield:
12 slices

1/2 cup shortening
1 cup sugar
2 eggs, slightly beaten
1 1/4 cups flour
1 teaspoon baking powder
1/4 teaspoon salt

1/2 cup milk
1/2 cup chopped walnuts
Grated peel of 1 lemon
1/4 cup sugar
Juice of 1 lemon

Approx
Per Slice:
Cal 256
Prot 3 g
Carbo 33 g
T Fat 13 g
45% Calories
from Fat
Chol 37 mg
Fiber 1 g
Sod 106 mg

Cream the shortening and 1 cup sugar in a medium bowl. Add the eggs and mix well. Sift the flour, baking powder and salt together. Add to the creamed mixture alternately with the milk, mixing well after each addition. Stir in the walnuts and lemon peel. Spoon into a greased 5x9-inch loaf pan. Bake at 350 degrees for 1 hour or until golden brown and a wooden pick inserted in the center comes out clean. Blend 1/4 cup sugar with the lemon juice. Drizzle over the hot bread.

Elaine Hinkle
Cook for the Kerper Family, Danielle 2000

Party Pull-Apart Bread

Yield:
20 servings

1 pound hot sausage
1 cup chopped green bell pepper
1 cup chopped onion
1/2 cup grated Parmesan cheese

1/2 cup melted margarine
3 (10-count) can refrigerator
   biscuits

Approx
Per Serving:
Cal 233
Prot 6 g
Carbo 18 g
T Fat 15 g
58% Calories
from Fat
Chol 12 mg
Fiber 1 g
Sod 680 mg

Brown the sausage in a large skillet, stirring frequently until crumbly; drain well. Add the green pepper and onion to the sausage and sauté until tender. Cool slightly. Mix in the Parmesan cheese. Cut the biscuits into quarters with scissors. Coat the biscuit pieces with the melted margarine. Alternate layers of the sausage mixture and the biscuits in a greased tube pan, starting with the sausage mixture and ending with the biscuits. Drizzle any remaining margarine over the biscuits. Bake at 350 degrees for 35 to 45 minutes or until golden brown. Cool in the pan on a wire rack for 10 to 15 minutes. Invert onto a serving platter.

Mrs. York E. Smith
Grandparent, Amber 2000

Peanut Butter Bread

Yield:
12 slices

1 3/4 cups flour
1 teaspoon baking powder
1 teaspoon baking soda
1/2 teaspoon salt
1 1/4 cups sugar

2 eggs
1 1/4 cups peanut butter
1 teaspoon vanilla extract
1 cup whole or skim milk

Approx
Per Slice:
Cal 330
Prot 10 g
Carbo 41 g
T Fat 15 g
40% Calories
from Fat
Chol 38 mg
Fiber 2 g
Sod 388 mg

Sift the flour, baking powder, baking soda and salt together and set aside. Combine the sugar and eggs in a large mixer bowl and beat until fluffy. Add the peanut butter and vanilla and beat until blended. Beat in the milk gradually. Beat at high speed for 2 minutes. Add the sifted dry ingredients and mix until well blended. Pour into a greased and floured 4x8-inch loaf pan. Bake at 350 degrees for 1 hour. Cool in the pan on a wire rack for 15 minutes. Remove to a wire rack to cool completely. This is great for school lunches.

Tristan 2003 and Shanda Gomes 2000

Pumpkin Bread

Yield:
36 slices

3 cups sugar
1 cup vegetable oil
4 eggs
1/2 (29-ounce) can pumpkin
1 teaspoon vanilla extract
2/3 cup water

3 cups flour
2 teaspoons baking soda
1 teaspoon ground nutmeg
1 teaspoon ground cinnamon
1/2 teaspoon salt
Raisins (optional)

Approx
Per Slice:
Cal 168
Prot 2 g
Carbo 26 g
T Fat 7 g
35% Calories
from Fat
Chol 24 mg
Fiber 1 g
Sod 110 mg

Blend the sugar and oil in a large bowl. Beat in the eggs, pumpkin, vanilla and water until smooth. Mix the next 5 ingredients together. Add to the pumpkin mixture and beat until well mixed. Stir in the raisins. Fill 3 greased loaf pans half full. Bake at 350 degrees for 1 to 1 1/4 hours or until a wooden pick inserted in the center comes out clean. Cool in the pans on wire racks.

Izzy Leverant
Parent, Andrea 2001 and Alex 2003
President, Parents' Association, 1996 to 1997
Board of Trustees, 1998 to present

Raisin and Walnut Pumpkin Bread

Yield:
12 slices

3/4 cup sugar
1/2 cup packed light brown sugar
1 cup canned pumpkin
1/2 cup vegetable oil
2 eggs
2 cups sifted flour
1 teaspoon baking soda

1/2 teaspoon salt
1/2 teaspoon ground nutmeg
1/2 teaspoon cinnamon
1/4 teaspoon ground ginger
1/2 cup golden raisins
1/2 cup chopped walnuts
1/4 cup chilled coffee

Approx
Per Slice:
Cal 303
Prot 4 g
Carbo 43 g
T Fat 13 g
38% Calories
from Fat
Chol 35 mg
Fiber 2 g
Sod 219 mg

Combine the first 5 ingredients in a large bowl and beat until well blended. Sift the flour, baking soda, salt, nutmeg, cinnamon and ginger together. Add to the pumpkin mixture and mix well. Stir in the raisins, walnuts and coffee. Spoon into a 5x9-inch loaf pan sprayed with nonstick cooking spray. Bake at 350 degrees for 1 to 1 1/4 hours or until a wooden pick inserted in the center comes out clean. Turn the loaf onto a wire rack to cool.

Gail Finegold
Parent, Jared 1997

Zucchini Bread

Yield:
16 slices

3 eggs
1 cup vegetable oil
2 cups sugar
1 teaspoon vanilla extract
2 to 3 cups grated peeled zucchini
2 cups flour

2 teaspoons baking soda
1 teaspoon salt
1 teaspoon cinnamon
1/4 teaspoon baking powder
1 cup chopped pecans

Approx
Per Slice:
Cal 345
Prot 4 g
Carbo 40 g
T Fat 20 g
50% Calories
from Fat
Chol 40 mg
Fiber 2 g
Sod 324 mg

Beat the eggs in a large bowl. Blend in the oil. Add the sugar and vanilla and blend well. Add the squash and mix well. Mix the flour, baking soda, salt, cinnamon and baking powder together. Add to the squash mixture and mix well. Stir in the pecans. Spoon into a greased and floured bundt pan. Bake at 350 degrees for 1 hour or until a wooden pick inserted in the center comes out clean.

Melinda Kanter
Parent, Jason 2003 and Rachel 2006

Caryl Spector's Chocolate Zucchini Bread

Yield:
15 servings

1/2 cup butter, softened
1/2 cup vegetable oil
1 3/4 cups sugar
2 eggs
1 teaspoon vanilla extract
1/2 cup buttermilk or sour milk
2 1/2 cups flour

1/4 cup baking cocoa
1 teaspoon baking soda
1/2 teaspoon ground cloves
1/2 teaspoon ground cinnamon
1/2 teaspoon salt
2 cups grated zucchini
1/2 cup semisweet chocolate chips

Approx
Per Serving:
Cal 333
Prot 4 g
Carbo 45 g
T Fat 16 g
43% Calories
from Fat
Chol 45 mg
Fiber 2 g
Sod 244 mg

Cream the butter, oil and sugar in a large bowl until light and fluffy. Add the eggs, vanilla and buttermilk and stir until well mixed. Mix the flour, cocoa, baking soda, cloves, cinnamon and salt together. Add to the creamed mixture and mix well. Stir in the zucchini. Spoon into a greased and floured 9x13-inch baking pan. Sprinkle with the chocolate chips. Bake at 350 degrees for 40 minutes or until a wooden pick inserted in the center comes out clean.

Dale Reeder
Dean of Students, Lower School, 1991 to present

British Scones

Serve these scones with tea on a Sunday afternoon and your accent will change.

Yield:
12 scones

2¹/₂ cups self-rising flour
2 teaspoons baking powder
¹/₄ teaspoon salt
1 tablespoon sugar

¹/₄ cup butter
¹/₂ cup currants
1 egg, beaten
¹/₂ cup milk

Approx
Per Scone:
Cal 175
Prot 4 g
Carbo 22 g
T Fat 5 g
26% Calories
from Fat
Chol 29 mg
Fiber 1 g
Sod 508 mg

Mix the first 4 ingredients in a bowl. Add the butter; rub until well mixed. Stir in the currants. Beat the egg with milk. Add to the flour mixture; mix until a soft dough forms. Knead several times on a lightly floured surface. Roll out ¹/₂ inch thick and cut into rounds. Arrange on a lightly greased baking sheet. Bake at 450 degrees for 10 minutes or until light brown.

John Finch
Director, Middle School, 1995 to present

Swiss Butterhorns

Yield:
36 rolls

2 cups flour
¹/₄ teaspoon salt
¹/₂ cup cold margarine
¹/₃ cup cold butter
1 egg yolk, lightly beaten
³/₄ cup sour cream

¹/₂ cup chopped pecans
¹/₂ cup sugar
1 teaspoon ground cinnamon
1 cup confectioners' sugar
2 tablespoons milk
¹/₄ teaspoon vanilla extract

Approx
Per Roll:
Cal 110
Prot 1 g
Carbo 12 g
T Fat 7 g
53% Calories
from Fat
Chol 13 mg
Fiber <1 g
Sod 66 mg

Mix the flour and salt in a large bowl. Cut in the margarine and butter until crumbly. Mix in the egg yolk and sour cream. Shape into a ball and wrap in plastic wrap. Chill for several hours to overnight. Divide the dough into 3 portions. Roll each portion into a 12-inch circle on a floured surface. Mix the pecans, sugar and cinnamon in a small bowl. Sprinkle ¹/₃ of the pecan mixture over each circle. Cut each circle into 12 wedges and roll up each wedge starting from the wide end. Arrange point side down on greased baking sheets. Bake at 350 degrees for 15 to 18 minutes or until light brown. Drizzle a mixture of the remaining ingredients over the warm rolls.

Dorothy Trexel
Grandparent, Mandy 2010

Jim's Cinnamon Rolls for Bread Machine

Yield:
18 rolls

5 tablespoons butter
$1/2$ cup packed brown sugar
$1/4$ to $1/2$ cup chopped pecans
1 cup minus 2 tablespoons buttermilk
1 egg
$1/4$ cup butter
3 cups bread flour
$1/4$ cup sugar
1 teaspoon salt
$1/4$ teaspoon baking soda
$1^{1/2}$ teaspoons dry yeast
1 tablespoon melted butter
2 tablespoons sugar
2 tablespoons brown sugar
1 tablespoon cinnamon
$1/2$ cup raisins

Approx
Per Roll:
Cal 229
Prot 4 g
Carbo 33 g
T Fat 9 g
36% Calories
from Fat
Chol 29 mg
Fiber 1 g
Sod 232 mg

Melt 5 tablespoons butter in a 9x13-inch baking pan. Sprinkle with $1/2$ cup brown sugar and pecans and set aside. Place the buttermilk, egg and $1/4$ cup butter in the bread machine pan. Add the flour, $1/4$ cup sugar, salt, baking soda and yeast. Select the Dough setting and press Start. When the dough has risen long enough, the machine will signal. Turn the dough onto a lightly floured surface. Pat or roll into a 9x18-inch rectangle. Brush with 1 tablespoon melted butter and sprinkle with a mixture of 2 tablespoons sugar, 2 tablespoons brown sugar, 1 tablespoon cinnamon and raisins. Roll as for jelly roll from the long edge. Score lightly into $1^{1/2}$-inch slices. Slide a piece of dental floss under the dough, cross the ends of the floss over a scored mark and pull in opposite directions to slice through. Arrange the slices cut side up in the prepared baking pan. Let rise, covered, for 30 to 45 minutes or until doubled in bulk. Bake at 350 degrees for 25 to 30 minutes or until golden brown. Invert onto a serving tray. Serve warm.

Jean Ilstrup
Library Staff, 1987 to 1993

Buttermilk Corn Bread

Yield:
12 servings

2 eggs
1/4 cup sugar
1 cup sifted flour
2/3 cup cornmeal
2 teaspoons baking powder

1/4 teaspoon baking soda
3/4 teaspoon salt
1 cup buttermilk
1/4 cup melted butter

Approx
Per Serving:
Cal 131
Prot 3 g
Carbo 18 g
T Fat 5 g
35% Calories
from Fat
Chol 46 mg
Fiber 1 g
Sod 326 mg

Beat the eggs in a large bowl. Add the sugar and mix well. Mix the flour with the cornmeal, baking powder, baking soda and salt. Add the mixed dry ingredients to the sugar mixture alternately with the buttermilk, mixing well after each addition. Stir in the melted butter. Pour into a buttered and floured 8x8-inch baking dish. Bake at 400 degrees for 25 minutes or until golden brown and a wooden pick inserted in the center comes out clean.

Carol Spaulding
Parent, Jessica 1999

Our Favorite Coffee Cake

Yield:
16 servings

1/2 cup sugar
1/2 cup chopped walnuts
1/2 cup semisweet chocolate chips
2 teaspoons ground cinnamon
1 (2-layer) package yellow or lemon cake mix

1 (4-ounce) package lemon instant pudding mix
4 eggs
1/2 cup vegetable oil
1 cup sour cream

Approx
Per Serving:
Cal 345
Prot 4 g
Carbo 43 g
T Fat 18 g
47% Calories
from Fat
Chol 60 mg
Fiber 1 g
Sod 332 mg

Combine the sugar, walnuts, chocolate chips and cinnamon in a small bowl, mix well and set aside. Combine the cake mix, pudding mix, eggs, oil and sour cream in a large mixer bowl. Beat at medium speed for 5 minutes. Pour half the batter into a greased and floured tube pan. Sprinkle with half the walnut mixture. Add layers of the remaining batter and walnut mixture. Bake at 350 degrees for 1 hour or until a wooden pick inserted in the center comes out clean. Cool in the pan on a wire rack for 10 minutes. Invert onto a serving plate.

Susan Small
Parent, Allison 1990

Apple Coffee Cake

1 envelope dry yeast
1 teaspoon sugar
3 tablespoons warm water
$1/2$ cup milk
2 tablespoons butter
2 tablespoons sugar
1 teaspoon salt
1 egg
2 to $2^{1}/2$ cups flour
3 or 4 tart apples, peeled, cored, sliced
1 cup sugar
$1^{1}/2$ teaspoons ground cinnamon
2 tablespoons butter, softened
1 egg yolk
$1/3$ cup cream

Approx
Per Serving:
Cal 269
Prot 4 g
Carbo 46 g
T Fat 8 g
26% Calories
from Fat
Chol 56 mg
Fiber 2 g
Sod 247 mg

Dissolve the yeast and 1 teaspoon sugar in the warm water. Let stand for 5 minutes or longer to proof. Combine the milk, 2 tablespoons butter, 2 tablespoons sugar and salt in a small saucepan. Heat until very warm, remove from the heat and cool to lukewarm. Combine the warm milk, egg and yeast in a large mixer bowl, stirring to mix. Add 2 cups of the flour gradually, beating until a soft dough forms. Knead in the remaining flour on a lightly floured surface until the dough will hold its shape. Place the dough in a greased bowl, turning to coat the surface. Let rise, covered, in a warm oven until doubled in bulk. Press the dough into a greased 9x13-inch baking pan. Top with the apple slices. Mix 1 cup sugar, cinnamon and 2 tablespoons softened butter until crumbly. Sprinkle over the apples. Let rise, loosely covered, for 30 minutes. Bake at 350 degrees for 20 minutes. Beat the egg yolk with the cream. Drizzle over the partially baked coffee cake. Bake for 10 minutes longer or until golden brown. Cool before cutting.

Mrs. William Griffith
Grandparent, Devin Ochoa 1999

Cream Cheese Coffee Cake

Yield:
12 servings

1/2 cup butter, softened
8 ounces cream cheese, softened
1 1/4 cups sugar
2 eggs
1 teaspoon vanilla extract
1 1/3 cups flour
1 teaspoon baking powder

1/2 teaspoon baking soda
1/4 teaspoon salt
1/4 cup milk
1 teaspoon cinnamon
1/2 cup chopped pecans or walnuts
1/3 cup sugar

Approx
Per Serving:
Cal 335
Prot 5 g
Carbo 39 g
T Fat 19 g
49% Calories
from Fat
Chol 78 mg
Fiber 1 g
Sod 289 mg

Cream the butter, cream cheese and 1 1/4 cups sugar in a large bowl until light and fluffy. Add the eggs and vanilla and beat well. Sift the flour, baking powder, baking soda and salt together. Add to the creamed mixture alternately with the milk, mixing well after each addition. Pour into a greased 9x13-inch baking pan. Mix the cinnamon, pecans and 1/3 cup sugar in a bowl. Sprinkle over the batter. Bake at 350 degrees for 40 minutes.

Ellen Shaffer
Librarian, Upper School, 1990 to present

Sour Cream Coffee Cake

Yield:
12 servings

1 cup butter, softened
2 cups sugar
2 eggs
1/2 teaspoon vanilla extract
1 cup sour cream
1 3/4 cups sifted cake flour

1 teaspoon baking powder
1/4 teaspoon salt
1/2 cup chopped pecans or walnuts
2 tablespoons dark brown sugar
1 1/2 teaspoons cinnamon

Approx
Per Serving:
Cal 411
Prot 3 g
Carbo 48 g
T Fat 24 g
51% Calories
from Fat
Chol 85 mg
Fiber 1 g
Sod 268 mg

Cream the butter and sugar in a bowl until light and fluffy. Beat in the eggs 1 at a time. Beat in the vanilla and sour cream until smooth. Sift the flour, baking powder and salt together. Mix into the sour cream mixture. Combine the pecans, brown sugar and cinnamon in a small bowl. Pour half the batter into a generously buttered bundt or tube pan. Sprinkle with half the pecan mixture. Repeat the layers. Bake at 350 degrees for 1 hour or until the coffee cake tests done. Cool in the pan on a wire rack. Remove from the pan and place on a serving plate with the pecan side up.

Rachel Staver
Parent, Anne 2002 and Ted 2007

Cheese Strata

Yield:
6 servings

10 slices bread
1/2 cup butter, softened
4 cups shredded Cheddar cheese
5 egg yolks
3 cups warm milk
1/2 teaspoon salt
5 egg whites
1 teaspoon Worcestershire sauce or pinch of dry mustard
Salt and pepper to taste
Paprika to taste

Canadian Bacon
1/2 cream/milk 1
cayanne pepper
green onions

Approx
Per Serving:
Cal 665
Prot 31 g
Carbo 23 g
T Fat 50 g
67% Calories
from Fat
Chol 314 mg
Fiber 1 g
Sod 1092 mg

Cut the crusts from the bread. Spread the bread generously with the butter and cut the slices into small squares. Alternate layers of the bread and cheese in a greased 9x13-inch baking dish, ending with the cheese. Beat the egg yolks with the warm milk and 1/2 teaspoon salt in a large bowl. Beat the egg whites in a small bowl until stiff peaks form. Fold the stiffly beaten egg whites into the milk mixture gently. Fold in the Worcestershire sauce and salt and pepper to taste. Pour the egg mixture over the bread and cheese layers. Sprinkle with paprika. Place the baking dish, covered, in the refrigerator. Chill for 1 hour or longer to allow the egg mixture to penetrate the layers completely. Bake at 350 degrees for 1 1/2 hours or until puffed and golden brown.

Gladis B. Innerst
Kindergarten, Lower School, 1953 to 1976

Death by Cheese

Yield:
16 servings

2 pounds Monterey Jack cheese
8 ounces cream cheese
12 eggs
1 cup flour
2 teaspoons baking powder
1/4 teaspoon salt
2 cups milk
16 ounces cream-style cottage cheese
1/4 cup butter

Approx
Per Serving:
Cal 419
Prot 25 g
Carbo 10 g
T Fat 31 g
67% Calories
from Fat
Chol 242 mg
Fiber <1 g
Sod 650 mg

Cut the Monterey Jack and cream cheeses into small cubes, place in sealable plastic bags or wrap tightly and refrigerate overnight. Beat the eggs in a large bowl. Mix the flour, baking powder and salt together. Add the flour mixture and milk to the eggs gradually, whisking constantly until smooth. Whisk in the cottage cheese; the mixture will appear lumpy from the curds. Add the cheese cubes and mix well to separate the cubes. Pour into a greased large baking dish. Dot with the butter. Bake at 325 degrees for 45 minutes or until puffed and golden brown. Let stand for 10 minutes before cutting. This recipe may be served as a side dish or appetizer also.

Joan Weiss
Parent, Jodi Semer 2001
Board of Trustees, 1996 to present

For over 100 years after San Diego was founded, the area constituting La Jolla was barren and undeveloped. Useless without a supply of fresh water, it remained a favorite picnic and bathing spot. Until 1887, all of the land in the area of La Jolla was owned by the City of San Diego and was referred to as pueblo land.

Hoppel Poppel

Yield:
12 servings

12 eggs or equivalent amount of egg
   substitute
1/2 cup finely chopped onion, or
   6 green onions, finely chopped

2 tomatoes, chopped
1 pound salami, cut into chunks
2 teaspoons salt
1/2 teaspoon pepper

Approx
Per Serving:
Cal 176
Prot 12 g
Carbo 3 g
T Fat 13 g
66% Calories
   from Fat
Chol 237 mg
Fiber <1 g
Sod 855 mg

Beat the eggs lightly in a large bowl. Add the onion, tomatoes, salami, salt and pepper and mix well. Pour into a greased 9x13-inch baking pan. Bake at 350 degrees for 30 minutes or until puffed and golden brown. Serve with fresh fruit and bagels or specialty breads.

Izzy Leverant
Parent, Andrea 2001 and Alex 2003
President, Parents' Association, 1996 to 1997
Board of Trustees, 1998 to present

Merry-Kerry Eggs

Yield:
6 servings

10 hard-cooked eggs
1 pound fresh mushrooms, sliced
Salt and pepper to taste
3 tablespoons butter
3 tablespoons flour
3 cups milk
1/2 cup cream

1/4 cup cognac or brandy
2 teaspoons instant chicken bouillon
2 teaspoons dillweed
1/2 cup crushed canned French-fried
   onions or buttered bread crumbs
1/4 cup (about) butter for muffins
6 English muffins, toasted

Approx
Per Serving:
Cal 814
Prot 26 g
Carbo 54 g
T Fat 52 g
58% Calories
   from Fat
Chol 434 mg
Fiber 3 g
Sod 1202 mg

Peel the eggs and cut into quarters. Arrange in a greased 9x13-inch baking dish. Sprinkle the mushrooms with salt and pepper. Sauté the mushrooms in 3 tablespoons butter in a large skillet until tender. Mix the flour into the mushroom mixture. Stir in the milk, cream, cognac, bouillon and dillweed. Cook until thickened, stirring constantly. Simmer for 10 minutes, stirring frequently. Adjust the seasonings. Pour the sauce over the eggs. Sprinkle the onions over the top. Bake at 350 degrees for 20 minutes. Serve over toasted and buttered English muffins.

Elizabeth R. Patton
Grandparent, Sanders 2001, Charlie 2004 and Amy

Aunt Jean's Spinach and Cheese Pie

Yield:
6 servings

1 (10-ounce) package frozen
   chopped spinach
6 eggs
3 ounces cream cheese, softened
1/4 cup shredded Cheddar cheese
2 tablespoons sliced green onions

1 tablespoon snipped fresh parsley
Salt and pepper to taste
1 unbaked (9-inch) pie shell
2 tablespoons grated Parmesan
   cheese

Approx
Per Serving:
Cal 323
Prot 13 g
Carbo 17 g
T Fat 23 g
63% Calories
from Fat
Chol 235 mg
Fiber 2 g
Sod 371 mg

Cook the spinach according to the package directions, drain and set aside. Beat the eggs lightly in a medium bowl. Add the cream cheese and Cheddar cheese and mix well. Stir in the spinach, green onions, parsley, salt and pepper. Pour into the pie shell. Sprinkle with the Parmesan cheese. Bake at 425 degrees for 25 minutes or until the filling is set near the edge. May serve as a supper dish or cut into very thin wedges as an appetizer also.

Jan Ann Kahler
Parent, Christopher 2002

Dorothy Lee's Cheese and Sausage Quiche

Yield:
8 servings

8 ounces sweet Italian turkey
   sausage
1 cup shredded Swiss cheese
1/2 cup chopped onion
1 (12-ounce) can Mexican-style
   corn, drained
1 (4-ounce) can chopped green
   chiles, drained

4 eggs or equivalent amount egg
   substitute
1/2 cup baking mix or low-fat baking
   mix
2 cups milk
1/4 teaspoon salt
1/8 teaspoon pepper

Approx
Per Serving:
Cal 221
Prot 13 g
Carbo 18 g
T Fat 11 g
44% Calories
from Fat
Chol 135 mg
Fiber 1 g
Sod 754 mg

Brown the sausage in a skillet, stirring until crumbly; drain well. Mix the sausage, cheese, onion, corn and chiles in a bowl. Spread the mixture in a greased 10-inch pie plate. Beat the eggs in a large mixer bowl. Add the remaining ingredients. Beat at high speed for 1 minute. Pour over the mixture in the pie plate. Bake at 350 degrees for 50 to 55 minutes or until set. Let stand for 5 minutes before cutting.

Jeannie Mershon
Parent, Chelsea Wonacott-Mershon 1997

Crustless Ham and Cheese Quiche

Yield:
6 servings

2 cups shredded Swiss cheese
1 cup chopped ham, or 1/2 cup
    crumbled crisp-fried bacon
1/4 cup chopped green onions
1/4 cup chopped onion
2 eggs

1 cup milk
1 tablespoon flour
1/2 teaspoon baking powder
1/2 teaspoon dry mustard
Salt and pepper to taste

Approx
Per Serving:
Cal 242
Prot 21 g
Carbo 5 g
T Fat 15 g
56% Calories
from Fat
Chol 131 mg
Fiber <1 g
Sod 191 mg

Sprinkle the cheese, ham, green onions and onion into a greased pie plate or quiche pan. Beat the eggs in a medium bowl. Beat in the milk. Mix the flour, baking powder, dry mustard, salt and pepper together. Add to the egg mixture and beat until well blended. Pour into the prepared pie plate. Bake at 350 degrees for 30 to 35 minutes or until set.

Meiling Hager
Secretary, Lower School, 1991 to present

Tuna Quiche

Yield:
6 servings

1 unbaked (10-inch) pie shell
1 cup sour cream
1/2 to 3/4 cup mayonnaise
1/4 cup finely chopped celery
2 tablespoons chives
2 tablespoons lemon juice

1 cup shredded Swiss or Colby
    cheese
4 eggs, well beaten
1 (9-ounce) can water-pack tuna,
    drained, flaked
1 (3-ounce) can French-fried onions

Approx
Per Serving:
Cal 714
Prot 25 g
Carbo 25 g
T Fat 57 g
72% Calories
from Fat
Chol 208 mg
Fiber 1 g
Sod 681 mg

Prick the pie shell over the bottom and around the side. Bake at 450 degrees for 5 minutes. Reduce the oven temperature to 350 degrees. Combine the sour cream, mayonnaise, celery, chives, lemon juice and cheese in a large bowl and mix well. Fold in the eggs, tuna and onions. Pour into the pie shell. Bake at 350 degrees for 45 to 50 minutes or until set. Let stand for 10 minutes before cutting into wedges.

Izzy Leverant
Parent, Andrea 2001 and Alex 2003
President, Parents' Association, 1996 to 1997
Board of Trustees, 1998 to present

Mexican French Toast

Yield:
8 slices

3 egg yolks
1 cup sugar
1 teaspoon salt
2 cups flour

1½ cups (about) milk
3 egg whites, stiffly beaten
Vegetable oil for deep-frying
8 slices bread

Approx
Per Slice:
Cal 358
Prot 10 g
Carbo 68 g
T Fat 5 g
13% Calories
from Fat
Chol 87 mg
Fiber 2 g
Sod 500 mg

Beat the egg yolks in a bowl until foamy. Add the sugar and salt and mix well. Add the flour and beat until smooth. Beat in enough milk to make the mixture the consistency of pancake batter. Fold in the stiffly beaten egg whites gently. Preheat the oil to 350 degrees in an electric skillet. Dip the bread slices into the batter and place in the hot oil. Deep-fry until puffed and golden brown, turning once. Drain on paper towels and remove to a heated platter. Serve with your favorite toppings.

Nutritional information for this recipe does not include oil for deep-frying.

Rosemary Harbushka
Parent, Alexandra 2001

California French Toast

Yield:
10 slices

2 eggs, beaten
1 cup orange juice
10 slices raisin bread

1½ cups crushed vanilla wafers
10 tablespoons butter or margarine

Approx
Per Slice:
Cal 257
Prot 4 g
Carbo 26 g
T Fat 16 g
54% Calories
from Fat
Chol 75 mg
Fiber 1 g
Sod 273 mg

Beat the eggs and orange juice together. Dip the bread slices into the egg mixture and coat with wafer crumbs. Cook each bread slice in 1 tablespoon butter in a large skillet until brown on both sides. Serve with additional butter and warm syrup accompanied by crisp-fried bacon slices and fresh fruit.

Shiloh Sarlin, Student, 1980 to 1986

Caramel French Toast

Serve for a Sunday or holiday brunch with baked sliced apples.

Yield:
10 servings

1¹/₂ cups packed brown sugar
³/₄ cup butter or margarine
6 tablespoons light corn syrup
10 (1³/₄-inch-thick) slices French bread
4 eggs, beaten
2¹/₂ cups milk or half-and-half
1 tablespoon vanilla extract
¹/₄ teaspoon salt
3 tablespoons sugar
1¹/₂ teaspoons ground cinnamon
¹/₄ cup melted butter or margarine

Approx
Per Serving:
Cal 476
Prot 7 g
Carbo 62 g
T Fat 23 g
43% Calories
from Fat
Chol 143 mg
Fiber 1 g
Sod 481 mg

Combine the brown sugar, ³/₄ cup butter and corn syrup in a medium saucepan. Cook over low heat for 5 minutes or until bubbly, stirring constantly. Pour the syrup into a lightly greased 9x13-inch baking dish. Arrange the bread slices in the prepared dish. Beat the eggs with the milk, vanilla and salt. Pour over the bread slices. Refrigerate, covered, for 8 hours or longer. Sprinkle with a mixture of sugar and cinnamon. Drizzle the melted butter over the top. Bake, uncovered, at 350 degrees for 45 to 50 minutes or until golden brown and bubbly. Serve immediately.

Cary Tremblay
Parent, Scott 1986 to 1992

Apple Pancake

Yield:
2 servings

3 large tart apples
2 to 3 tablespoons butter
3 eggs
$1/4$ teaspoon salt
$1/2$ cup milk
$1/2$ cup flour
3 tablespoons melted butter
$1/3$ cup cinnamon-sugar

Approx
Per Serving:
Cal 833
Prot 15 g
Carbo 191 g
T Fat 45 g
33% Calories
from Fat
Chol 420 mg
Fiber 5 g
Sod 767 mg

Peel, core and slice the apples into $1/4$-inch-thick slices. Sauté the apples in 2 to 3 tablespoons butter in a 10- to 12-inch ovenproof skillet until tender. Beat the eggs in a medium bowl. Add the salt, milk and flour and beat until smooth. Pour over the sautéed apples. Bake at 500 degrees for 10 minutes or until the pancake puffs and browns slightly around the edge. Remove the pancake from the oven. Drizzle the melted butter around the edge and over the pancake. Sprinkle the cinnamon-sugar over the top. Bake for 5 minutes longer or until the sugar is caramelized.

Jackie and Barry Seidman
Parents, David 1996 and Steven 2001

Education is not preparation for life,
education is life itself.

John Dewey, **Democracy in Education** (1903)

Blueberry Pancakes

Yield:
4 servings

2 cups pancake mix
1 cup skim milk
1/4 cup reduced-fat sour cream
1/2 cup packed dark brown sugar

1 tablespoon vanilla extract
1 egg or 1/4 cup egg substitute
1 cup fresh blueberries

Approx
Per Serving:
Cal 433
Prot 11 g
Carbo 88 g
T Fat 4 g
8% Calories
from Fat
Chol 59 mg
Fiber 1 g
Sod 1038 mg

Combine the pancake mix, milk, sour cream, brown sugar, vanilla and egg in a large bowl and mix until smooth. Fold in the blueberries gently. Ladle the desired amount of batter onto a hot greased griddle. Bake until bubbles form and the edge appears dry, turn the pancake over and bake until brown. Repeat the process with the remaining batter.

Brad and Nancy Smith
Parents, Jade 2004

Blueberry Sauce

Yield:
36 tablespoons

1/4 cup sugar
2 teaspoons cornstarch
2 teaspoons lemon juice

1/3 cup water
2 cups blueberries

Approx
Per Tablespoon:
Cal 11
Prot <1 g
Carbo 3 g
T Fat <1 g
2% Calories
from Fat
Chol 0 mg
Fiber <1 g
Sod 1 mg

Combine the sugar, cornstarch, lemon juice and water in a medium saucepan and mix well. Add the blueberries. Cook over medium heat until the juices are clear and thickened, stirring constantly. Serve on pancakes, waffles, ice cream or yogurt.

Gail Finegold
Parent, Jared 1997

Cran-Sorbet Super Drink

Yield:
4 servings

1/2 large orange
2 scoops vanilla ice cream
2 cups cranapple juice

1 orange gelatin snack cup
1 red gelatin snack cup
2 cups ice cubes

Approx
Per Serving:
Cal 198
Prot 2 g
Carbo 40 g
T Fat 4 g
16% Calories
from Fat
Chol 15 mg
Fiber 1 g
Sod 51 mg

Combine the orange, ice cream, cranapple juice, gelatin snack cups and ice cubes in a blender container. Process until smooth and creamy. Pour into glasses and serve immediately.

Ryan Hitchcock 2006

Fruit Smoothies

The fun of making a smoothie is that you rarely make a mistake by mixing and matching different combinations of fresh fruit and yogurt flavors. Experiment and enjoy.

Yield:
4 servings

Nutritional
information for
this recipe is
not available.

1 (8-ounce) carton strawberry, peach, mixed fruit, blueberry or lemon yogurt
1 banana, frozen
1 scoop vanilla ice cream
1 cup orange juice
2 tablespoons honey

Fresh fruit (1 orange, 6 to 8 strawberries, 1/2 cup fresh raspberries, 1 cup fresh blueberries or 1 cup cantaloupe chunks)
Coconut flakes (optional)
Protein powder (optional)

Combine the yogurt, banana, ice cream, orange juice, honey, fresh fruit, coconut and protein powder in a blender container. Process until smooth and creamy. Serve immediately.

Sanders 2001 and Charlie Patton 2004

Desserts

No one can become really educated without having
pursued some study in which he took no interest.
For it is part of education to interest ourselves in
subjects for which we have no aptitude.

T. S. Elliot,
author

Desserts

~~~~~~

Quinoa Apple Cake

Quinoa is a high-protein flour that has a wonderful nutty flavor. It is available at health food stores and large supermarkets.

Yield:
9 servings

1 cup quinoa flour
1/4 teaspoon salt
1 teaspoon baking soda
3/4 cup honey
1 tablespoon vegetable oil
2 egg whites
1/4 cup apple juice
1 medium apple, grated
1/2 cup toasted almonds
1/2 cup currants

Approx
Per Serving:
Cal 224
Prot 5 g
Carbo 40 g
T Fat 7 g
25% Calories
from Fat
Chol 0 mg
Fiber 3 g
Sod 222 mg

Mix the quinoa flour, salt and baking soda together and set aside. Combine the honey, oil, egg whites, apple juice, grated apple, almonds and currants in a large bowl and mix well. Add the quinoa flour mixture to the honey mixture and mix well. Pour into an oiled 8-inch-square cake pan. Bake at 350 degrees for 30 minutes or until a wooden pick inserted in the center comes out clean.

Marsha Boston
Art, Upper School, 1989 to present

Banana Chocolate Chip Cakes

Yield:
20 servings

1 cup sugar
1/2 cup butter, softened
2 eggs
3 bananas, mashed
1/2 cup sour cream
1/2 teaspoon vanilla extract
2 cups flour
1 teaspoon baking soda
1 1/4 cups semisweet chocolate chips

Approx
Per Serving:
Cal 211
Prot 3 g
Carbo 31 g
T Fat 10 g
39% Calories
from Fat
Chol 36 mg
Fiber 1 g
Sod 121 mg

Cream the sugar and butter in a large bowl until light and fluffy. Add the eggs, bananas, sour cream and vanilla and mix until smooth. Mix the flour and baking soda together, add to the banana mixture and mix well. Stir about 3/4 of the chocolate chips into the batter. Divide the batter between 2 greased foil loaf pans. Sprinkle the remaining chocolate chips on top. Bake at 350 degrees for 50 to 60 minutes or until a wooden pick inserted in the center comes out clean.

Michele and Arnold Zousmer
Parents, Alexandra 2002 and Maxwell 2005

Without education, you are not going anywhere in this world.

Malcolm X, speech (1964)

Banana Walnut Bundt Cake

Yield:
20 servings

1²/₃ cups sugar
1 cup butter, softened
2 eggs
1 teaspoon vanilla extract
2¹/₂ cups flour
1 teaspoon salt
1 teaspoon baking soda
1 teaspoon baking powder
1¹/₂ to 2 cups mashed bananas
¹/₂ cup sour cream
1 cup semisweet chocolate chips
1 cup chopped walnuts

Approx
Per Serving:
Cal 322
Prot 4 g
Carbo 41 g
T Fat 17 g
47% Calories
from Fat
Chol 49 mg
Fiber 2 g
Sod 309 mg

Cream the sugar and butter in a large bowl until light and fluffy. Beat in the eggs and vanilla. Mix the flour, salt, baking soda and baking powder together. Add to the creamed mixture and mix well. Fold in the bananas and sour cream. Add the chocolate chips and walnuts and stir until well mixed. Pour the batter into a greased and floured 12-inch bundt pan. Bake at 350 degrees for 1 hour or until a wooden pick inserted in the center comes out clean. Cool on a wire rack for 10 to 15 minutes. Invert onto a wire rack or serving plate to cool completely.

Barbara Mulligan
Parent, Matthew 2007 and Amanda 2009

Carrot Cake

Yield:
8 servings

2 cups flour
2 teaspoons baking powder
2 teaspoons baking soda
2½ teaspoons ground cinnamon
1 teaspoon nutmeg
1 teaspoon salt
2 cups sugar
1¼ cups vegetable oil
4 eggs
2⅓ cups grated carrots
½ cup chopped walnuts (optional)
½ cup raisins (optional)
1 (8-ounce) can crushed pineapple, drained
1 cup shredded coconut
Cream Cheese Frosting

Approx
Per Serving:
Cal 1154
Prot 9 g
Carbo 144 g
T Fat 63 g
48% Calories
from Fat
Chol 169 mg
Fiber 3 g
Sod 980 mg

Combine the flour, baking powder, baking soda, cinnamon, sugar, nutmeg and salt in a large bowl and mix well. Add the oil and mix well. Add the eggs and stir until well mixed. Stir in the carrots, walnuts, raisins, pineapple and coconut. Pour the batter into a greased and floured 9x13-inch cake pan. Bake at 350 degrees for 1 hour or until a wooden pick inserted in the center comes out clean. Cool completely before frosting with the Cream Cheese Frosting.

Cream Cheese Frosting

8 ounces cream cheese or Neufchâtel cheese, softened
½ cup butter, softened
1 teaspoon vanilla extract
1 (1-pound) package confectioners' sugar

Cream the cheese and butter in a large bowl. Mix in the vanilla. Add the confectioners' sugar gradually, beating until smooth and creamy.

Lisa Braun-Glazer
Parent, Julia 2001

Easter Carrot Cake

Yield:
16 servings

4 eggs, beaten
2 cups sugar
2¹/₂ cups flour
2 teaspoons baking soda
2 teaspoons ground cinnamon
1 teaspoon salt
1¹/₂ cups vegetable oil
3 (4-ounce) jars baby food carrots
¹/₂ cup coarsely chopped walnuts
8 ounces cream cheese, softened
¹/₂ cup butter or margarine, softened
¹/₂ teaspoon vanilla extract
3¹/₂ cups confectioners' sugar

Approx
Per Serving:
Cal 601
Prot 5 g
Carbo 69 g
T Fat 35 g
52% Calories
from Fat
Chol 84 mg
Fiber 1 g
Sod 435 mg

Combine the eggs and sugar in a large bowl and beat until blended. Sift the flour, baking soda, cinnamon and salt together, add to the egg mixture and mix well. Add the oil, carrots and walnuts and stir until mixed but do not overmix. Pour into a greased 9x13-inch cake pan. Bake at 350 degrees for 30 to 40 minutes or until a wooden pick inserted in the center comes out clean. Cool on a wire rack. Beat the cream cheese and butter in a bowl until light and fluffy. Add the vanilla and confectioners' sugar and beat until of spreading consistency. Frost the cooled cake. Decorate with "nests" of green-tinted shredded coconut filled with jelly bean "eggs." Garnish with a sprinkle of chopped walnuts or toasted shredded coconut for a non-Easter treat.

Mary Doyle
Director, Public Relations, 1993 to present

Chocolate Cake with Fudge Frosting

Yield:
12 servings

1³/₄ cups sugar
¹/₂ cup butter, softened
6 tablespoons baking cocoa
5 tablespoons boiling water
4 egg yolks, beaten
1³/₄ cups cake flour
1 teaspoon (or more) baking powder
¹/₂ cup milk
1 teaspoon vanilla extract
4 egg whites, stiffly beaten
Fudge Frosting

Approx
Per Serving:
Cal 405
Prot 5 g
Carbo 73 g
T Fat 12 g
25% Calories
from Fat
Chol 97 mg
Fiber 2 g
Sod 160 mg

Cream the sugar and butter in a large bowl until light and fluffy. Dissolve the cocoa in the boiling water and blend into the creamed mixture. Add the egg yolks and blend well. Sift the flour and baking powder together. Blend the milk and vanilla together. Add the flour mixture alternately with the milk mixture, mixing well after each addition. Fold in the stiffly beaten egg whites gently. Pour into a greased 9x13-inch cake pan. Bake at 350 degrees for 35 to 40 minutes or until a wooden pick inserted in the center comes out clean. Cool on a wire rack. Frost the cooled cake with the Fudge Frosting. Serve with ice cream.

Fudge Frosting

1¹/₂ cups sugar
1 tablespoon butter
1 tablespoon baking cocoa
¹/₂ cup milk

Combine the sugar, butter, cocoa and milk in a saucepan. Bring to a boil stirring constantly. Cook to 240 degrees on a candy thermometer, soft-ball stage. Beat until smooth and of spreading consistency.

Angela West, 1997

Headmaster's Chocolate Cake

Yield:
16 servings

2 cups flour
1³/₄ cups sugar
1 tablespoon baking powder
1 teaspoon salt
¹/₂ cup vegetable oil
7 egg yolks
2 teaspoons vanilla extract
1 cup water
7 egg whites
¹/₂ teaspoon cream of tartar
3 ounces unsweetened baking chocolate, grated

Approx
Per Serving:
Cal 264
Prot 5 g
Carbo 36 g
T Fat 12 g
40% Calories
from Fat
Chol 93 mg
Fiber 1 g
Sod 265 mg

Sift the flour, sugar, baking powder and salt into a medium bowl. Add the oil, unbeaten egg yolks, vanilla and water and beat until smooth. Beat the egg whites with the cream of tartar in a large bowl until very stiff peaks form; do not underbeat. Pour the egg yolk mixture over the stiffly beaten egg whites gradually, folding gently until blended; do not stir. Fold in the grated chocolate gently. Pour into an ungreased tube pan. Bake at 325 degrees for 55 minutes. Increase the oven temperature to 350 degrees. Bake for 10 minutes longer. Invert the cake on an inverted funnel to cool completely. Loosen the cake from the side of the pan. Invert onto a serving plate.

John and Barbara Neiswender
John, Headmaster, 1992 to present
Director, Upper School, 1990 to 1992

Quick Chocolate Cake

Yield:
9 servings

2 ounces unsweetened baking chocolate
1/4 cup butter
1/2 cup boiling water
1/4 cup milk
3/4 teaspoon baking soda
1 teaspoon vinegar
1 cup flour
1 cup sugar
1 egg

Approx
Per Serving:
Cal 227
Prot 3 g
Carbo 35 g
T Fat 10 g
36% Calories
from Fat
Chol 38 mg
Fiber 1 g
Sod 169 mg

Place the baking chocolate and butter in a bowl. Add the boiling water and stir until the chocolate and butter melt. Mix the milk, baking soda and vinegar together. Add the flour, sugar, milk mixture and egg to the chocolate mixture, mixing well after each addition. Pour into a greased 9-inch-square cake pan. Bake at 350 degrees for 20 minutes or until a wooden pick inserted in the center comes out clean. Frost with a favorite chocolate frosting.

Don Leavenworth
Parent, Laurie 1970 and Julie 1973
Headmaster, 1957 to 1972

The La Jolla Country Day School was founded as The Balmer School in 1926, with a small cottage serving as the schoolhouse on Coast Boulevard in downtown La Jolla. The school was opened by Louise C. Balmer with an enrollment of four students. Today, the La Jolla Country Day School has an annual student population of over 1000 students who occupy a beautiful 24-acre site.

Fabulous Chocolate Pecan Cake

Yield:
12 servings

6 ounces bittersweet chocolate, chopped
³/4 cup unsalted butter, chopped
¹/2 cup sugar
4 egg yolks
1 cup ground toasted pecans
2 tablespoons flour or matzo meal
4 egg whites
¹/4 teaspoon cream of tartar
¹/4 cup sugar
8 ounces bittersweet chocolate, chopped
2 ounces white chocolate

Approx
Per Serving:
Cal 458
Prot 4 g
Carbo 27 g
T Fat 36 g
70% Calories
from Fat
Chol 117 mg
Fiber 2 g
Sod 23 mg

Butter a deep 9-inch cake pan or springform pan and line with waxed paper or baking parchment. Melt 6 ounces chocolate and butter in a double boiler over hot water; cool slightly. Combine ¹/2 cup sugar and egg yolks in a large bowl and beat until light. Add the melted chocolate mixture and blend well. Add the ground pecans and flour and mix well. Beat the egg whites with the cream of tartar in a small mixer bowl until soft peaks form. Add ¹/4 cup sugar gradually, beating until stiff peaks form. Stir ¹/3 of the stiffly beaten egg whites into the chocolate mixture. Fold in the remaining egg whites. Spoon gently into the prepared cake pan. Bake at 350 degrees for 35 to 40 minutes or until a wooden pick inserted in the center comes out slightly moist. Cool on a wire rack; the cake will fall. Press the edges of the cooled cake down to level the top. Invert onto a serving plate. Brush off loose crumbs. Heat 8 ounces chocolate with the whipping cream in a double boiler over hot water, blending well. Cool slightly and pour over the cake, tilting to glaze the top. Let stand until firm. Melt the white chocolate in a double boiler over hot water. Drizzle in concentric circles over the top of the cake.

Ruthi Warburg
Parent, Jeremy 2004

Forty-Year-Favorite Chocolate Roll

Yield:
10 servings

1/2 cup flour
1/2 teaspoon baking powder
1/4 teaspoon salt
4 eggs, at room temperature
3/4 cup sugar
1 teaspoon vanilla extract
2 tablespoons sugar
1/4 teaspoon baking soda
3 tablespoons cold water
2 ounces unsweetened baking chocolate, melted
1 cup whipping cream
1/2 cup semisweet chocolate chips
2 tablespoons butter or margarine

Approx
Per Serving:
Cal 293
Prot 5 g
Carbo 30 g
T Fat 19 g
55% Calories
from Fat
Chol 124 mg
Fiber 2 g
Sod 174 mg

Grease a 10x15-inch jelly roll pan and line with waxed paper. Sift the flour, baking powder and salt together and set aside. Combine the eggs and 3/4 cup sugar in a large mixer bowl and beat at high speed until thick and pale yellow. Fold in the flour mixture and vanilla. Blend 2 tablespoons sugar, baking soda, cold water and melted chocolate until thick and light. Stir the chocolate mixture into the egg mixture. Pour into the prepared pan. Bake at 375 degrees for 15 to 20 minutes or until the top springs back when touched lightly. Sprinkle a linen towel generously with sugar. Invert the cake onto the sugared towel and peel off the waxed paper. Let cool for exactly 5 minutes. Fold the edge of the towel over the edge of the cake and roll the cake and towel as for a jelly roll. Place on a wire rack to cool completely. Whip the cream in a chilled bowl using chilled beaters. Unroll the cake and spread with the whipped cream. Reroll the cake without the towel. Place on a serving plate. Melt the chocolate chips with the butter in a double boiler over hot water. Spread over the cake roll.

Roxy Ackerberg
Grandparent, Sanders 2001, Charlie 2004 and Amy Patton

Trudy's Red Devil's Food Cake

<hr />

Yield:
16 servings

1½ cups sugar
½ cup butter, softened
2 eggs
1 teaspoon vanilla extract
2 (1-ounce) bottles red food coloring
2 cups cake flour
2 tablespoons baking cocoa
1 teaspoon salt
1 cup buttermilk
1 teaspoon baking soda
1 teaspoon vinegar
Favorite seven-minute or cream cheese frosting

Approx
Per Serving:
Cal 203
Prot 3 g
Carbo 33 g
T Fat 7 g
30% Calories
from Fat
Chol 43 mg
Fiber 1 g
Sod 307 mg

Cream the sugar and butter in a large bowl until light and fluffy. Add the eggs, vanilla and food coloring and beat until smooth. Sift the flour, cocoa and salt together. Add to the creamed mixture alternately with the buttermilk, beating well after each addition. Mix the baking soda and vinegar together and beat into the batter. Pour into 2 greased and floured 8- or 9-inch cake pans. Bake at 350 degrees for 25 minutes or until a wooden pick inserted in the center comes out clean. Cool on wire racks. Spread frosting between the layers and over the top and side of cake.

Nutritional information does not include frosting.

Rosemary Harbushka
Parent, Alexandra 2001

Grapefruit Cake

Yield:
16 servings

^{2}/3 cup butter, softened
1^3/4 cups sugar
2 eggs
3 cups sifted cake flour
2^1/2 teaspoons baking powder
^{1}/2 teaspoon salt

^{1}/2 cup grapefruit juice
^{3}/4 cup milk
1 teaspoon grated grapefruit peel
1^1/2 teaspoons vanilla extract
Grapefruit Frosting

Approx
Per Serving:
Cal 318
Prot 3 g
Carbo 58 g
T Fat 9 g
25% Calories
from Fat
Chol 49 mg
Fiber <1 g
Sod 268 mg

Beat the butter in a large mixer bowl at medium speed until creamy. Add the sugar gradually, beating until light and fluffy. Beat in the eggs 1 at a time. Mix the flour, baking powder and salt together. Add the flour mixture to the sugar mixture alternately with the grapefruit juice, beginning and ending with the flour mixture and mixing well after each addition. Add the milk gradually, beating constantly. Stir the grapefruit peel and vanilla into the batter. Pour into 2 greased and floured 9-inch cake pans. Bake at 350 degrees for 25 minutes or until the layers test done. Cool in the pans on a wire rack. Remove from the pans. Spread the Grapefruit Frosting between the layers and over the top and side of the cake.

Grapefruit Frosting

1^1/2 cups sugar
2 egg whites
1 tablespoon light corn syrup

^{1}/8 teaspoon salt
^{1}/3 cup grapefruit juice
1 tablespoon grated grapefruit peel

Combine the sugar, egg whites, corn syrup, salt and grapefruit juice in a double boiler. Beat with an electric mixer at low speed for 30 seconds or just until blended. Place over boiling water and beat at high speed for 7 minutes or until stiff peaks form. Remove from the heat. Add the grapefruit peel and beat for 1 to 2 minutes or until the frosting is of spreading consistency.

Charlotte Garfield
Parent, Brian 2008 and Jim 1996

One-Step Lemon Pound Cake

Yield:
16 servings

2¼ cups flour
2 cups sugar
1 cup butter, softened
3 eggs
1 cup sour cream
1 teaspoon vanilla extract
1½ teaspoons lemon extract
½ teaspoon baking soda
½ teaspoon salt

Approx
Per Serving:
Cal 307
Prot 4 g
Carbo 39 g
T Fat 16 g
45% Calories
from Fat
Chol 77 mg
Fiber <1 g
Sod 249 mg

Combine the flour, sugar, butter, eggs, sour cream, vanilla and lemon extracts, baking soda and salt in a large mixer bowl. Beat at low speed until blended. Beat at medium speed for 3 minutes. Pour into a buttered and floured bundt pan. Bake at 325 degrees for 60 to 70 minutes or until a wooden pick inserted in the center comes out clean. Cool in the pan on a wire rack. Invert onto a serving plate.

Katey Alexander
English, Middle School, 1992 to present

To be fond of learning is to be near to knowledge.

Tze-Sze, **The Doctrine of the Mean** (5th C.B.C.)

Poppy Seed Cake

Yield:
16 servings

1 (2-layer) package yellow cake mix
1 (4-ounce) package French vanilla instant pudding mix
1 cup sour cream
1/3 cup poppy seeds
1/2 cup sherry
4 eggs
1/2 teaspoon almond extract
1/2 cup vegetable oil
3 ounces cream cheese, softened
1/4 cup butter, softened
1/2 teaspoon vanilla extract
1/2 (1- pound) package confectioners' sugar

Approx
Per Serving:
Cal 394
Prot 4 g
Carbo 47 g
T Fat 21 g
47% Calories
from Fat
Chol 74 mg
Fiber 1 g
Sod 374 mg

Combine the cake mix, pudding mix, sour cream, poppy seeds, sherry, eggs, almond extract and oil in a large mixer bowl. Beat at low speed for 1 minute or until blended. Beat at high speed for 3 minutes. Pour into a lightly greased and floured bundt pan. Bake at 350 degrees for 45 minutes or until a wooden pick inserted in the center comes out clean. Cool in the pan on a wire rack for several minutes. Invert onto a serving plate. Combine the cream cheese, butter, vanilla and confectioners' sugar in a large bowl and beat until smooth and creamy. Spread over the slightly warm cake.

Pam Kurz
Parent, Daniel 2000

Moist Pumpkin Cake

Yield:
15 servings

2 (1-layer) packages spice cake mix
1 (30-ounce) can pumpkin pie mix
2 eggs
¹/₃ cup water
2 teaspoons baking soda
8 ounces whipped topping
¹/₄ cup packed light brown sugar
1 teaspoon vanilla extract

Approx
Per Serving:
Cal 269
Prot 3 g
Carbo 46 g
T Fat 8 g
26% Calories
from Fat
Chol 37 mg
Fiber 1 g
Sod 518 mg

Combine the cake mix, pumpkin pie mix, eggs, water and baking soda in a bowl and mix until well blended. Pour into a greased 9x13-inch cake pan. Bake at 325 degrees for 35 to 40 minutes or until a wooden pick inserted in the center comes out clean. Cool in the pan on a wire rack. Blend the whipped topping with the brown sugar and vanilla. Spread over the cooled cake. Store in the refrigerator.

Cathy Blake
Third Grade, Lower School, 1987 to present

Pineapple Upside-Down Cake

My mother-in-law made this recipe for Neil on every one of his birthdays until the day she died, and now Neil makes it for us. He loves it, and so do the girls.

$1/4$ cup butter
1 cup packed brown sugar
1 cup pineapple rings or crushed pineapple, apricots or peaches
$1^1/4$ cups flour
$1^1/4$ teaspoons baking powder
$3/4$ cup sugar
1 egg, well beaten
$1/2$ cup milk
1 teaspoon vanilla extract

Melt the butter in a large cast-iron skillet or 9x9-inch cake pan. Spread the brown sugar evenly over the butter. Arrange the pineapple slices over the brown sugar. Remove from the heat. Sift the flour and baking powder together and set aside. Beat the sugar and egg in a large bowl. Add the flour mixture alternately with the milk, mixing well after each addition. Blend in the vanilla. Pour the batter carefully over the pineapple slices. Bake at 350 degrees for 30 minutes or until the cake tests done. Invert onto a cake plate. Let stand until cool.

Sharron and Neil Derrough, Trustee, 1996 to present
Parents, Rebecca 2005 and Althea 2010

Pig-Picking Cake

Yield:
16 servings

1 (2-layer) package yellow cake mix
2/3 cup vegetable oil
4 eggs
1 (11-ounce) can mandarin oranges
1 (20-ounce) can crushed pineapple
1 (4-ounce) package vanilla instant pudding mix
16 ounces whipped topping

Approx
Per Serving:
Cal 391
Prot 3 g
Carbo 49 g
T Fat 20 g
46% Calories
from Fat
Chol 54 mg
Fiber 1 g
Sod 322 mg

Combine the cake mix, oil, eggs and undrained mandarin oranges in a large bowl. Beat at low speed for 1 minute or until well mixed. Beat at high speed for 3 minutes. Pour into 3 greased and floured 8- or 9-inch cake pans. Bake and cool according to the package directions. Combine the undrained pineapple and pudding mix in a large bowl and mix well. Fold in the whipped topping. Spread the pineapple mixture between the layers and over the top and side of the cake. Store in the refrigerator.

Virginia Bial
Fourth Grade, Lower School, 1993 to present

Almond Toffee

Yield:
5 pounds
(80 ounces)

5 cups coarsely chopped almonds
9 (1-ounce) milk chocolate candy bars
1½ pounds butter
3 cups sugar
5 ounces water
1½ tablespoons vanilla extract

Approx
Per Ounce:
Cal 144
Prot 2 g
Carbo 10 g
T Fat 11 g
68% Calories
from Fat
Chol 18 mg
Fiber 1 g
Sod 69 mg

Sprinkle half the almonds evenly over the bottom of a 12x17-inch pan. Unwrap the candy bars and place near the prepared pan. Combine the butter, sugar, water and vanilla in a large heavy saucepan. Cook over medium heat. Cook for 40 to 50 minutes or to 300 to 320 degrees on a candy thermometer or until golden brown, stirring constantly. Pour the mixture evenly over the almonds in the prepared pan. Arrange the candy bars over the hot toffee and spread evenly over the top when melted. Sprinkle with the remaining almonds. Let stand for 20 minutes or until cool. Refrigerate until completely chilled. Break the toffee into pieces with the tip of a strong-bladed knife. Store in the refrigerator.

Betty Higgins
Grandparent, Hillary 2005 and Hunter 2010

After a good dinner, one can forgive anybody,
even one's own relatives.

Oscar Wilde, playwright and author (1854–1900)

Double-Decker Meltaway Fudge

Yield:
96 pieces

1 cup semisweet chocolate chips
3 1/2 cups sugar
1 (12-ounce) can evaporated milk
1/2 cup butter
2 tablespoons light corn syrup
1 tablespoon white vinegar
2 1/2 cups creamy or chunky peanut butter
1 (7-ounce) jar marshmallow creme
1/2 cup semisweet chocolate chips

Approx
Per Piece:
Cal 102
Prot 2 g
Carbo 13 g
T Fat 5 g
45% Calories
from Fat
Chol 3 mg
Fiber 1 g
Sod 47 mg

Place 1 cup chocolate chips in a large heatproof bowl. Combine the sugar, evaporated milk, butter, corn syrup and vinegar in a 4-quart saucepan. Bring to a boil over medium heat, stirring constantly. Boil for 5 minutes, stirring constantly. Remove from the heat and add the peanut butter and marshmallow creme. Stir until blended. Pour half the mixture over the chocolate chips in the bowl and stir until smooth. Pour the chocolate mixture into a foil-lined 9x13-inch pan. Top with the remaining peanut butter mixture. Sprinkle with 1/2 cup chocolate chips. Let stand for a minute or two until the chips melt. Swirl with a knife to marbleize. Let stand until cool or refrigerate until firm. Cut into squares.

Charlotte Garfield
Parent, Brian 2008 and Jim 1996

Minty Christmas Fudge

Yield:
28 ounces

18 ounces mint chocolate chips
1 (14-ounce) can sweetened condensed milk
$1/8$ teaspoon salt
$1^1/2$ teaspoons vanilla extract
$1/2$ cup chopped walnuts

Approx
Per Ounce:
Cal 147
Prot 2 g
Carbo 20 g
T Fat 8 g
45% Calories
from Fat
Chol 5 mg
Fiber 1 g
Sod 31 mg

Combine the chocolate chips and condensed milk in a large heavy saucepan. Cook over low heat until melted, shiny and smooth, stirring constantly. Remove from the heat and stir in the salt, vanilla and walnuts. Spread evenly in an 8-inch-square pan lined with waxed paper. Chill for 2 to 3 hours or until firm. Turn the fudge onto a cutting board and cut into squares. Store in a tightly covered container in the refrigerator.

Sue Harman
Parent, Kristi 2000

In 1955 while plans were being made to move the school campus from downtown La Jolla to a more spacious location, The Balmer School board approved the new name La Jolla Country Day School as fitting for a private, preparatory day school with the highest of academic standards.

Peanut Butter Balls

Yield:
10 candies

2 tablespoons peanut butter
2 tablespoons butter, softened
1/2 teaspoon vanilla extract
2 tablespoons light corn syrup
1/2 cup confectioners' sugar
1 tablespoon milk
4 ounces vanilla wafers

Approx
Per Candy:
Cal 125
Prot 1 g
Carbo 18 g
T Fat 6 g
40% Calories
from Fat
Chol 7 mg
Fiber <1 g
Sod 80 mg

Combine the peanut butter, butter, vanilla, corn syrup, confectioners' sugar and milk in a bowl and mix until blended. Crush the vanilla wafers into fine crumbs. Add 1 cup of the crumbs to the peanut butter mixture and mix well. Shape into 1-inch balls and roll in the remaining wafer crumbs to coat.

Shanta Sarlin, Student 1983 to 1986

Apricot Bars

Yield:
36 bars

1 cup packed brown sugar
3/4 cup butter, softened
1/2 teaspoon salt
1 1/2 cups flour
1 cup rolled oats
Apricot Filling

Approx
Per Bar:
Cal 106
Prot 1 g
Carbo 17 g
T Fat 4 g
42% Calories
from Fat
Chol 10 mg
Fiber <1 g
Sod 74 mg

Cream the brown sugar and butter in a medium bowl. Add the salt, flour and oats and mix well. Press 2/3 of the mixture over the bottom of a greased 9x13-inch baking pan. Spread the Apricot Filling over the oats mixture in the prepared pan. Sprinkle with the remaining oats mixture and press lightly. Bake at 350 degrees for 30 to 35 minutes or until golden brown. Cool on a wire rack. Cut into bars.

Apricot Filling

1 1/3 cups finely chopped dried
   apricots
1/2 cup water

1 tablespoon lemon juice
1/2 cup sugar

Combine the apricots, water, lemon juice and sugar in a small saucepan. Cook over medium heat until thick and smooth, stirring occasionally. Set aside to cool slightly.

Nancy Winslow
Parent, Sally 2002 and John 2004

Molasses Macadamia Nut Biscotti

Yield:
40 biscotti

3/4 cup butter or margarine, softened, or safflower oil
1 cup sugar
1/4 cup light molasses
1 egg
2 cups sifted flour
2 teaspoons baking soda
1/2 teaspoon ground cloves
1/2 teaspoon ground ginger
1 teaspoon ground cinnamon
1/2 teaspoon salt
1 cup coarsely chopped raw macadamia nuts
1/2 cup raisins
1/2 cup sugar
1/2 cup ground macadamia nuts

Approx
Per Biscotto:
Cal 134
Prot 1 g
Carbo 16 g
T Fat 8 g
50% Calories
from Fat
Chol 15 mg
Fiber 1 g
Sod 131 mg

Combine the butter, sugar, molasses and egg in a large bowl and beat until smooth. Mix the flour, baking soda, cloves, ginger, cinnamon and salt together. Add to the molasses mixture and mix well. Fold in the chopped macadamia nuts and raisins. Divide into 2 portions. Shape each into a log 12 to 14 inches long and 2 inches in diameter. Sprinkle 1/2 cup sugar and the ground macadamia nuts on a strip of foil. Roll each log in the mixture until coated. Place on an ungreased baking sheet. Bake at 350 degrees for 30 minutes. Cut the logs diagonally into 11/2-inch slices with a sharp knife or cleaver. Arrange the slices cut side down on the baking sheets. Bake for 15 minutes longer and remove to wire racks to cool completely. Store in an airtight container.

Tom Cooper
Uncle, Jade Smith, 2004

Brownies

Yield:
60 brownies

2 cups semisweet chocolate chips
3/4 cup butter
1 cup sugar
4 eggs, beaten
1 teaspoon vanilla extract
1 cup flour
1 teaspoon baking powder
1/8 teaspoon salt
Whole pecans to taste

Approx
Per Brownie:
Cal 73
Prot 1 g
Carbo 9 g
T Fat 4 g
51% Calories
from Fat
Chol 20 mg
Fiber <1 g
Sod 41 mg

Melt the chocolate chips and butter in a large saucepan over low heat, stirring occasionally. Remove from the heat. Add the sugar, eggs and vanilla and mix well. Mix the flour, baking powder and salt together. Add to the chocolate mixture gradually, mixing until smooth. Spread half the mixture in a buttered 9x13-inch baking pan. Arrange the pecans over the top. Spread the remaining batter carefully over the pecans. Bake at 350 degrees for 25 minutes or until the brownies pull from the side of the pan. Cool on a wire rack. Cut into squares.

Izzy Leverant
Parent, Andrea 2001 and Alex 2003
President, Parents' Association, 1996 to 1997
Board of Trustees, 1998 to present

Walnut Brownies

Yield:
60 brownies

6 ounces unsweetened baking chocolate
3/4 cup butter or margarine
3 cups sugar
1/2 teaspoon salt
1 tablespoon vanilla extract
3 eggs
1 1/2 cups flour
1 1/2 cups chopped walnuts

Approx
Per Brownie:
Cal 109
Prot 1 g
Carbo 14 g
T Fat 6 g
47% Calories
from Fat
Chol 17 mg
Fiber 1 g
Sod 47 mg

Melt the chocolate and butter in a double boiler over hot water. Remove from the heat. Add the sugar, salt, vanilla, eggs and flour and mix until smooth. Stir in the walnuts. Spread evenly in a greased 9x13-inch baking pan. Bake at 325 degrees for 35 minutes or until the brownies pull from the side of the pan. Cool on a wire rack. Cut into squares.

Elaine Hinkle
Cook for Kerper Family, Danielle 2004

Fudgy Brownies

Yield:
60 brownies

1¹/₂ cups packed brown sugar
1¹/₂ cups sugar
³/₄ cup butter, melted
4¹/₂ ounces unsweetened baking chocolate, melted
3 eggs
1 tablespoon vanilla extract
1¹/₂ cups flour
³/₈ teaspoon salt

Approx
Per Brownie:
Cal 87
Prot 1 g
Carbo 13 g
T Fat 4 g
37% Calories
from Fat
Chol 17 mg
Fiber <1 g
Sod 44 mg

Combine the brown sugar, sugar and melted butter in a large bowl and blend well. Add the melted chocolate and mix well. Beat the eggs with the vanilla, add to the chocolate mixture and mix well. Mix in the flour and salt. Pour into 2 greased 8- or 9-inch-square baking pans. Bake at 375 degrees for 25 to 30 minutes or until the edges pull from the sides of the pans. Cool slightly before cutting into squares. Cool completely before eating.

Katey Alexander
English, Middle School, 1992 to present

Accomplishment will prove to be a journey, not a destination.

Dwight D. Eisenhower

Desserts

Oma's Grasshoppers

Yield:
60 brownies

1 (22-ounce) package brownie mix
3 cups confectioners' sugar
6 tablespoons butter, softened
2 tablespoons milk
1 teaspoon mint extract
2 or 3 drops of green food coloring
4 ounces unsweetened baking chocolate
1 ounce semisweet chocolate
1/4 cup butter
1 teaspoon vanilla extract

Approx
Per Brownie:
Cal 129
Prot 1 g
Carbo 20 g
T Fat 5 g
36% Calories
from Fat
Chol 11 mg
Fiber 1 g
Sod 70 mg

Prepare and bake the brownie mix according to the package directions. Combine the confectioners' sugar, butter, milk, mint extract and food coloring in a mixer bowl and beat until smooth and creamy. Spread over the baked brownies. Chill in the refrigerator. Melt the unsweetened and semisweet chocolates and the butter in a small saucepan over low heat, stirring constantly. Blend in the vanilla. Spread over the mint frosting. Let stand until set. Cut into squares.

Susan Middleton
Parent, Sean 2004 and Amberley 2000
Head Librarian, Lower School, 1985 to present

Buffalo Chip Cookies

Yield:
60 cookies

2 cups butter, melted
2 cups sugar
2 cups packed brown sugar
4 eggs
4 teaspoons vanilla extract
2 cups rolled oats
2 cups cornflakes
2 cups semisweet chocolate chips
2 cups chopped walnuts or pecans
4 cups flour
1 tablespoon baking soda
1 tablespoon baking powder

Approx
Per Cookie:
Cal 210
Prot 3 g
Carbo 27 g
T Fat 11 g
45% Calories
from Fat
Chol 31 mg
Fiber 1 g
Sod 167 mg

Combine the melted butter, sugar, brown sugar, eggs and vanilla in a large bowl and mix well. Stir in the oats, cornflakes, chocolate chips and walnuts. Mix the flour, baking soda and baking powder together. Add to the oats mixture and mix well. Use an ice cream scoop to place 6 large scoops on a cookie sheet, no more than 6 to a cookie sheet as the cookies will spread. Bake at 350 degrees for 13 to 15 minutes or until golden brown. Cool on the cookie sheet for 1 minute. Remove to a wire rack to cool completely.

Lori Long
Fourth Grade, Lower School, 1996 to present

Great-Grandmother's Cowboy Cookies

Yield:
60 cookies

$^1/_2$ cup butter or margarine, softened
$^1/_2$ cup shortening
1 cup packed brown sugar
1 cup sugar
2 eggs
2 cups flour
1 teaspoon baking soda
$^1/_2$ teaspoon baking powder
$^1/_2$ teaspoon salt
1 teaspoon vanilla extract
2 cups semisweet chocolate chips
1 cup chopped pecans (optional)

Approx
Per Cookie:
Cal 100
Prot 1 g
Carbo 14 g
T Fat 5 g
44% Calories
from Fat
Chol 11 mg
Fiber <1 g
Sod 64 mg

Cream the butter, shortening, brown sugar and sugar in a large bowl until light and fluffy. Mix in the eggs 1 at a time. Mix the flour, baking soda, baking powder and salt together. Add to the creamed mixture and mix well. Stir in the vanilla. Stir in the chocolate chips and pecans. Drop by teaspoonfuls onto an ungreased cookie sheet. Bake at 350 degrees for 10 to 12 minutes or until golden brown. Cool on the cookie sheet for 1 minute. Remove to a wire rack to cool completely.

Libby Keller
Music, Lower School, 1994 to present

Cowgirl Cookies

Yield:
72 cookies

1 cup sugar
1 cup packed brown sugar
1 cup vegetable oil
2 eggs
2 cups flour
1 teaspoon baking soda
1/2 teaspoon baking powder
1/2 teaspoon salt
2 cups semisweet chocolate chips
2 cups rolled oats

Approx
Per Cookie:
Cal 95
Prot 1 g
Carbo 13 g
T Fat 5 g
43% Calories
from Fat
Chol 6 mg
Fiber 1 g
Sod 41 mg

Combine the sugar, brown sugar and oil in a large bowl and beat until blended. Beat in the eggs. Sift the flour, baking soda, baking powder and salt into the egg mixture and mix well. Stir in the chocolate chips and oats. Drop by teaspoonfuls onto an ungreased cookie sheet. Bake at 350 degrees for 15 minutes; the cookies will not become very brown so do not overbake. May substitute 1/2 cup wheat germ for 1/2 cup of the flour.

Emily Maxon, 1990

La Jolla Country Day School is recognized as one of the premier college preparatory schools in the United States. La Jolla Country Day School has a history of sending over 97% of its graduating seniors to accredited four-year colleges. Each year over 85% of the senior class has successfully passed one or more Advanced Placement examinations, which will enable the student to earn college course credit while attending Country Day.

Amazing Low-Fat Cookies

Yield:
60 cookies

1 cup applesauce
3/4 cup sugar
3/4 cup packed brown sugar
1/2 cup egg substitute, or 3 egg whites
1 teaspoon (or more) vanilla extract
3 1/4 cups flour
1 teaspoon baking soda
1 teaspoon salt
4 cups semisweet chocolate chips
2 1/2 cups chopped pecans (optional)

Approx
Per Cookie:
Cal 102
Prot 1 g
Carbo 18 g
T Fat 4 g
29% Calories
from Fat
Chol <1 mg
Fiber 1 g
Sod 66 mg

Combine the applesauce, sugar and brown sugar in a large bowl and mix well. Add the egg substitute and vanilla and mix until smooth. Sift the flour, baking soda and salt together. Add to the applesauce mixture and mix well; the dough will be stiff. Mix in the chocolate chips and pecans. Drop by rounded tablespoonfuls onto ungreased cookie sheets. Bake at 325 degrees for 15 to 18 minutes or until light golden brown; do not overbake.

Angela West, 1997

Czechoslovakian Cookies

Yield:
60 cookies

1 cup butter, softened
1 cup sugar
2 eggs
1 teaspoon vanilla extract
2 cups flour
1 cup finely chopped walnuts
1 cup favorite jam or jelly

Approx
Per Cookie:
Cal 83
Prot 1 g
Carbo 10 g
T Fat 5 g
47% Calories
from Fat
Chol 15 mg
Fiber <1 g
Sod 36 mg

Cream the butter and sugar in a bowl until light and fluffy. Beat in the eggs and vanilla. Add the flour and walnuts and stir gently until mixed. Press 2/3 of the dough into an ungreased 9x13-inch baking pan. Spread the jam evenly in the prepared pan. Top with the remaining dough. Bake at 325 degrees for 35 minutes or until golden brown. Cool on a wire rack. Cut into squares.

Karen Morikawa
Parent, Evan 2006 and Megan 2008

Knowledge is power.

Francis Bacon, **Meditationes Sacrae** (1597)

Date Sticks

I have this recipe on a tattered, torn and stained recipe card in my grandmother's own handwriting. Date Sticks are our Christmas tradition.

Yield:
100 cookies

1 cup sugar
1 tablespoon butter, softened
1 tablespoon hot water
2 eggs, well beaten
1 pound pitted dates, finely chopped
1/2 cup chopped walnuts
1 cup flour
1 teaspoon baking powder
1 cup (or more) confectioners' sugar

Approx
Per Cookie:
Cal 36
Prot <1 g
Carbo 8 g
T Fat 1 g
15% Calories
from Fat
Chol 5 mg
Fiber <1 g
Sod 8 mg

Cream the sugar and butter in a bowl. Add the hot water and eggs and mix well. Add the dates and walnuts and mix well. Sift the flour and baking powder together 2 times, add to the date mixture and mix well. Spread in a greased 9x13-inch baking pan. Bake at 350 degrees for 25 minutes. Cool in the pan on a wire rack. Cut into 2-inch-long sticks. Roll in confectioners' sugar to coat. Store in an airtight container.

Susan Middleton
Parent, Sean 2004 and Amberley 2000
Head Librarian, Lower School, 1985 to present

Date Walnut Bars

Yield:
20 bars

1¼ cups flour
⅓ cup sugar
½ cup butter, softened
⅓ cup packed brown sugar
⅓ cup sugar
2 eggs
1 teaspoon vanilla extract
2 tablespoons flour
1 teaspoon baking powder
½ teaspoon salt
¼ teaspoon nutmeg
2 tablespoons chopped walnuts
8 ounces pitted dates, chopped
1 to 2 tablespoons confectioners' sugar

Approx
Per Bar:
Cal 158
Prot 2 g
Carbo 26 g
T Fat 6 g
31% Calories
from Fat
Chol 34 mg
Fiber 1 g
Sod 138 mg

Combine 1¼ cups flour and ⅓ cup sugar in a bowl and mix well. Cut in the butter until crumbly. Mix with fingers until a dough forms. Press evenly over the bottom of a greased 9-inch-square baking pan. Bake at 350 degrees for 20 minutes. Combine the brown sugar, ⅓ cup sugar, eggs and vanilla in a bowl and mix until smooth. Mix the flour, baking powder, salt and nutmeg together, add to the egg mixture and mix well. Stir in the walnuts and dates. Spread the date mixture over the baked layer. Bake for 20 minutes longer. Cool on a wire rack. Sprinkle with the confectioners' sugar. Cut into bars.

Izzy Leverant
Parent, Andrea 2001 and Alex 2003
President, Parents' Association, 1996 to 1997
Board of Trustees, 1998 to present

Lemon Bars

Yield:
20 bars

¹/₂ cup butter, softened
1 cup sifted flour
¹/₄ cup confectioners' sugar
2 eggs
1 cup sugar
¹/₄ teaspoon salt
3 tablespoons lemon juice
¹/₂ teaspoon baking powder
2 tablespoons flour

Approx
Per Bar:
Cal 117
Prot 1 g
Carbo 17 g
T Fat 5 g
39% Calories
from Fat
Chol 34 mg
Fiber <1 g
Sod 95 mg

Beat the butter in a bowl. Add 1 cup flour and confectioners' sugar and mix well. Press into an 8-inch-square baking pan. Bake at 350 degrees for 18 to 20 minutes or until light golden brown. Beat the eggs with the sugar, salt, lemon juice and a mixture of baking powder and 2 tablespoons flour. Spoon over the baked layer. Bake for 30 minutes longer or until light brown. Cool on a wire rack. Garnish with a sprinkle of additional confectioners' sugar. Cut into bars.

Pat Konkle
Parent, Scott 1997

Lemon Squares

Yield:
16 squares

1/2 cup butter or margarine, softened
1 cup flour
1/4 cup confectioners' sugar
2 eggs
1/4 cup sugar
1/2 teaspoon baking powder
2 teaspoons lemon juice

Approx
Per Square:
Cal 108
Prot 2 g
Carbo 11 g
T Fat 6 g
53% Calories
from Fat
Chol 42 mg
Fiber <1 g
Sod 82 mg

Combine the butter, flour and confectioners' sugar in a bowl and mix until a dough forms. Press evenly over the bottom of an ungreased 9-inch baking pan. Bake at 350 degrees for 20 minutes. Combine the eggs, sugar, baking powder and lemon juice in a mixer bowl. Beat for 3 minutes or until light and fluffy. Pour over the hot baked layer. Bake for 25 minutes longer or until no imprint remains when lightly touched in the center. Cool on a wire rack. Cut into squares.

Elizabeth Hill
Grandparent, Andrew 2009

In 1869 the first recorded sale of land in La Jolla occurred. Samuel Sizer bought 80 acres of beautiful oceanfront property for $1.25 an acre. The early residents of the area had fresh water hauled in twice a week from San Diego. Any visitors to La Jolla either walked, rode a horse, or came by carriage to the jewel on the Pacific Ocean located 12 miles north of San Diego.

Lemon Poppy Seed Cookies

Yield:
36 cookies

3 cups flour
1 teaspoon baking powder
$1/4$ teaspoon baking soda
$1/4$ teaspoon salt
1 cup sugar
3 eggs
$1/2$ cup vegetable oil
1 teaspoon vanilla extract
1 teaspoon lemon juice
1 tablespoon (or more) poppy seeds

Approx
Per Cookie:
Cal 94
Prot 2 g
Carbo 14 g
T Fat 4 g
35% Calories
from Fat
Chol 18 mg
Fiber <1 g
Sod 44 mg

Sift the flour, baking powder, baking soda and salt into a large bowl. Add the sugar, eggs, oil, vanilla and lemon juice. Mix well with a fork. Knead lightly, adding the poppy seeds. Shape into a ball. Refrigerate, covered, for 15 to 30 minutes or until firm. Divide into 4 equal portions. Refrigerate the unused portions. Roll one portion at a time on a lightly floured surface, cut with a round cookie cutter and place on an ungreased cookie sheet. Bake at 350 degrees for 10 minutes or until light golden brown. Cool on the cookie sheet for 1 minute and remove to a wire rack to cool completely.

Helene Ziman
Parent, Jared 2000

Nanaimo Bars

Yield:
48 bars

1/2 cup melted butter
1/4 cup sugar
1/3 cup unsweetened baking cocoa
1 egg
2 cups graham cracker crumbs
1 cup flaked coconut
1/2 cup chopped walnuts
1/4 cup butter, softened
2 tablespoons custard powder
1 teaspoon vanilla extract
3 tablespoons milk
2 cups sifted confectioners' sugar
3 ounces semisweet chocolate
1 tablespoon butter

Approx
Per Bar:
Cal 98
Prot 1 g
Carbo 12 g
T Fat 6 g
51% Calories
from Fat
Chol 13 mg
Fiber 1 g
Sod 68 mg

Combine the melted butter, sugar, cocoa and egg in a bowl and mix until smooth. Add the graham cracker crumbs, coconut and walnuts and mix well. Press evenly over the bottom of a lightly greased 9-inch-square baking pan. Refrigerate while making the filling. Cream the softened butter, custard powder and vanilla in a bowl. Add the milk and confectioners' sugar alternately, mixing until smooth and creamy. Reserve 1/4 cup of the mixture. Spread the remaining mixture over the crust. Chill until firm. Melt the chocolate and 1 tablespoon butter in a small saucepan over low heat, stirring constantly. Spread over the chilled layers. Chill until firm. Cut into bars. Decorate with the reserved mixture. (Editorial Note: Because the bars are not cooked, we recommend that pasturized egg substitute be substituted for the fresh egg.)

Diane de Sequera
Science, Middle School, 1991 to present

Ché Café Monster Cookies

These cookies are HUGE and yummy—don't substitute any ingredients. Turbinado sugar may be hard to find—it is raw sugar that has been cleaned with steam and is light brown in color with a molasses flavor.

Yield:
25 cookies

7 cups margarine, softened
3 cups turbinado sugar
4$^{1}/_{2}$ cups packed brown sugar
6 eggs or equivalent egg substitute
2 tablespoons vanilla extract
2 tablespoons baking powder
9 cups whole wheat flour
2 tablespoons ground cinnamon
$^{1}/_{2}$ teaspoon ground nutmeg
18 cups rolled oats
11 cups chocolate chips

Approx
Per Cookie:
Cal 1438
Prot 20 g
Carbo 180 g
T Fat 79 g
47% Calories
from Fat
Chol 51 mg
Fiber 16 g
Sod 648 mg

Cream the margarine, turbinado sugar and brown sugar in a very large bowl until light and fluffy. Add the eggs and vanilla and mix well. Mix the flour, cinnamon and nutmeg together, add to the egg mixture and mix well. Stir in the oats and chocolate chips. Divide into 25 portions. Place 1 or 2 portions at a time on a cookie sheet. Mash lightly if larger cookies are desired. Bake at 350 degrees for 15 minutes. Cool on the cookie sheet for 2 to 3 minutes and remove to wire racks to cool completely.

Michael Amiel, 1986

Dagney's Oatmeal Cookies

Mark's grandfather was Swedish and a member of the Vasa Order of America, Vineland Lodge of Cape Cod, Massachusetts. This is one of their recipes.

Yield:
60 servings

1/2 cup sugar
1 cup butter, softened
2 teaspoons vanilla or lemon extract
1 1/4 cups flour
1/2 teaspoon baking soda
1 1/4 cups quick-cooking oats

Approx
Per Serving:
Cal 51
Prot 1 g
Carbo 5 g
T Fat 3 g
56% Calories
from Fat
Chol 8 mg
Fiber <1 g
Sod 31 mg

Cream the sugar and butter in a bowl until light and fluffy. Blend in the vanilla. Add the flour, baking soda and oats and mix well. Shape into small balls, arrange on a cookie sheet and flatten with a fork dipped in cold water. Decorate with tinted sugar, nuts or candied cherries. Bake at 350 degrees for 8 to 10 minutes or until golden brown. Cool on the cookie sheet for 1 minute and remove to a wire rack to cool completely.

Althea T. Johnson
Grandparent, Mark Wischkaemper 1997

I have never let my schooling interfere with my education.

Mark Twain (1835–1910)

Famous Oatmeal Cookies

I don't know how many millions of these I've made for LJCDS students over the years.

Yield:
30 cookies

3/4 cup shortening
1 cup packed brown sugar
1/2 cup sugar
1 egg
1/4 cup water
1 teaspoon vanilla extract
1 cup sifted flour
1 teaspoon salt
1/2 teaspoon baking soda
3 cups rolled oats
2 cups chocolate chips

Approx
Per Cookie:
Cal 187
Prot 2 g
Carbo 26 g
T Fat 9 g
42% Calories
from Fat
Chol 7 mg
Fiber 2 g
Sod 105 mg

Combine the shortening, brown sugar, sugar, egg, water and vanilla in a large bowl and beat until creamy. Sift in the flour, salt and baking soda and mix well. Stir in the oats and chocolate chips. Add any desired amounts of nuts, raisins or shredded coconut at this point. Drop by teaspoonfuls onto a greased cookie sheet. Bake at 350 degrees for 12 to 15 minutes or until golden brown. Cool on the cookie sheet for 1 to 2 minutes and remove to a wire rack to cool completely.

Dara Hensley
English, Upper School, 1981 to 1986; 1989 to 1995

Raisin and Oatmeal Cookies

Yield:
36 cookies

1 cup butter, softened
1 cup packed brown sugar
$1/2$ cup sugar
2 eggs
2 tablespoons milk
2 teaspoons vanilla extract
$1^3/4$ cups flour
1 teaspoon baking soda
$1/2$ teaspoon salt
$2^1/2$ cups rolled oats
2 cups chocolate chips
1 cup raisins

Approx
Per Cookie:
Cal 184
Prot 2 g
Carbo 26 g
T Fat 9 g
40% Calories
from Fat
Chol 26 mg
Fiber 1 g
Sod 128 mg

Cream the butter, brown sugar and sugar in a large bowl until light and fluffy. Beat in the eggs, milk and vanilla. Mix the flour, baking soda and salt together and mix into the creamed mixture. Stir in the oats, chocolate chips and raisins. Drop by spoonfuls onto a lightly greased cookie sheet. Bake at 375 degrees for 10 minutes or until golden brown. Cool on the cookie sheet for 1 minute and remove to a wire rack to cool completely. May increase the granulated sugar to $1^1/2$ cups, add $1/4$ to $1/3$ cup molasses and omit the brown sugar.

Brooke Donahoe Roberts
History, Upper School, 1994 to 1996

Great-Grandmother Esther's Oatmeal Cookies

Yield:
36 cookies

1 cup sugar
1 cup packed brown sugar
1 cup butter, softened
2 eggs
1 teaspoon vanilla extract
1½ cups flour
1 teaspoon salt
1 teaspoon baking soda
2 tablespoons water
3 cups rolled oats
1½ cups chopped walnuts or pecans

Approx
Per Cookie:
Cal 171
Prot 3 g
Carbo 21 g
T Fat 9 g
46% Calories
from Fat
Chol 26 mg
Fiber 1 g
Sod 158 mg

Cream the sugar, brown sugar and butter in a large bowl until light and fluffy. Beat in the eggs and vanilla. Add the flour ½ cup at a time, mixing well after each addition. Mix in the salt. Add the baking soda dissolved in the water and mix well. Stir in the oats and walnuts. Drop by tablespoonfuls onto a lightly greased cookie sheet. Bake at 350 degrees for 8 minutes or until golden brown. The cookies will look slightly runny while baking and will appear lacy. Cool on the cookie sheet for 1 minute. Remove to a wire rack to cool completely. Store in an airtight container.

Tracy Katkov
Parent, Ryan 1998

'Tis an ill cook that cannot lick his own fingers.

Shakespeare, **Romeo and Juliet** (1564–1616)

Daddy's Oatmeal Cookies

Yield:
48 cookies

$^3/_4$ cup butter
1 cup sugar
$^1/_2$ cup packed brown sugar
1 egg
1 teaspoon vanilla extract
2 tablespoons molasses
1$^1/_2$ cups flour
1 teaspoon baking soda
1 teaspoon baking powder
1$^1/_2$ teaspoons ground cinnamon
1 teaspoon ground nutmeg
1 cup shredded coconut
1$^1/_2$ cups rolled oats

Approx
Per Cookie:
Cal 85
Prot 1 g
Carbo 12 g
T Fat 4 g
38% Calories
from Fat
Chol 12 mg
Fiber <1 g
Sod 72 mg

Cream the butter, sugar and brown sugar in a large bowl until light and fluffy. Add the egg, vanilla and molasses and mix well. Mix the flour, baking soda, baking powder, cinnamon and nutmeg together. Add to the creamed mixture and mix well. Add the coconut and oats and mix well. Shape into small balls and arrange on a lightly greased cookie sheet. Bake at 350 degrees for 10 to 12 minutes or until golden brown. Cool on the cookie sheet for 1 minute and remove to a wire rack to cool completely.

Catherine Blair
Parent, Meaghan 2006, Darcie 2008 and Evan 2010

Shortbread Cookies

Yield:
12 cookies

3/4 cup margarine, softened
1 cup flour

1/2 cup cornstarch
1/2 cup confectioners' sugar

Approx
Per Cookie:
Cal 179
Prot 1 g
Carbo 18 g
T Fat 11 g
57% Calories
from Fat
Chol 0 mg
Fiber <1 g
Sod 134 mg

Beat the margarine in a bowl. Add the flour, cornstarch and confectioners' sugar and mix well. Shape into balls and arrange on a cookie sheet. Flatten with a glass dipped in flour or make an indentation with your thumb and fill the indentation with jam. Bake at 325 degrees for 20 to 25 minutes or until light golden brown. Cool on the cookie sheet for 1 minute and remove to a wire rack to cool completely.

Elaine Hinkle
Cook for the Kerper Family, Danielle 2004

Snowballs

Yield:
36 cookies

1 cup margarine, softened
1/2 cup sugar
1/2 teaspoon salt
2 teaspoons vanilla extract

2 cups flour
1 cup chopped walnuts or pecans
1 cup (or more) confectioners' sugar

Approx
Per Cookie:
Cal 115
Prot 1 g
Carbo 12 g
T Fat 7 g
55% Calories
from Fat
Chol 0 mg
Fiber <1 g
Sod 92 mg

Cream the margarine and sugar in a bowl until light and fluffy. Beat in the salt and vanilla. Add the flour gradually, mixing well after each addition. Mix in the walnuts. Shape into 1-inch balls and arrange on an ungreased cookie sheet. Bake at 350 degrees for 12 to 15 minutes or until light brown. Let cool slightly. Roll in confectioners' sugar while warm and place on wire racks to cool completely.

Lu Ann Hall
Parent, Lurline Sweet 2002

Sugar Cookies

Yield:
36 cookies

1 cup sugar
1/2 cup butter, softened
2 eggs
2 tablespoons milk
2 1/4 cups flour
1 1/2 teaspoons baking powder
1/4 teaspoon salt
1/2 teaspoon nutmeg
1/2 cup (about) sugar

Approx
Per Cookie:
Cal 88
Prot 1 g
Carbo 14 g
T Fat 3 g
30% Calories
from Fat
Chol 19 mg
Fiber <1 g
Sod 67 mg

Cream 1 cup sugar and butter in a large bowl until light and fluffy. Beat in the eggs 1 at a time. Blend in the milk. Mix the flour, baking powder, salt and nutmeg together. Add to the creamed mixture and mix well. Chill, covered, for 2 hours. Roll the dough on a lightly floured surface and cut with cookie cutters. Arrange on an ungreased cookie sheet. Sprinkle with 1/2 cup sugar. Bake at 400 degrees for 8 to 10 minutes or until light brown. Cool on the cookie sheet for 1 minute and remove to a wire rack to cool completely.

Nancy Winslow
Parent, Sally 2002 and John 2004

School colors: Blue and white
Sports teams: The Torres
School mascot: A Torrey pine tree
School motto: Scientia Pacifica (Latin: Peaceful Knowledge)
The school spirit of the Country Day student is like a symphony,
each note building to a crescendo of enthusiastic joy.

Madeleine's Swedish Spice Cookies

A Swedish friend gave this recipe to the family in the 1940s. These are soft cookies that stay fresh for a long time and are especially nice to mail to college students.

Yield:
60 cookies

2 cups raisins
1½ cups water
1 cup margarine, softened
2 cups packed brown sugar
2 eggs
3½ cups flour
¼ to ½ teaspoon salt
1 teaspoon ground cloves
1 teaspoon ground cinnamon
1 teaspoon ground nutmeg
1 teaspoon baking soda

Approx
Per Cookie:
Cal 98
Prot 1 g
Carbo 17 g
T Fat 3 g
29% Calories
from Fat
Chol 7 mg
Fiber <1 g
Sod 82 mg

Combine the raisins and water in a saucepan. Simmer for 10 minutes, stirring occasionally. Set aside to cool. Cream the margarine and brown sugar in a large bowl until light and fluffy. Beat in the eggs. Mix the flour, salt, cloves, cinnamon and nutmeg together. Add to the creamed mixture and mix well. Stir the baking soda into the raisins and add to the flour mixture. Drop by teaspoonfuls onto a lightly greased cookie sheet. Bake at 325 degrees for 15 minutes or until light brown.

Marian Randall
Third Grade, Lower School, 1989 to present

Sue's Apple Pie

This is perhaps the best apple pie recipe ever! I have been using it for nearly 27 years. It was given to me in confidence, by Sue Armstrong of Minneapolis, Minnesota, a close family friend, who enjoyed this recipe as a child in Oklahoma. The recipe is over 100 years old. With much love, I thank you, Sue!

Yield:
8 servings

12 or 13 Jonathan, Winesap or McIntosh apples
1 cup (or more) sugar
1 teaspoon (or more) ground cinnamon
1/4 teaspoon ground nutmeg
1/4 teaspoon salt
Pie Pastry
5 teaspoons (or more) lemon juice
3 tablespoons butter, chopped
Cinnamon-sugar to taste

Approx
Per Serving:
Cal 474
Prot 3 g
Carbo 72 g
T Fat 21 g
39% Calories
from Fat
Chol 12 mg
Fiber 5 g
Sod 263 mg

Peel, core and thinly slice the apples. Mix the sugar, 1 teaspoon cinnamon, nutmeg and salt together. Fit one of the pastry rounds into a 10-inch pie plate. Sprinkle with a generous layer of the sugar mixture. Alternate layers of the apples and sugar mixture until all the ingredients are used. Drizzle the lemon juice over the top. Dot with 2 tablespoons of the butter. Top with the remaining pie pastry, sprinkle lightly with cinnamon-sugar and dot with the remaining butter. Seal the edge and cut vents. Line the bottom of the oven with heavy-duty foil as the pie is sure to run over. Place the pie in a preheated 450-degree oven. Bake for 12 minutes. Reduce the temperature to 350 degrees. Bake for 1 hour longer or until the juices run over and the whole place smells heavenly. Turn off the oven and let the pie to cool in the oven. Serve with vanilla ice cream or a sharp Cheddar cheese.

Pie Pastry

1 1/2 cups sifted flour
1/2 teaspoon salt
8 to 10 tablespoons shortening
5 tablespoons ice water

Mix the flour and salt in a bowl. Cut in the shortening with a pastry blender until crumbly. Add the ice water and toss with a fork until the dough clings together. Divide into 2 portions and roll into rounds on a lightly floured surface.

Shelley Ackerberg-Patton
Parent, Sanders 2001 and Charlie 2004
Cookbook Editor

Best Apple Pie Ever

Yield:
8 servings

8 McIntosh apples, peeled, sliced
1²/₃ cups sour cream
1 cup sugar
¹/₃ cup flour
¹/₂ teaspoon salt

1 egg
2 teaspoons vanilla extract
Cider Pastry
Walnut Topping

Approx
Per Serving:
Cal 876
Prot 9 g
Carbo 105 g
T Fat 50 g
49% Calories
from Fat
Chol 126 mg
Fiber 5 g
Sod 660 m

Combine the apples, sour cream, sugar, flour, salt, egg and vanilla in a large bowl and mix well. Spoon into the pie plate lined with the Cider Pastry. Place the pie in a preheated 450-degree oven. Bake for 10 minutes. Reduce the oven temperature to 350 degrees. Bake for 40 minutes or until the filling is slightly puffed and golden brown. Sprinkle the Walnut Topping over the top. Bake for 15 minutes longer.

Cider Pastry

1³/₄ cups flour
¹/₄ cup sugar
1 teaspoon ground cinnamon

¹/₂ teaspoon salt
³/₄ cup butter
¹/₄ cup apple cider or water

Mix the flour, sugar, cinnamon and salt in a bowl. Cut in the butter until crumbly. Add the cider and toss the mixture with a fork until the mixture holds together. Shape into a ball and roll on a lightly floured surface. Fit the pastry into a 10-inch pie plate.

Walnut Topping

1 cup chopped walnuts
¹/₂ cup flour
¹/₃ cup packed brown sugar
¹/₃ cup sugar

1 tablespoon ground cinnamon
¹/₈ teaspoon salt
¹/₂ cup butter, softened

Combine the walnuts, flour, brown sugar, sugar, cinnamon and salt in a bowl. Add the softened butter and mix until crumbly.

Miriam Robbins
Parent, Monica 2001

Cream Cheese Pie

~~~~~~

Yield:
8 servings

6 graham crackers, ground
1/4 cup sugar
1/4 cup melted butter
9 ounces cream cheese, softened
1/2 cup sugar
3 eggs
Juice of 1 orange
1 teaspoon vanilla extract
1 cup sour cream
2 tablespoons confectioners' sugar
1/2 teaspoon vanilla extract

Approx
Per Serving:
Cal 363
Prot 6 g
Carbo 29 g
T Fat 25 g
62% Calories
from Fat
Chol 143 mg
Fiber <1 g
Sod 224 mg

Combine the graham cracker crumbs, 1/4 cup sugar and melted butter in a bowl and mix well. Press the mixture over the bottom and up the side of a 9-inch pie plate. Bake at 375 degrees for 8 minutes. Let stand until cool. Reduce the oven temperature to 350 degrees. Combine the cream cheese, 1/2 cup sugar, eggs, orange juice and 1 teaspoon vanilla in a food processor and process until smooth. Pour into the cooled graham cracker crust. Bake at 350 degrees for 25 minutes. Cool for 20 minutes. Increase the oven temperature to 450 degrees. Blend the sour cream with the confectioners' sugar and 1/2 teaspoon vanilla. Pour over the cream cheese mixture. Bake for 10 minutes leaving the oven door ajar.

Beverly Silldorf
Parent, David 1999 and Mark 2003

Tartlets

Yield:
12 (2-tartlet)
servings

3 ounces cream cheese, softened
1/2 cup butter or margarine, softened
1 cup flour
1 egg, beaten
3/4 cup packed brown sugar
1/4 teaspoon (about) vanilla extract
1 cup chopped walnuts or pecans
1 tablespoon butter
Confectioners' sugar to taste

Approx
Per Serving:
Cal 253
Prot 4 g
Carbo 23 g
T Fat 17 g
58% Calories
from Fat
Chol 46 mg
Fiber 1 g
Sod 111 mg

Blend the cream cheese and 1/2 cup butter in a bowl. Add the flour and mix well. Shape into 24 small balls. Press each ball over the bottom and up the side of a miniature muffin cup. Beat the egg with the brown sugar and vanilla. Add the walnuts and 1 tablespoon butter, mixing well. Spoon into the pastry-lined cups. Do not fill the cups completely to prevent overflow during baking. Bake at 375 degrees for 20 minutes or until set and brown. Sprinkle lightly with confectioners' sugar. Remove the tartlets to a wire rack to cool.

Denyse Pierre-Pierre
Grandparent, Michelle 1999 and Zack 2001

The development of the area known as La Jolla came long after the word La Jolla. What does La Jolla mean? Quite simply, it means jewel. Although there is no word in the Spanish dictionary La Jolla, there is a Spanish word joya (phonetically pronounced hoya), which means jewel. Situated a breeze away from the magnificent Pacific Ocean, La Jolla Country Day School is certainly a jewel.

Chocolate Angel Pie

This recipe is submitted in memory of Michelle's great-grandmother and of her grandmother, Bernice Newkirk. It is well worth the nearly four hours it requires from start to ready-to-eat.

Yield:
8 servings

2 egg whites
1/8 teaspoon cream of tartar
1/8 teaspoon salt
1/2 cup sifted sugar
1/2 cup finely chopped walnuts or pecans
1/2 teaspoon vanilla extract
1 (6-ounce) package German's sweet chocolate, chopped
3 tablespoons water
1 teaspoon vanilla extract
1 cup whipping cream, whipped

Approx
Per Serving:
Cal 299
Prot 4 g
Carbo 27 g
T Fat 21 g
63% Calories
from Fat
Chol 41 mg
Fiber 1 g
Sod 62 mg

Beat the egg whites in a large bowl until foamy. Add the cream of tartar and salt and mix well. Add the sugar gradually, beating until very stiff peaks form. Fold in the walnuts and 1/2 teaspoon vanilla. Spread the meringue over the bottom and up the side of a lightly greased 8-inch pie plate, forming a shell 1/2 inch above the edge of the pie plate. Bake at 300 degrees for 50 to 55 minutes or until dry to the touch. Let stand until completely cool. Combine the chocolate and water in a small saucepan over low heat. Heat until the chocolate is melted and the mixture is well blended, stirring constantly. Cool until thickened. Blend in 1 teaspoon vanilla. Fold the chocolate mixture into the whipped cream. Spoon into the meringue shell. Chill for 2 hours before serving.

Nancy Ann Marshall
Parent, Michelle 2002

Chocolate Pecan Pie

Yield:
8 servings

2/3 cup evaporated milk
2 tablespoons butter
2 cups semisweet chocolate chips
2 cups broken pecans
1/4 teaspoon vanilla extract
2 eggs, slightly beaten
1 cup sugar
1 unbaked (9-inch) pie shell or chocolate crumb pie shell

Approx
Per Serving:
Cal 686
Prot 9 g
Carbo 70 g
T Fat 46 g
57% Calories
from Fat
Chol 64 mg
Fiber 5 g
Sod 192 mg

Combine the evaporated milk, butter and chocolate chips in a 1-quart saucepan over low heat. Heat until the chocolate melts and the mixture is well blended, stirring constantly. Remove from the heat and stir in the pecans and vanilla. Beat the eggs with sugar and stir into the chocolate mixture. Pour into the pie shell. Bake at 375 degrees for 35 minutes or until a knife inserted in the center comes out clean. Cool before cutting.

Julie Sugarman
Parent, Eli 1998

Key Lime Pie

Yield:
8 servings

4 egg yolks, beaten
1 (14-ounce) can sweetened condensed milk
6 tablespoons Key lime juice
Grated zest of 1 lime
1 (8- or 9-inch) graham cracker pie shell
1 cup whipping cream, whipped

Approx
Per Serving:
Cal 440
Prot 7 g
Carbo 48 g
T Fat 25 g
51% Calories
from Fat
Chol 164 mg
Fiber 1 g
Sod 260 mg

Combine the egg yolks and condensed milk and beat until well blended. Stir in the lime juice and zest until smooth and creamy. Pour into the pie shell. Bake at 350 degrees for 10 minutes. Chill until serving time. Top with the whipped cream just before serving.

Ellen Person
Parent, Jeff 2000

Lemon Meringue Pie

Yield:
8 servings

1 cup sugar
1/4 cup flour
3 tablespoons cornstarch
1/4 teaspoon salt
2 cups water
3 egg yolks, beaten
1 tablespoon butter
1/4 cup lemon juice
Grated peel of 1 lemon
1 baked (9-inch) pie shell
Meringue

Approx
Per Serving:
Cal 321
Prot 4 g
Carbo 52 g
T Fat 11 g
31% Calories
from Fat
Chol 84 mg
Fiber 1 g
Sod 233 mg

Combine the sugar, flour, cornstarch and salt in a large saucepan. Stir in the water gradually. Cook over medium heat until smooth and thickened, stirring constantly. Stir a small amount of the hot mixture into the beaten egg yolks; stir the egg yolks into the hot mixture. Cook for 2 minutes longer, stirring constantly. Remove from the heat and blend in the butter, lemon juice and peel. Cool slightly and pour into the pie shell. Let stand until cool. Top with the Meringue, sealing to the edge of the pie shell. Bake at 425 degrees for 5 to 6 minutes or until the meringue is golden brown.

Meringue

3 egg whites
1/4 teaspoon cream of tartar
6 tablespoons sugar

Beat the egg whites in a mixer bowl until light and frothy. Add the cream of tartar and beat until stiff peaks form. Add the sugar gradually, beating until the peaks are stiff and glossy.

Elizabeth Hill
Grandparent, Andrew 2009

Fresh Peach and Raspberry Pie

Yield:
8 servings

1 recipe (2-crust) pie pastry
1 egg white, beaten
4 cups sliced peeled peaches
3/4 cup sugar
1/3 cup flour
1 tablespoon fresh lemon juice
1/2 teaspoon grated lemon peel
1/2 teaspoon ground cinnamon
1 cup fresh raspberries

Approx
Per Serving:
Cal 349
Prot 4 g
Carbo 53 g
T Fat 14 g
36% Calories
from Fat
Chol 0 mg
Fiber 4 g
Sod 224 mg

Prepare and roll the pie pastry according to recipe directions. Fit one of the pastries into a buttered 9-inch pie plate and brush with the beaten egg white. Reserve the second pastry. Combine the peaches, sugar, flour, lemon juice and peel and cinnamon in a large bowl and mix gently. Fold in the raspberries. Spoon the fruit mixture into the prepared pie shell. Top with the reserved pie pastry, sealing the edge and cutting vents. Sprinkle the top with additional sugar. Bake at 425 degrees for 40 to 45 minutes or until golden brown. Cool before cutting.

Rebecca Wood, 1970

Pecan Pie

Yield:
8 servings

1 cup packed light brown sugar
1/2 cup sugar
1 tablespoon flour
2 eggs, beaten
2 tablespoons milk
1 teaspoon vanilla extract
1/2 cup melted butter
1 cup pecans
1 (9-inch) pie shell

Approx
Per Serving:
Cal 487
Prot 4 g
Carbo 53 g
T Fat 30 g
54% Calories
from Fat
Chol 85 mg
Fiber 1 g
Sod 268 mg

Mix the brown sugar, sugar and flour in a large bowl. Add the eggs, milk, vanilla and butter and beat until well blended. Fold in the pecans. Pour into the pie shell. Place a baking sheet on the oven rack below the pie to catch any boil-over. Bake at 375 degrees for 40 to 50 minutes or until a knife inserted in the center comes out clean. Serve slightly warm either plain or with whipped cream.

Susan Roberts
Parent, Tesse 1994, Brad 1997 and Volker, a German exchange student 1996

In 1929 Mrs. Balmer, founder of La Jolla Country Day School, stated "The purpose of a school is to keep the priceless qualities inherent in childhood pure, strong and unsullied by prejudices, indoctrination and the stress of living." These goals continue to be valued seventy years later by the educators at La Jolla Country Day School.

Incredible Yogurt Pie

Yield:
8 servings

1 cup ricotta cheese
1 cup plain yogurt
3 tablespoons honey
$1/2$ teaspoon vanilla extract
1 envelope unflavored gelatin
$1^{1}/2$ to $1^{3}/4$ cups sliced fruit of choice (do not use fresh pineapple or kiwifruit)
Almond Crumb Pie Shell
$1/3$ cup apricot, peach or strawberry preserves or chocolate sauce

Approx
Per Serving:
Cal 310
Prot 8 g
Carbo 35 g
T Fat 17 g
47% Calories
from Fat
Chol 40 mg
Fiber 1 g
Sod 219 mg

Combine the ricotta cheese, yogurt, honey, vanilla, dry gelatin and $1/2$ to $3/4$ cup of the fruit in a food processor. Process until smooth and creamy. Pour into the pie shell. Chill for 2 hours or longer. Arrange the remaining sliced fruit on top. Heat the preserves and drizzle over the fruit. Serve immediately.

Almond Crumb Pie Shell

$2/3$ to 1 cup graham cracker crumbs
$1/3$ to $1/2$ cup ground toasted almonds
2 to 3 tablespoons brown sugar
$1/3$ cup melted butter

Combine the graham cracker crumbs, almonds, brown sugar and butter in a bowl and mix well. Press over the bottom and up the side of a 9-inch pie plate or quiche pan. Bake at 375 degrees for 5 minutes and let stand until completely cooled or do not bake and chill in the refrigerator for 1 hour.

Nutritional information for this recipe does not include the fruit.

Lisa Braun-Glazer
Parent, Julia 2001

Ginger Pecan Layered Pumpkin Pie

Yield:
8 servings

1 pint vanilla or vanilla bean ice cream, softened
3 tablespoons chopped crystallized ginger
1 baked (9-inch) pie shell or graham cracker or vanilla wafer pie shell
1 cup canned pumpkin
1 cup sugar
1 teaspoon pumpkin pie spice
$1/2$ teaspoon ground ginger
$1/2$ teaspoon salt (optional)
$1/2$ cup chopped pecans (optional)
1 cup whipping cream, whipped

Approx
Per Serving:
Cal 413
Prot 4 g
Carbo 51 g
T Fat 22 g
48% Calories
from Fat
Chol 55 mg
Fiber 2 g
Sod 164 mg

Fold the softened ice cream and crystallized ginger together and spread in the cooled pie shell. Freeze until the ice cream is firm. Combine the pumpkin, sugar, pie spice, ground ginger, salt and pecans in a bowl and mix well. Fold in the whipped cream gently. Pour over the ice cream layer. Freeze for several hours to overnight.

Teresa M. Laneville
Grandparent of Amy Marie Watkins (deceased), class of 1987
In her memory, the Amy Marie Watkins Memorial Poetry Contest is held annually.

Angel Cream Melba

Yield:
12 servings

3 envelopes unflavored gelatin
1 cup sugar
$3/4$ teaspoon salt
4 cups milk
4 teaspoons vanilla extract
4 cups whipping cream
Melba Sauce

Approx
Per Serving:
Cal 441
Prot 6 g
Carbo 34 g
T Fat 32 g
65% Calories
from Fat
Chol 120 mg
Fiber 1 g
Sod 222 mg

Mix the gelatin, sugar, salt and 2 cups of the milk in a 2-quart saucepan. Cook over medium heat until the gelatin is completely dissolved, stirring constantly. Remove from the heat and stir in the remaining 2 cups milk and vanilla. Chill in the refrigerator for 30 to 50 minutes or until the mixture mounds slightly when dropped from a spoon. Whip the whipping cream in a large bowl until soft peaks form. Fold the gelatin mixture gently into the whipped cream. Spoon the mixture into a bundt pan or 12 dessert dishes. Chill for 3 hours to overnight or until firm. Unmold the Angel Cream onto a chilled platter. Spoon a small amount of the Melba Sauce over the mold. Arrange the peach slices over the top and serve with the remaining Melba Sauce.

Melba Sauce

1 (10-ounce) package frozen blueberries, or 1 to 2 cups fresh blueberries
1 (16-ounce) can sliced peaches
1 tablespoon cornstarch
1 tablespoon water

Reserve a few spoonfuls of whole blueberries. Purée the remaining blueberries in a food processor. Drain the peaches, reserving the juice. Combine the reserved juice and the puréed blueberries in a saucepan over medium heat. Bring the mixture to a boil, stirring frequently. Dissolve the cornstarch in the water and stir into the blueberry mixture. Cook until thickened, stirring constantly.

Meiling Hager
Secretary, Lower School, 1991 to present

Apple Crisp

Yield:
6 servings

1/2 cup sugar
Cinnamon to taste
1/4 cup butter
4 or 5 large tart Granny Smith or Pippin apples, sliced
1 cup packed brown sugar
1 cup flour
1/4 cup butter

Approx
Per Serving:
Cal 477
Prot 3 g
Carbo 84 g
T Fat 16 g
29% Calories
from Fat
Chol 41 mg
Fiber 3 g
Sod 173 mg

Sprinkle the sugar over the bottom of a 9-inch-square baking pan. Sprinkle with cinnamon and dot with 1/4 cup butter. Arrange the apple slices in the prepared pan. Mix the brown sugar, flour and 1/4 cup butter in a small bowl until crumbly. Sprinkle over the apples. Bake at 350 degrees for 1 hour.

Ellen Person
Parent, Jeff 2000

Vermont Apple Delight

Yield:
8 servings

6 or 7 very tart McIntosh, Pippin or Granny Smith apples, sliced
1 teaspoon ground cinnamon
1/2 cup walnuts
1/2 cup raisins
3/4 cup pure maple syrup (no substitution)
1/2 cup shredded sharp Cheddar cheese
1 1/4 cups unbleached flour
1 cup packed brown sugar
1/2 teaspoon cinnamon
1/4 cup butter

Approx
Per Serving:
Cal 461
Prot 6 g
Carbo 84 g
T Fat 13 g
25% Calories
from Fat
Chol 23 mg
Fiber 4 g
Sod 119 mg

Combine the apple slices, 1 teaspoon cinnamon, walnuts, raisins and maple syrup in a 9x13-inch baking pan. Sprinkle with the cheese. Mix the flour, brown sugar, 1/2 teaspoon cinnamon and butter in a bowl until crumbly. Sprinkle over the apple mixture. Bake, covered with foil, at 350 degrees for 30 minutes. Bake, uncovered, for 15 to 30 minutes longer or until brown and bubbly. Serve hot with vanilla ice cream.

Lisa Braun-Glazer
Parent, Julia 2001

Never eat more than you can lift.

Miss Piggy (Jim Henson)

Basque Cake (Pastel Vasco)

This popular dessert is one of the few that Basque people traditionally serve. Jacqueline's family on her mother's side is from the St. Jean Pied de Port in the French Pyrenees.

Yield:
4 servings

1¹/₂ cups flour, sifted
¹/₂ cup sugar
¹/₈ teaspoon salt
¹/₂ cup butter, softened
2 egg yolks

1 teaspoon baking powder
Grated peel of 1 lemon
Pastry Cream
1 egg, beaten

Approx
Per Serving:
Cal 853
Prot 17 g
Carbo 113 g
T Fat 38 g
40% Calories
from Fat
Chol 504 mg
Fiber 2 g
Sod 592 mg

Sift the flour into a large bowl and make a well in the center. Add the sugar, salt, butter, egg yolks, baking powder and lemon peel to the well. Mix together until a dough forms. Divide the dough into 2 portions with one portion slightly larger than the other. Roll the larger portion on a lightly floured surface. Fit into a greased and floured 8- or 9-inch springform pan to cover the bottom and up the side of the pan. Fill with Pastry Cream but do not allow the Cream to touch the side of the pan. Roll the remaining dough on a lightly floured surface and place on top of the Cream. Brush with the beaten egg. Bake at 350 degrees for 35 minutes or until golden brown. Let stand until cool. Remove the side of the pan carefully. Store in the refrigerator.

Pastry Cream

³/₄ cup sugar
5 egg yolks
¹/₃ cup flour, sifted
¹/₈ teaspoon salt

1 teaspoon vanilla extract
2 cups milk
Dark rum to taste

Beat the sugar and egg yolks in a bowl until smooth and light colored. Add the flour and salt and stir just enough to mix. Add the vanilla to the milk in a saucepan. Heat the milk mixture to scalding. Stir a small amount of the hot mixture into the beaten egg mixture; stir the egg mixture into the hot milk mixture. Cook until the mixture reaches the boiling point, stirring vigorously. Boil for about 2 minutes and remove from the heat. Stir in the rum. Strain the mixture into a bowl. Let stand until cool, stirring occasionally to prevent a crust from forming.

Annette Tribble
Parent, Jacqueline 2002

My Sister Marie's Cheesecake

Yield:
8 servings

16 ounces cream cheese, softened
3/4 cup sugar
1 teaspoon vanilla extract
2 eggs
1 recipe graham cracker crust
1 cup sour cream
2 tablespoons sugar
1 teaspoon vanilla extract

Approx
Per Serving:
Cal 510
Prot 8 g
Carbo 44 g
T Fat 35 g
60% Calories
from Fat
Chol 128 mg
Fiber <1 g
Sod 370 mg

Cream the cream cheese, 3/4 cup sugar and 1 teaspoon vanilla in a bowl until smooth. Beat in the eggs. Press the graham cracker crust mixture over the bottom and up the side of a springform pan or pie plate. Spoon the cream cheese mixture into the crust. Bake at 375 degrees for 20 minutes. Cool for 15 minutes. Increase the oven temperature to 425 degrees. Mix the sour cream, 2 tablespoons sugar and 1 teaspoon vanilla in a bowl until smooth. Spread evenly over the cream cheese mixture. Bake at 425 degrees for 10 minutes. Let stand until cool. Chill for 4 to 5 hours before serving.

Betsy McCallum
Parent, Jason 2010 and Kaitlin 2012
Mathematics, Middle School, 1994 to present

The population of La Jolla in 1900 was a mere 300 residents. Today, the community of La Jolla boasts a population of over 35,000.

New York Cheesecake

Yield:
16 servings

32 ounces whipped cream cheese
2 cups sour cream
$1/2$ cup unsalted butter
5 eggs
2 tablespoons cornstarch
$1^{1}/_{4}$ cups sugar
$1^{1}/_{4}$ teaspoons vanilla extract
1 teaspoon lemon juice

Approx
Per Serving:
Cal 398
Prot 7 g
Carbo 19 g
T Fat 33 g
74% Calories
from Fat
Chol 157 mg
Fiber <1 g
Sod 202 mg

Let the cream cheese, sour cream, butter and eggs stand at room temperature for 1 hour. Combine the cream cheese, sour cream and butter in a bowl and beat until creamy. Add the cornstarch, sugar, vanilla and lemon juice and beat at high speed until blended. Add the eggs 1 at a time and beat until very smooth. Pour into a greased springform pan. Place the pan in a larger pan. Add warm water to half the depth of the springform pan. Bake at 375 degrees for 1 hour or until golden brown. Turn off the oven. Let the cheesecake stand in the oven with the door ajar for 1 hour. Let the cheesecake stand at room temperature for 2 hours. Refrigerate, covered, for 6 hours to overnight. Place the pan on a serving plate and remove the side of the pan.

Michele Zousmer
Parent, Alexandra 2002 and Maxwell 2005

Sour Cream Cheesecake

Yield:
16 servings

1³/4 cups graham cracker crumbs
1 teaspoon ground cinnamon
¹/2 cup melted unsalted butter
16 ounces cream cheese, softened
1 cup sugar
2 teaspoons vanilla extract
3 eggs, beaten
3 cups sour cream

Approx
Per Serving:
Cal 360
Prot 6 g
Carbo 25 g
T Fat 27 g
66% Calories
from Fat
Chol 106 mg
Fiber <1 g
Sod 197 mg

Mix the graham cracker crumbs, cinnamon and melted butter in a bowl. Press over the bottom and up the side of a 9-inch springform pan. Bake at 375 degrees for 10 minutes. Chill in the refrigerator. Combine the cream cheese, sugar, vanilla and eggs in a large bowl and beat until fluffy. Blend in the sour cream. Pour into the chilled crust. Bake at 350 degrees for 40 minutes or until set; the filling will be soft. Let stand until cool. Chill for 4 to 5 hours. Place on a serving plate and remove the side of the pan. Garnish with fruit or chocolate curls.

Joan Weiss
Parent, Jodi Semer 2001
Board of Trustees, 1996 to present

Frozen White Chocolate Mousse Tarts

Yield:
24 servings

2 (12-ounce) packages chocolate wafers
3/4 cup melted unsalted butter
1 cup whipping cream
24 ounces white chocolate
8 egg yolks
1 tablespoon white crème de cacao
6 cups whipping cream, chilled
8 egg whites
1/2 teaspoon salt
1/4 teaspoon cream of tartar
1 1/2 cups sugar

Approx
Per Serving:
Cal 650
Prot 7 g
Carbo 53 g
T Fat 46 g
63% Calories
from Fat
Chol 187 mg
Fiber 1 g
Sod 281 mg

Process the chocolate wafers in a food processor or blender until coarse crumbs form. Mix the crumbs with the melted butter. Press over the bottoms and up the sides of two 10-inch springform pans. Bake at 375 degrees for 8 minutes. Let stand until cool. Combine the whipping cream and white chocolate in a double boiler over simmering water. Heat until the chocolate melts, stirring frequently. Let stand until cool. Add the egg yolks 1 at a time to the white chocolate mixture, beating with an electric mixer after each addition and then beating until smooth. Blend in the crème de cacao. Let stand until completely cool. Whip the cream until soft peaks form. Place in the refrigerator. Beat the egg whites in a chilled mixer bowl until foamy. Add the salt and cream of tartar and beat until stiff peaks form. Add the sugar gradually, beating constantly at medium speed. Beat at high speed until the mixture is firm but not stiff. Fold the egg whites gently into the white chocolate mixture. Fold in the whipped cream gently. Pour into the cooled crusts. Freeze for 1 hour. Seal tightly in plastic wrap. Store in the freezer. Serve frozen.

Jody Sutton
Lower School, 1985 to 1997

Fruit Cobbler

Yield:
8 servings

½ cup butter
1 cup milk
1 cup flour
1 teaspoon baking powder

1 cup sugar
2½ cups fruit of choice
Brown sugar to taste

Nutritional information for this recipe is not available.

Beat the butter in a bowl. Add the milk gradually and mix well. Add a mixture of the flour and baking powder and mix well. Mix in the sugar. Pour into a buttered 8-inch-round or -square baking pan. Spoon the fruit over the top and sprinkle with brown sugar. Bake at 350 degrees for 1 hour or until the fruit is tender and the top is brown.

Izzy Leverant
Parent, Andrea 2001 and Alex 2003
President, Parents Association 1996 to 1997
Board of Trustees, 1998 to present

Simply Delicious

Yield:
15 servings

16 ounces whipped topping
1 (14-ounce) can sweetened
   condensed milk
1 (20- to 30-ounce) can raspberry,
   cherry or strawberry pie filling

1 (20-ounce) can crushed pineapple,
   drained
1½ cups miniature marshmallows
½ cup pecans

Approx
Per Serving:
Cal 304
Prot 3 g
Carbo 48 g
T Fat 8 g
24% Calories
from Fat
Chol 9 mg
Fiber 1 g
Sod 41 mg

Blend the whipped topping and condensed milk in a large bowl. Fold in the pie filling, pineapple, marshmallows and pecans. Serve immediately or chill until serving time. Use low-fat ingredients for a healthier version.

Drs. William and Linda Lewis
Parents, Bryce 2008

Flan

Yield:
12 servings

1 cup sugar
6 eggs
2 (14-ounce) cans sweetened condensed milk
2 (12-ounce) cans evaporated milk
1 teaspoon vanilla extract
1 cup sugar

Approx
Per Serving.
Cal 454
Prot 12 g
Carbo 75 g
T Fat 12 g
24% Calories
from Fat
Chol 138 mg
Fiber 0 g
Sod 173 mg

Caramelize 1 cup sugar in a heavy saucepan over medium heat until light golden in color, stirring frequently. Pour the caramelized sugar into a 10-inch tube mold and tilt to coat the inside of the mold with the sugar. Combine the eggs, condensed and evaporated milk, vanilla and 1 cup sugar in a blender container. Process until smooth. (The amount will probably require processing in batches.) Pour the egg mixture into the prepared mold. Place the mold in a large pan with about 1 inch of water. Bake at 350 degrees for 1 hour or until a knife inserted in the center comes out clean. Refrigerate the flan overnight. Dip the mold into very hot water and invert the flan onto a serving platter.

Miriam Robbins
Parent, Monica 2001

Education's purpose is to replace an empty
mind with an open one.

Malcolm S. Forbes

Galatobouriko (Custard Pastry)

Yield:
36 servings

2 cups sugar
2 cups water
1 lemon wedge
5 cups milk
1$^{1}/_{2}$ cups sugar
1 tablespoon butter
1 cup cream of wheat or wheat hearts
6 eggs, beaten
1 teaspoon vanilla extract
$^{1}/_{2}$ teaspoon grated orange peel
1 pound phyllo
$^{1}/_{2}$ cup melted butter

Approx
Per Serving:
Cal 189
Prot 4 g
Carbo 31 g
T Fat 6 g
27% Calories
from Fat
Chol 48 mg
Fiber <1 g
Sod 118 mg

Combine the 2 cups sugar, 2 cups water and lemon wedge in a large saucepan. Bring to a boil, stirring until the sugar dissolves completely. Set the syrup aside to cool completely. Combine the milk, 1$^{1}/_{2}$ cups sugar and 1 tablespoon butter in a large saucepan. Heat the mixture to the simmering point, stirring until the sugar dissolves. Stir the cream of wheat in gradually. Cook until thickened, stirring constantly. Cool for 5 minutes. Stir a small amount of the hot mixture into the beaten eggs; stir the eggs into the hot mixture and mix until smooth. Stir in the vanilla and orange peel. Cool completely. Alternate layers of half the phyllo and the melted butter in a buttered 11x16-inch baking pan, leaving phyllo overhang on all sides. Spoon the custard mixture into the prepared pan and spread evenly. Fold the overhang over the custard. Alternate layers of the remaining phyllo and butter over the custard. Score through half the top phyllo layers in 6 or 7 rows to form diamonds. Bake at 375 degrees for 45 minutes or until puffed and golden brown and a knife inserted in the center comes out clean. Remove from the oven. Pour the cooled syrup carefully over the hot pastry. Let stand until cool. Cut along the score lines. Store in the refrigerator.

Ann Brizolis
Parent, Alex 2001

Baked Indian Pudding

This very old family recipe, better than the pudding served at Boston's Durgin Park, has been handed down to me through many generations. My parents currently live in the old family farmhouse, built circa 1780.

Yield:
8 servings

4 cups milk
1/2 cup packed brown sugar
1/8 teaspoon salt
2 tablespoons butter
7 tablespoons cornmeal
1/2 cup molasses
1/2 teaspoon ground nutmeg
1 teaspoon ground ginger
1 cup raisins
1 cup cold water

Approx
Per Serving:
Cal 285
Prot 5 g
Carbo 53 g
T Fat 7 g
22% Calories
from Fat
Chol 24 mg
Fiber 1 g
Sod 143 mg

Scald the milk in a 2-quart saucepan. Add the brown sugar, salt and butter. Mix the cornmeal with the molasses, nutmeg and ginger. Stir into the hot milk mixture. Add the raisins and cook over low heat for several minutes, stirring frequently. Pour into a baking dish. Place the mixture in a slow oven. (Try to cook the pudding when the oven is on for a roast or something that requires long cooking at low temperature.) When the pudding is hot, add the cold water; do not stir. A syrup will develop as the pudding continues baking for 2 1/2 to 3 hours total baking time.

Susanne Strong Schissel
Earth Science, Middle School, 1983 to present

Grannie's Iced Tea

Grannie Hinrichs served this tea in the shade of a California pepper tree in the 1940s after Sunday badminton. It is as tasty and welcome today, especially with one of these delectible desserts to enhance it.

Yield:
8 servings

5 teabags
Several sprigs of mint
2 cups boiling water
1 cup sugar
Juice of 4 lemons
1 quart ginger ale, chilled

Approx
Per Serving:
Cal 144
Prot 0 g
Carbo 39 g
T Fat 0 g
0% Calories
from Fat
Chol 0 mg
Fiber 0 g
Sod 8 mg

Steep the teabags and mint in the boiling water for 5 minutes. Strain the tea over the sugar and stir until the sugar dissolves. Add the lemon juice. Pour into a large pitcher. Add enough ice and water to measure 2 quarts. Add the ginger ale just before serving. Pour into tall glasses and garnish with a sprig of mint.

Carol Hinrichs
Parent, David 1984 and Daniel 1985
Lower School, 1971 to present

Etcetera

Tell me and I'll forget. Show me, and I
may not remember. Involve me and
I'll understand.

Native American saying

Nutritional Profile Guidelines

The editors have attempted to present these family recipes in a format that allows approximate nutritional values to be computed. Persons with dietary or health problems or whose diets require close monitoring should not rely solely on the nutritional information provided. They should consult their physicians or a registered dietitian for specific information.

Abbreviations for Nutritional Profile

Cal —
Calories
T Fat —
Total Fat
Chol —
Cholesterol
Sod —
Sodium
Carbo —
Carbohydrates
Fiber —
Dietary Fiber
Prot —
Protein
g —
grams
mg —
milligrams

Nutritional information for these recipes is computed from information derived from many sources, including materials supplied by the United States Department of Agriculture, computer databanks, and journals in which the information is assumed to be in the public domain. However, many specialty items, new products, and processed foods may not be available from these sources or may vary from the average values used in these profiles. More information on new and/or specific products may be obtained by reading the nutrient labels. Unless otherwise specified, the nutritional profile of these recipes is based on all measurements being level.

* **Artificial sweeteners** vary in use and strength so should be used "to taste," using the recipe ingredients as a guideline. Sweeteners using aspartame (NutraSweet and Equal) should not be used as a sweetener in recipes involving prolonged heating, which reduces the sweet taste. For further information on the use of these sweeteners, refer to the package.
* **Alcoholic ingredients** have been analyzed for the basic information. Cooking causes the evaporation of alcohol, which decreases alcoholic and caloric content.
* **Buttermilk, sour cream,** and **yogurt** are the types available commercially.
* **Cake mixes** which are prepared using package directions include 3 eggs and 1/2 cup oil.
* **Chicken,** cooked for boning and chopping, has been roasted; this method yields the lowest caloric values.
* **Cottage cheese** is cream-style with 4.2% creaming mixture. Dry curd cottage cheese has no creaming mixture.
* **Eggs** are all large. To avoid raw eggs that may carry salmonella, as in eggnog or 6-week muffin batter, use an equivalent amount of commercial egg substitute.
* **Flour** is unsifted all-purpose flour.
* **Garnishes,** serving suggestions, and other optional information and variations are not included in the profile.
* **Margarine** and **butter** are regular, not whipped or presoftened.
* **Milk** is whole milk, 3.5% butterfat. Low-fat milk is 1% butterfat. Evaporated milk is whole milk with 60% of the water removed.
* **Oil** is any type of vegetable cooking oil. **Shortening** is hydrogenated vegetable shortening.
* **Salt** and other ingredients to taste as noted in the ingredients have not been included in the nutritional profile.
* If a choice of ingredients has been given, the profile reflects the first option. If a choice of amounts has been given, the profile reflects the greater amount.

Culinary Math

The following numbers are given to help interpret the nutritional profile included with each recipe.

	Per day for a 120-pound person	Per day for a 170-pound person
Calories	1,800	2,550
Protein	Min. 44 g	Min. 62 g
Fat*	Max. 60 g	Max. 85 g
Carbohydrate	Min. 248 g	Min. 351 g
Sodium**	Max. 6,000 mg	Max. 6,000 mg
Cholesterol	Max. 300 mg	Max. 300 mg

*An easy way to limit fat consumption to the recommended 30 percent of calories is to divide your level weight in half. This number is an estimate of the allowed fat in grams per day for a moderately active person. The above values are given as a reference only, since calories needed to maintain ideal body weight vary from person to person.

**Unlike fat, there is no general consensus for healthy people to reduce sodium below this moderate level.

Saving Fat and Calories

- A mixture of equal parts of nonfat yogurt and ricotta cheese blended in a food processor makes a good base for dips.

- To reduce fat, cholesterol and calories in your favorite baked goods, substitute an equal amount of applesauce for the oil called for in the recipe. For the average recipe, you will reduce the calories by half and the fat by more than three quarters.

- Bake guilt-free brownies by replacing the 1/2 cup oil and 2 eggs called for in the brownie mix with 1/2 cup nonfat yogurt and about 4 tablespoons of unsweetened applesauce.

- A low-calorie substitute for sour cream is 1 cup low-fat cottage cheese mixed with a teaspoon of vinegar and 1/4 cup skim milk. Process the mixture in a blender or food processor until smooth.

- Use dairy products made from nonfat or low-fat milk to reduce fat and calories in the diet. Evaporated nonfat milk can be substituted for cream in many recipes.

- Use yogurt in your favorite recipes in place of other dairy products in order to reduce fat. You can use it as a cooking ingredient if you protect against curdling and separating by blending 2 tablespoons flour or 1 tablespoon cornstarch into each cup of yogurt.

- Save calories by topping desserts with lightly sweetened nonfat sour cream instead of whipped cream.

- To reduce calories and cholesterol in pasta dishes, substitute chicken broth with 1 tablespoon of cream for the whole cream used to thicken sauces.

- A leaf of lettuce dropped into a soup pot will absorb the grease from the top of the soup. Discard the leaf immediately.

- Instead of sautéing vegetables in butter, margarine, or oil, "sweat" them in a covered heavy saucepan over very low heat for 10 minutes or longer.

- Save time by purchasing cheeses already shredded, but save fat by using the finely shredded cheeses. It will require less to achieve satisfying color and flavor results.

- There are a lot of wonderful fat-free salad dressings. Keep trying them until you find one you like and stick to it.

- Change from whole or 2% milk to nonfat. It has all the calcium as whole milk but just takes a little getting used to. You can save a lot of fat this way.

- Use nonfat sour cream, cream cheese, cottage cheese, cheese, ricotta, etc., in your recipes. After a time or two, you will not know the difference.

- Use nonstick cooking sprays (Pam, etc.) instead of greasing pans.

- You can use mashed ripe bananas as a substitute for fat when baking muffins and brownies.

- Instead of using whole eggs all the time, use some egg substitute from time to time. It is very good and cooks in recipes well.

- Think of chicken or vegetable broth as a substitute for oil. Anytime you need to sauté in a recipe use broth. (Substitute chicken or vegetable broth instead of oil. It works beautifully when cooking onions or garlic to add to chili, spaghetti, etc.)

Suggested Substitutions

Instead of	Try
1 whole egg	$1/4$ cup egg substitute; 1 egg white and 1 teaspoon oil; 2 egg whites
1 tablespoon butter	1 tablespoon low-fat butter
1 cup whole milk	1 cup nonfat milk
1 cup light cream	3 tablespoons oil and skim milk equal to 1 cup; 1 cup evaporated nonfat milk
1 cup sour cream	1 cup fat-free sour cream; $3/4$ cup buttermilk and $1/4$ cup oil; 1 cup plain low-fat yogurt; 1 cup blended low-fat cottage cheese
1 ounce hard cheese	1 ounce of fat-free or low-fat cheese; 1 ounce fat-free mozzarella cheese; 2 tablespoons ricotta cheese (skim)
1 ounce (1 square) baking chocolate	3 tablespoons cocoa and 1 tablespoon oil
Shortening or lard	Vegetable oil or a margarine made with a mono-saturated vegetable oil such as canola, olive, or peanut
Ground beef	Ground turkey; ground chuck; ground round
Sautéed vegetables	Raw or steamed vegetables
Bread crumbs	Crushed high-fiber cereal flakes

Children's Art Contributors

The Parents' Association would like to thank Ann Caitlin, Middle School Art Director, for coordinating the student art submitted for the cookbook. A special thank you goes to the lower and middle school students for their artwork contributions.

1st Grade—Class of 2008

Ariel Abbott
Grant Alter
Lauren Armstrong
Dana Barshop
Stephanie Berger
Darcie Blair
Darren Blake
Beau Brand
Tracy Burnett
Justin Carson
Laurel Casey
Cameron Chapman
Nancy Cherashore
Matthew Cordell
Trevor Dorne
Allison Dorr
William Duncan
Elizabeth Ellison
Kenna Foltz
Neva Fowler-Gerace

Brian Garfield
Stephanie Gerretsen
Emily Goldberg
Taylor Green
Amanda Haworth
Tatiana Henry
Jennifer Herring
Kimberly Higgins
James Hopp
Nyla Iqbal
Melanie Kaplan
Alyson Kennon
Daniel Kwittken
Sophie Laing
Bryce Lewis
Jeanette Maynard
Michael McKenna
Megan Morikawa
Tommy Morris
Matthew Mulvey

Waleed Najm
Annette Ochoa
Charlotte Ostrow
Samantha Parry
Joseph Peterson
Rebecca Poliner
Brian Price
Elizabeth Richardson
Zachary Ritchken
Sam Rogers
Adam Saven
Erica Schild
Samantha Schlossberg
Clark Schulman
Sierra Shapery
Zachary Tonks
Scott Wadlington
Jotaro Wakabayashi
Alexandra Weiss
Tyler Wolfson

2nd Grade—Class of 2007

Connor Ajan-Lee
Maya Babla
Nikolas Behar
Cameron Bell
Kate Bell
Hillary Buckner
Stephen Burns
Yumi Chung
Lauren Coden
James Coleman
Rachel Cromidas

Michelle Crow
Natalie Dobke
Max Doshay
Taylor Essex
Bella Estes
Benjamin Fleischhacker
Christopher Frace
Adam Francis
Philip Gachot
Linda Gain
Tanya Grewal

Gregory Hirshman
Danielle Ito
Claire Kaufinan
Ajexandra M. Kretowicz
Tamara Louie
Nathan Meinert
Benjamin Michlin
Matthew Mulligan
Erin Nelson
Matteo Padovani
Lauren Pischel

Ashley Pollack
Lindsey Pope
Stephanie Riedler
Grace Royer
Tanya Schulz
Timmy Sedwitz
Victoria Shaw

Oren Siegel
Kimberly Small
Miquele Smith
Ted Staver
Philip Stewart
Gavin Teutli-Vadheim
Collin Tuck

Jonathan Volfson
Katie Wachsman
Alexandra Williams
Sabrina Wilson
Michelle Wolfe
Jonathan Yip

3rd Grade—Class of 2006

Logan Abbott
Preet Anand
Rupert Barshop
Meaghan Blair
Sara Blasingame
Kevin Brinig
Rachel Brooks
Andrew Buckley
Brittany Carson
Valerie Christy
Daniel Deuprey
Lauren Dodson
Kirsten Dorr
Amanda Edelson
Frantz Farreau
Kristy Foster
Adam Freeman
Katharine Friedgen
Jeffrey Fronek
Ravi Gupta

Ryan Hart
Ryan Hitchcock
Hallie Huston
Hana Justice
Rachel Kanter
Jordan Kobernick
Chelsea Krant
Mitchell Kroener
Benjamin Kwittken
Sarah Lebovitz
Sean Lindenberger
Krista Liskevych
Austin Lyman
Aya Maekawa
Samantha Mark
Alexia Melville
Bijan Moallemi
Chase Mohseni
Andrew Moir
Evan Morikawa

Sammy Morris
Phillip Neeley
Ashley O'Dell
Mathilda O'Neill
Maggie Ogle
Lancey Pratt
Shelley Pressman
Kathy Salehizadeh
Larisa Salmon
Erin Saven
Kelley Schiffman
Amanda Shaffer
Katelyn Sigeti
Stephen Stiefel
Chad Vogt
Yotaro Wakabayashi
Alex Watrous
Justin Weiss
Katherine Wright
Morgan Zemen

4th Grade—Class of 2005

Nicholas Alessandro
Jeremy Batter
Jennifer Brainerd
Brendan Brinig
Elizabeth Buckley
William Cherashore
Michael Cordell

Alissa Crestani
Brian Davis
Andrea Dawson
Tyler Delbert
Nikki Demeter
Rebecca Derrough
Lauren Evarts

Andrew Fischer
Kelly Foltz
Stephanie Gachot
Brendan Gardner
Michelle Geffen
Jean-Philippe Gerretsen
Alexander Gill

Children's Contributor List

Scott Glasberg
Whitney Goodman
Amy Graeber
Ryan Grimes
Mari Gromkowski
Max Guise
Rishu Gupta
Jason Hendershaw
Hillary Higgins
Matthew Hodgson
Sean Hofman
Cristina Hussong
Aumna Iqbal
Alexandra Jackson

Justin Jameson
Lauren Kessler
Alexander Kiefhaber
Benjamin Killmer
Jesse Kobernick
Jonas Krant
Hunter May
Eric Mothander
Christopher Muto
Carley O'Neill
Elissa Osterland
David Pratt
Jennifer Rosen
Stephanie Russell-Kraft

Brian Sedwitz
Tyler Sgueglia
Sage Shapery
Jeffrey Steinborn
Alison Tebo
Andrew Teutli-Vadheim
Jonathan Thompson
Lindsay Ullman
Jacquelyn Vadnais
Alexandra Watkins
Evan White
Samantha Wilson
Alexander Blane-Zimberg
Maxwell Zousmer

5th Grade—Class of 2004

Jonathan Acord
Taylor Alan-Lee
Alexander Alessandro
Lindsley Baker-Baum
Benjamin Bartlett
Rebecca Blasingame
Whitney Brodie
Lauren Browar
Jennifer Campbell
Nicole Chayet
Dennis Dawson
Jennifer Deuprey
Lara Durrant
Ashley Estes
Kristina Friedgen
Gabriel Fries-Briggs
Stefan Georgi
Kathryn Goepner
Melissa Goldman
Sonia Gupta
William Gwyn
Spencer Hirsch

Michael Hirshman
Garrett Iaco
Jonathan James
Andrew Jorgensen
Allen Kessler
Cynthia Khoury
Risa Kirihara
Yuanyuan Kong
Cameron Lange
Stefanie Lenz
Jacqueline Mark
Philip Marks
Scott McCracken
Sean Middleton
Takuro Mizoguchi
Shayla Mulvey
Niccolo Padovani
Kaitlyn Page
Charlie Patton
Raquel Perlman
Michel Poucet
Mindy Pressman

Jessica Robertson
Vanessa Rutman
Clara Saks
Katherine Santohigashi
Daniel Skaggs
Jade Smith
David Smith
Michael Song
Desirea Soumekh
Stephen Steger
Kathleen Sullivan
Kimberly Traube
Brandon Vogt
Rosemarie Wagner
Jeremy Warburg
Sarah Wheeler
Gerald Whitney
Katherine Wingert
John Winslow
Shawn Wolfe
Nicholas Wright
Jared Zeidman

Recipe Contributors

The Parents' Association would like to thank all of the people who helped in making this book possible, including the hundreds of people who submitted their favorite recipes. The support and contributions were overwhelming. It is our sincere hope that no one has been inadvertently overlooked.

Carolyn Ackerberg
Roxy Ackerberg
Katey Alexander
Kathleen Allenbach
Michael Amiel
Nancy Anderson
Luis Arellano
Sue Armstrong
Hayley Atchison-Buettner
Jean Bartlett
Pat Bartlett
Janice Batter
Katrina Beers
Suzanne Berol
Virginia Bial
Cathy Blake
Ann Blankenship
Laurie Blasingame
Marsha Boston
Kate Bradbury
Lisa Braun-Glazer
Judy Braunstein
Anne Brickley
Ann Brizolis
Mary Anne Brower
Joyce Browning-Summers
Jenn Buckner
JoAnn Burchfiel
Mary Burns
Becky Candra
Jack Carpenter
Julie Cary
Michele Cass
Debra Charles

Joan Mann Chesner
Parvine Chowfla
Silvana Christy
Shani Clarke
Hazel Coelho
Gerry Coleman
Renee Comeau
Tom Cooper
Phyllis Crady
Joy Davis
Jo Ann DeMartini
Diane Demeter
Neil Derrough
Sharron Derrough
Diana de Sequera
Dorothy Dickinson
Joan Diener
Brooke Donahoe-Roberts
Mary Doyle
Marian Duncan
Genean Dunn
Cathy Ellison
Virginia Erickson
Ruth Evans
Joan Faue-Durrant
Moreen Fielden
John Finch
Gail Finegold
Debbie Fischer
Kay Foltz
Wanda Foltz
Frances Frace
Lolie Fromm
Helane Fronek

Charlotte Garfield
Marlene Gelber
Rita Gittes
Julie Goldberg
Sam Goldberg
Tristan Gomes
Kristin Gridley
Mrs. William Griffin
Marla Griswold
Terry Gulden
Meiling Hager
Judy Haidinger
Tim Haidinger
Amy Haimsohn
Lu Ann Hall
Lynne Hansen
Rosemary Harbushka
Sue Harman
Helen Hauer
Kathleen Healy
Lesa Heebner
Keith Heldman
Dara Hensley
Susan Herman
Dawn Herring
Kathy Hewitt
Gwen Hiatt
Jo Higgins
Sue Higgins
Elizabeth Hill
Rosa Hill
Elaine Hinkle
Carol Hinrichs
Greg Hirsch

Kathy Hirsch
Jana Hirschenbein
Seth Hirschenbein
Ryan Hitchcock
Sharon Horan
Eileen Huffman
Lillian Hurwitz
Sally Huzyak
Rama Iaco
Jean Ilstrup
Gladis Innerst
Nancy James
Harvey Jetmore
David Johns
Althea Johnson
Kelly Justus
Lorraine Kaa
Jan Kahler
Melinda Kanter
Tracy Katkov
Libby Keller
Kay Kennard
Carole Kerr
Pat Konkle
Peggy Kratzmier
Lerena Kreiss
Susan Kroviak
Pam Kurz
Mary Landa
Teresa Laneville
Diana Larson
Mrs. John Laun, Jr.
Claudia Law-Greenberg
Don Leavenworth
Cherry Lee
Izzy Leverant
Linda Lewis
Nanci Lewis
William Lewis

Karen Lon
Lori Long
Debbie Lynn
Pam Madigan
Lesa Malécot
Michel Malécot
Mark Marcus
Nancy Marshall
Emily Maxon
Heather May
Betsy McCallum
Ferne McCuen
Vicki McGhee
Candace McKenna
Peggy Meehl
Ruthann Mercer
Jeannie Mershon
Mrs. Ralph Michael, Jr.
Silvana Michan
Susan Middleton
Micki Mighdoll
Lisa Moallemi
Karen Morikawa
Susan Morris
Diane Mothander
Peter Mothander
Shari Mount-Essex
Linda Moyer
Debbie Moyneur
Barbara Mulligan
Gertrude Nebeling
Barbara Neiswender
John Neiswender
Nancy Nevin
Newnham Family
Kris Ochoa-Keane
Susie Olson
Terri Orr
Vera Osterland

Julie Page
Charlie Patton
Elizabeth Patton
Sanders Patton
Shelley Ackerberg-Patton
Ryan Peavey
Ellen Person
Rachel Petrella
Edna Phillips
Denyse Pierre-Pierre
Chan Pike
Carol Pratt
Chick Pyle
Marian Randall
Dale Reeder
Charles Renshaw
Elynor Renshaw
Brenda Riedler
Deborah Ritchken
Bonnie Robbins
Miriam Robbins
Susan Roberts
Gaylee Rogers
Vera Rotenberg
Sandra Rovira
Reico Saito
Joel Salberg
Gloria Salem
Lauren Salomon
Julie Sanderson
Marilyn Sarlin
Minda Sarlin
Shanta Sarlin
Shiloh Sarlin
Renata Saven
Lee Sawyer
Vina Saycocie
Susanne Schissel
Eileen Schwartz

Marissa Schwartz-Brooks
Barry Seidman
Jackie Seidman
Ellen Shaffer
Beverly Silldorf
Billy Simms
Ellen Simms
Susan Small
Brad Smith
June Smith
Nancy Smith
Mrs. York Smith
Moira Solomon
Carol Spaulding
Dorothy Stanziano
Rachel Staver
Cheryl Stewart

Karen Stewart
Pat Stickels
Julie Sugarman
Joanne Sullivan
Jody Sutton
Fumiko Tachibana
Susan Taylor
Laura Temmer
Cary Tremblay
Dorothy Trexel
Annette Tribble
Barbara Trigueros
Nancy Ullman
Debbie Valentine
Sage Valenzuela
Cameron Volker
Helen Voorhees

Sue Waggener
Ruthi Warburg
Roger Weaver
Barbara Weinstein
Joan Weiss
Angela West
Patricia Wild
Beth Wilkie-Dowding
Nancy Winslow
Pamela Wischkaemper
Rebecca Wood
Kathryn Woods
Margaret Yost
Sarah Youtkus
Ronni Zeidman
Helene Ziman
Michele Zousmer

A heartfelt thank you must go to Brad, my husband, and to Sanders,
Charlie and Amy, my children, who endured months of my emotional absence while
the cookbook was produced. To my friends Rama, Jackie, Gloria and
Ruth Ann, I thank each of you for enduring my anxiety over completion of this
cookbook, and for your continuing and supportive friendship.

Index

Index

Order Information

La Jolla Country Day School Parents' Association

9490 Genesee Avenue
La Jolla, CA 92037
619–453–3440

All orders must be prepaid.

Please make check or money order payable to LJCDS Parents' Association and send with completed form to the address above.

Name

Address

City   State   Zip

I would like to order _____ cookbooks at $19.95 each   _____

Postage and Handling

   To U.S. addresses, $5.00 per book (First Class/Priority)   _____

   To Canada and Mexico addresses, $8.50 per book (First Class)   _____

   To all other countries, $10.95 per book (U.S. Global Priority)   _____

Total   _____

Photocopies of this form will be accepted.

La Jolla Country Day School Parents' Association

9490 Genesee Avenue
La Jolla, CA 92037
619–453–3440

All orders must be prepaid.

Please make check or money order payable to LJCDS Parents' Association and send with completed form to the address above.

Name

Address

City   State   Zip

I would like to order _____ cookbooks at $19.95 each   _____

Postage and Handling

   To U.S. addresses, $5.00 per book (First Class/Priority)   _____

   To Canada and Mexico addresses, $8.50 per book (First Class)   _____

   To all other countries, $10.95 per book (U.S. Global Priority)   _____

Total   _____

Photocopies of this form will be accepted.